THE CFO MBA

Your Blueprint to Financial Excellence

By

Robert N. Jacobs

All rights reserved
Copyright © Robert N. Jacobs, 2025
The right of Robert N. Jacobs to be identified as the author of this
work has been asserted in accordance with Section 78
of the Copyright, Designs and Patents Act 1988
The book cover is copyright to Robert N. Jacobs
This book is published by
Growth Seeker Publishing Ltd.
www.growthseekerpublishing.com

This book is sold subject to the conditions that it shall not, by way of
trade or otherwise, be lent, resold, hired out or otherwise circulated
without the author's or publisher's prior consent in any form of binding
or cover other than that in which it is published and
without a similar condition including this condition being imposed
on the subsequent purchaser.
This book is a work of fiction. Any resemblance to
people or events, past or present, is purely coincidental.
ISBN: 9798282478273

As you open these pages, you're stepping onto a path I've travelled myself, a path of extraordinary challenge, immense responsibility, and unmatched opportunity. The role of CFO isn't just about numbers or compliance; it's about being the visionary leader who shapes the future of an organisation. You have the potential to drive innovation, inspire excellence, and transform complexity into clarity. My goal is to equip you with the strategies, insights, and confidence to thrive in this demanding role. Let this book be your trusted companion as you elevate your skills, expand your vision, and unlock your fullest potential. Your journey to financial leadership excellence begins now. Believe deeply, lead boldly, and remember—your impact can be extraordinary.

Robert N. Jacobs

Introduction

The role of a Chief Financial Officer has evolved far beyond what it once was. We're no longer just stewards of numbers and guardians of compliance. Today, we are strategists, visionaries, and leaders tasked with driving innovation, managing complexity, and charting the future of the organisations we serve. Whether you are aspiring to become a CFO or looking to refine your expertise as one, I wrote The CFO MBA to help you succeed.

I know firsthand that not everyone has the time or resources to pursue a traditional MBA, which can cost tens of thousands of pounds and require years of study. The truth is that you don't need a formal degree to master the core principles of finance and leadership. This book is designed to serve as your comprehensive guide, offering everything you need to understand, grow, and thrive as a CFO.

What sets this book apart is its practicality. I've taken the complexities of financial management and leadership and translated them into actionable insights. It's not about abstract theories; it's about the real world. From mastering financial statements and managing risk to building effective teams and embracing digital transformation, each chapter provides step-by-step guidance and real-world examples. You'll find case studies drawn from the challenges and successes I've seen throughout my career, making this book as relatable as it is informative.

I wrote The CFO MBA with a deep understanding of the challenges you face today. Whether it's navigating the uncertainties of a merger, adopting emerging technologies, or balancing the tension between short-term results and long-term goals, I want this book to be a resource you can rely on. It's a blueprint to help you not only meet those challenges but to rise above them.

If you're an ambitious professional preparing for the leap into the C-suite or a seasoned CFO seeking a fresh perspective, I invite you to join me on this journey. I've poured my experiences, lessons, and insights into this book so you can benefit from them. My hope is that it becomes a trusted companion, guiding you as you lead your organisation to new heights.

Let's get started. Your journey to financial excellence begins here.

You've got this!

Robert Jacobs
Curious By Design

Table of Contents

Chapter 1
The CFO's Role And Responsibilities 1

1.1 - Evolution Of The CFO Role 2

1.2 - Strategic vs. Operational CFOs 4

1.3 - Key Skills Every CFO Needs 7

1.4 - Understanding Financial Statements 10

1.5 - Financial Reporting and Compliance Basics 12

1.6 - Ethics and Integrity in Finance 15

1.7 - Relationship Management with the C-Suite 18

1.8 - The CFO's Role in Corporate Governance 21

1.9 - Setting Financial Goals for the Organisation 23

1.10 - Overview of the CFO Career Path 27

Chapter 2
Mastering Financial Planning and Analysis (FP&A) 30

2.1 - Introduction to FP&A 30

2.2 - Budgeting Techniques and Best Practices 33

2.3 - Forecasting Fundamentals 36

2.4 - Financial Modelling 101 39

2.5 - Scenario Analysis and Stress Testing 43

2.6 - Leveraging Data for Decision-Making 46

2.7 - Aligning Financial Plans with Business Goals 49

2.8 - Communication of Financial Insights 52

2.9 - Tools and Software for FP&A 56

2.10 - Case Study: Successful Budgeting in a Crisis 58

Chapter 3
Corporate Finance Essentials 64
- 3.1 - Capital Structure Fundamentals 64
- 3.2 - Equity vs. Debt Financing 67
- 3.3 - Managing Working Capital 69
- 3.4 - Investment Appraisal Techniques 73
- 3.5 - The CFO's Role in Mergers and Acquisitions 75
- 3.6 - Raising Capital in Private vs. Public Markets 79
- 3.7 - Treasury Management Basics 82
- 3.8 - Foreign Exchange and Risk Management 85
- 3.9 - Dividend Policy and Shareholder Returns 87
- 3.10 - Case Study: Navigating a Complex M&A 91

Chapter 4
Cost Management and Optimisation 95
- 4.1 - Understanding Cost Drivers 95
- 4.2 - Fixed vs. Variable Costs 98
- 4.3 - Activity-Based Costing (ABC) 101
- 4.4 - Lean Finance Principles 104
- 4.5 - Identifying Inefficiencies 107
- 4.6 - Strategies for Cost Reduction 111
- Proactive vs. Reactive Cost Reduction 111
- 4.7 - Balancing Cost-Cutting with Growth 114
- 4.8 - Managing Overhead Costs 117
- 4.9 - Vendor and Supply Chain Cost Optimisation 119
- 4.10 - Case Study: Implementing Cost Controls 123

Chapter 5
Strategic Decision-Making 127

    5.1 - Strategic vs. Tactical Financial Decisions 127

    5.2 - Role of CFO in Business Strategy 130

    5.3 - Evaluating Market Opportunities 133

    5.4 - Resource Allocation Strategies 136

    5.5 - Navigating Competitive Landscapes 139

    5.6 - Creating Value for Stakeholders 143

    5.7 - Long-Term vs. Short-Term Decision-Making 145

    5.8 - Crisis Management and Recovery 149

    5.9 - Aligning Strategy Across Teams 151

    5.10 - Case Study: Leading Through Uncertainty 154

Chapter 6
Technology and Digital Transformation 158

    6.1 - Role of Technology in Modern Finance 158

    6.2 - AI and Machine Learning in Financial Analytics 161

    6.3 - Blockchain and Its Impact on Finance 164

    6.4 - Cybersecurity Risks and Mitigation 167

    6.5 - Implementing Financial Automation 170

    6.6 - Understanding Cloud-Based Solutions 174

    6.7 - Big Data and Predictive Analytics 177

    6.8 - Driving Innovation in Finance Departments 180

    6.9 - CFO's Role in Organisational Digital Transformation 183

    6.10 - Case Study: Leading a Digital Finance Revolution 187

Chapter 7
Risk Management and Compliance 193
    7.1 - Identifying Financial Risks 193

    7.2 - Enterprise Risk Management (ERM) Frameworks 196

    7.3 - Regulatory Compliance Overview 199

    7.4 - Building a Risk-Aware Culture 203

    7.5 - Managing Credit Risk 205

    7.6 - Mitigating Operational Risks 209

    7.7 - Financial Fraud Detection and Prevention 212

    7.8 - Role of Internal Controls 216

    7.9 - Navigating Legal and Tax Risks 219

    7.10 - Case Study: Overcoming a Risk Management Challenge 222

Chapter 8
Building and Leading High-Performance Teams 229
    8.1 - Importance of Leadership in Finance 229

    8.2 - Hiring and Retaining Top Talent 231

    8.3 - Developing Future Finance Leaders 233

    8.4 - Managing Diverse Teams 235

    8.5 - Building a Culture of Collaboration 238

    8.6 - Communication Skills for CFOs 240

    8.7 - Conflict Resolution in Finance Teams 244

    8.8 - Leading Through Change 246

    8.9 - Recognizing and Rewarding Success 250

    8.10 - Case Study: Transforming a Finance Team 253

Chapter 9

Global CFO Challenges 260

    9.1 - Managing Multinational Operations 260

    9.2 - Understanding Global Financial Markets 263

    9.3 - Addressing Cultural Differences in Finance 266

    9.4 - Taxation Challenges Across Borders 269

    9.5 - Global Supply Chain Management 272

    9.6 - Exchange Rate Volatility 274

    9.7 - Political and Economic Risks 277

    9.8 - Sustainability and ESG (Environmental, Social, Governance) 280

    9.9 - Corporate Social Responsibility (CSR) Reporting 283

    9.10 - Case Study: Leading in a Globalised Economy 286

Chapter 10

Becoming a Visionary CFO 294

    10.1 - The CFO as a Change Agent 294

    10.2 - Developing a Personal Leadership Style 296

    10.3 - Long-Term Value Creation 299

    10.4 - Navigating Disruptive Trends 302

    10.5 - Balancing Stakeholder Expectations 305

    10.6 - Continuous Learning and Growth 308

    10.7 - Building a Legacy as a CFO 311

    10.8 - Mentorship and Giving Back 314

    10.9 - Future of the CFO Role 317

    10.10 - Case Study: Inspiring Leadership in Finance 319

Final Word   327

Inspiring a New Era of CFO Leadership 327

"Finance is not merely about numbers; it's the lifeblood of business, the strategic force that transforms dreams into reality, vision into success, and aspirations into lasting impact."

Robert N. Jacobs

Chapter 1

The CFO's Role And Responsibilities

> *"The modern CFO wears two hats: one of precision, ensuring the books balance, and one of ambition, charting the course for sustainable growth."*
>
> **Robert N. Jacobs**

The Chief Financial Officer (CFO) is often seen as the cornerstone of a company's financial health and strategic direction. As businesses navigate a world of increasing complexity, the role of the CFO has expanded far beyond the traditional responsibilities of budgeting and compliance. Modern CFOs are not only financial stewards but also visionaries who drive strategy, manage risks, and foster innovation. This chapter explores this transformation in depth, highlighting how technological advancements, globalisation, and shifting stakeholder expectations have redefined the expectations placed on today's CFOs. By understanding the nuances of this role, readers will gain a comprehensive view of what it takes to excel as a financial leader in an ever-changing corporate landscape.

1.1 - Evolution Of The CFO Role

The Chief Financial Officer (CFO) role has transformed dramatically over the decades, evolving from a purely financial steward to a critical strategic leader within organisations. Historically, CFOs were primarily concerned with overseeing financial reporting, managing budgets, and ensuring regulatory compliance. Their work was largely transactional and backwards-looking, focused on recording and presenting historical financial performance. Today, however, CFOs are expected to drive organisational strategy, manage risk, and act as key decision-makers alongside other members of the C-suite.

The transition of the CFO role can be traced to several key factors, including technological advancements, globalisation, regulatory changes, and shifting stakeholder expectations. In the past, finance was a siloed function responsible for bookkeeping and financial reporting. CFOs of that era were the custodians of the company's financial health, ensuring numbers were accurate and aligned with legal requirements. While these responsibilities remain crucial, the role has expanded to include forward-thinking activities, such as strategic planning, risk mitigation, and innovation.

Technology has been one of the primary drivers of this transformation. Tools such as enterprise resource planning (ERP) systems, artificial intelligence, and advanced analytics have revolutionised the finance function. These innovations enable CFOs to access real-time data, improve forecasting accuracy, and make more informed decisions. For example, a retail CFO can now use predictive analytics to forecast consumer trends and optimise pricing strategies. This strategic use of data elevates the CFO's position from a support function to a driving force behind organisational success.

Globalisation has also significantly impacted the CFO role. With companies expanding into international markets, CFOs must manage complexities such as currency fluctuations, diverse regulatory environments, and cross-border tax compliance. This requires a deep understanding of global financial markets and the ability to navigate cultural differences in business practices. A CFO at a multinational corporation, for instance, must balance the need for standardisation with local market adaptations, ensuring financial stability while fostering growth.

In addition to technological and global challenges, modern CFOs are increasingly called upon to address environmental, social, and governance (ESG) concerns. Stakeholders now expect businesses to operate ethically and sustainably, and CFOs play a pivotal role in aligning financial goals with these broader values. For instance, a CFO in the manufacturing sector might work on reducing the company's carbon footprint by investing in greener technologies and balancing environmental goals with financial constraints.

The qualifications required for today's CFOs reflect this evolution. While traditional finance certifications such as Certified Public Accountant (CPA) or Chartered Financial Analyst (CFA) remain valuable, many CFOs now pursue advanced degrees like an MBA to develop strategic and leadership skills. Practical experience in financial planning, treasury management, and corporate strategy is also essential. Furthermore, a successful CFO often gains cross-functional experience, working closely with marketing, operations, and IT teams to understand the business holistically.

The modern CFO role is not without its challenges. Balancing the dual responsibilities of financial stewardship and strategic leadership can be daunting. CFOs must manage competing priorities, ensure compliance, and drive growth, all while navigating an ever-changing business landscape. To thrive in this role, CFOs must be adaptable, forward-thinking, and willing to embrace change.

In conclusion, the evolution of the CFO role reflects the dynamic nature of the business world. From financial steward to strategic leader, the modern CFO is a multifaceted professional tasked with ensuring organisational success. By embracing technological advancements, understanding global markets, and aligning with societal expectations, CFOs are uniquely positioned to drive growth and innovation.

1.2 - Strategic vs. Operational CFOs

The distinction between strategic and operational CFOs is a useful framework for understanding the diverse approaches CFOs can take in fulfilling their responsibilities. While these two orientations are not mutually exclusive, they represent different focuses that can significantly influence how a CFO contributes to an organisation's success. Strategic CFOs prioritise long-term planning, innovation, and growth, while operational CFOs concentrate on ensuring day-to-day financial processes run smoothly and efficiently.

An operational CFO is often described as the "guardian of the numbers." This type of CFO thrives in environments where efficiency, accuracy, and control are paramount. Operational CFOs are deeply involved in the mechanics of financial management, overseeing activities such as budgeting, cash flow management, and compliance. Their primary focus is on maintaining stability and ensuring that the organisation operates within its financial means. For instance, an operational CFO in a logistics company might implement a detailed cost-control programme to improve profitability. Their success is often measured in terms of operational efficiency, such as reducing overhead costs or improving the accuracy of financial reporting.

In contrast, strategic CFOs are forward-looking, with a strong emphasis on aligning financial goals with the organisation's broader objectives. These CFOs often work closely with the CEO and other executives to identify growth opportunities, mitigate risks, and drive value creation. For example, a strategic CFO at a technology firm might lead an initiative to secure venture capital funding, presenting a compelling vision of the company's future to potential investors. Strategic CFOs are often seen as innovators, using financial data to inform decisions that shape the organisation's trajectory.

The ability to balance these two perspectives, strategic and operational, is what sets exceptional CFOs apart. Consider the case of Anna, the CFO of a mid-sized retail chain. When Anna joined the company, she identified inefficiencies in the supply chain that were causing unnecessary expenses. By adopting an operational focus, she streamlined processes and negotiated better terms with suppliers, achieving significant cost savings. Once the organisation's finances stabilised, Anna shifted her focus to strategy, spearheading an e-commerce initiative that allowed the company to expand its market reach and increase revenue by 40% over three years.

However, the dual nature of the CFO role can be challenging to navigate. Operational CFOs may find it difficult to step back from immediate financial concerns to think strategically, while strategic CFOs might overlook critical operational details. To address this, many organisations encourage CFOs to develop a flexible approach, adjusting their focus based on the company's needs. Building a strong finance team is another crucial strategy, as it allows CFOs to delegate operational tasks and concentrate on higher-level initiatives.

It's also important to recognise that an organisation's stage of development often dictates whether it needs a more operational or strategic CFO. Startups, for example, may require a strategic CFO to secure funding and drive growth, while established companies in highly regulated industries might benefit from an operational CFO who can ensure compliance and maintain stability.

In conclusion, the distinction between strategic and operational CFOs highlights the diverse ways CFOs can contribute to organisational success. While some CFOs naturally gravitate towards one approach, the best CFOs are those who can adapt their focus to meet the needs of their organisation. By balancing operational efficiency with strategic vision, CFOs can ensure both short-term stability and long-term growth.

1.3 - Key Skills Every CFO Needs

The modern CFO role demands a wide-ranging skill set that extends far beyond financial expertise. While a deep understanding of finance and accounting remains essential, today's CFOs must also master strategic thinking, leadership, and adaptability. They are not only responsible for ensuring financial stability but also for driving innovation, managing risks, and shaping the organisation's long-term vision. Developing these skills is critical for aspiring CFOs who wish to navigate the complexities of this dynamic role.

At the heart of every successful CFO's skill set lies financial expertise. This includes mastery of accounting principles, financial reporting standards, and regulatory compliance. CFOs must be able to interpret complex financial data, identify trends, and use these insights to inform decision-making. For instance, a CFO at a retail company might analyse revenue patterns to determine the profitability of individual store locations. By leveraging this financial acumen, they can make recommendations on whether to expand, relocate, or close specific outlets.

However, financial knowledge alone is no longer sufficient. Strategic thinking is increasingly a cornerstone of the CFO role. A modern CFO must look beyond the numbers, considering broader market dynamics, competitive landscapes, and long-term business objectives. This requires the ability to see the "big picture" and connect financial insights with overall strategy. For example, a CFO in the pharmaceutical industry might analyse trends in healthcare regulations and use this knowledge to guide investment in research and development, ensuring the company remains competitive.

In the digital age, technological proficiency is another indispensable skill. CFOs must be comfortable using advanced financial tools and technologies, such as enterprise resource planning (ERP) systems, data analytics platforms, and artificial intelligence. These tools enable CFOs to automate routine tasks, improve forecasting accuracy, and identify opportunities for efficiency. For instance, a CFO might use AI-powered analytics to predict customer purchasing behaviour, helping the marketing team tailor campaigns and maximise return on investment.

Beyond technical skills, leadership and communication are crucial for CFOs, as they often work closely with diverse stakeholders. They must inspire confidence in their teams, build strong relationships with the C-suite, and effectively communicate financial information to non-financial audiences. Consider Jane, a CFO at a mid-sized manufacturing firm, who successfully implemented a new budgeting system despite initial resistance. By clearly explaining the benefits, addressing concerns, and providing comprehensive training, she gained buy-in from her team and ensured a smooth transition.

Another essential trait for modern CFOs is adaptability and resilience. The business environment is constantly changing, and CFOs must be prepared to navigate economic downturns, technological disruptions, and shifting stakeholder expectations. During the COVID-19 pandemic, for example, many CFOs played a central role in crisis management, ensuring liquidity, managing costs, and helping their organisations adapt to new market realities.

Finally, ethical integrity is a non-negotiable quality for any CFO. As the guardians of an organisation's financial health, CFOs must uphold the highest standards of transparency and honesty. This includes fostering a culture of accountability and ensuring that all financial practices align with legal and ethical guidelines. Ethical lapses, as demonstrated by high-profile scandals like Enron, can have devastating consequences for both the organisation and its leaders.

Developing these skills requires a combination of education, experience, and continuous learning. Traditional qualifications such as a Certified Public Accountant (CPA) or Chartered Financial Analyst (CFA) designation provide a strong foundation in finance, while an MBA can help aspiring CFOs build leadership and strategic skills. Gaining cross-functional experience, working in departments like operations, marketing, or IT, can also provide valuable insights into the broader business landscape.

In conclusion, the key skills required for modern CFOs go far beyond financial expertise. By mastering strategic thinking, technological proficiency, leadership, adaptability, and ethical integrity, CFOs can position themselves as indispensable leaders within their organisations. These skills not only enable CFOs to navigate current challenges but also empower them to drive innovation and shape the future of their businesses.

1.4 - Understanding Financial Statements

A comprehensive understanding of financial statements is fundamental to the CFO role. These documents provide a snapshot of an organisation's financial health, enabling leaders to make informed decisions and communicate performance to stakeholders. While many CFOs come from accounting or finance backgrounds, the ability to interpret and leverage financial statements effectively remains one of the most critical aspects of their responsibilities.

The balance sheet is perhaps the most well-known financial statement, offering a detailed view of an organisation's assets, liabilities, and equity at a specific point in time. This document helps CFOs assess the organisation's financial position and determine its capacity to meet short-term and long-term obligations. For example, a CFO evaluating a company's liquidity might examine current assets like cash and accounts receivable against current liabilities such as accounts payable. By doing so, they can identify potential cash flow challenges and take proactive measures to address them.

The income statement, also known as the profit and loss statement, provides an overview of revenues, expenses, and net income over a specific period. This document is essential for evaluating profitability and operational performance. A CFO at a service-based company, for instance, might use the income statement to identify which service lines are the most profitable and allocate resources accordingly. By analysing trends in revenue and expenses, they can also identify opportunities for cost reduction or revenue growth.

The cash flow statement is equally vital, offering insights into how cash flows into and out of the organisation. Unlike the income statement, which includes non-cash items such as depreciation, the cash flow statement focuses solely on actual cash transactions. This document is particularly important for CFOs managing liquidity and ensuring the organisation has enough cash to fund operations, investments, and debt obligations. For example, a CFO in the retail industry might use the cash flow statement to plan inventory purchases during peak sales seasons, ensuring they have adequate stock without overextending resources.

In addition to these primary financial statements, CFOs often rely on supplementary reports such as the statement of changes in equity and financial ratio analyses. These tools provide additional context, helping CFOs assess performance and benchmark against industry standards.

Interpreting financial statements is only part of the equation. CFOs must also use this information to guide strategic decision-making. For instance, if the balance sheet reveals a high level of debt, the CFO might prioritise debt repayment to improve the company's financial stability. Alternatively, if the income statement shows declining margins, the CFO could investigate potential inefficiencies in the supply chain or pricing strategy.

Communicating financial insights to non-financial stakeholders is another critical aspect of this responsibility. CFOs must translate complex data into clear, actionable insights, ensuring that board members, investors, and other leaders understand the organisation's financial performance and its implications. Visual aids like charts and graphs can be particularly effective in simplifying complex information.

In conclusion, financial statements are the foundation of the CFO's work, providing the data needed to assess financial health, drive strategy, and communicate with stakeholders. A deep understanding of these documents enables CFOs to make informed decisions, anticipate challenges, and seize opportunities. By mastering the art of financial analysis and interpretation, CFOs can ensure their organisations remain financially sound and strategically positioned for success.

1.5 - Financial Reporting and Compliance Basics

Financial reporting and compliance are fundamental to the role of a CFO, serving as the bedrock of trust between an organisation and its stakeholders. In an increasingly regulated and transparent business environment, ensuring accurate and timely financial reporting is not just a legal obligation but also a strategic necessity. CFOs play a pivotal role in maintaining the integrity of financial information, ensuring that their organisation adheres to both internal policies and external regulatory frameworks.

At its core, financial reporting involves preparing and presenting financial statements that provide a clear picture of an organisation's financial health. These reports include the balance sheet, income statement, and cash flow statement, along with accompanying disclosures. Together, they allow stakeholders, such as investors, board members, and regulators, to assess the organisation's performance and make informed decisions. For example, a CFO might oversee the preparation of quarterly financial reports for shareholders, ensuring they comply with International Financial Reporting Standards (IFRS) or Generally Accepted Accounting Principles (GAAP), depending on the organisation's jurisdiction.

Compliance, on the other hand, refers to adhering to the laws, regulations, and standards that govern financial practices. These regulations vary across industries and regions but often include requirements for transparency, accuracy, and ethical conduct. In the UK, for instance, CFOs must ensure compliance with the Companies Act 2006 and other regulations enforced by bodies such as the Financial Reporting Council (FRC). Failure to meet these requirements can lead to legal penalties, reputational damage, and loss of investor confidence.

One of the most significant challenges in financial reporting and compliance is the complexity of modern regulations. Frameworks such as Sarbanes-Oxley (SOX) in the United States or GDPR in the European Union require organisations to implement robust internal controls and ensure the security of financial data. For CFOs, this means not only understanding these regulations but also embedding them into the organisation's processes. A practical example would be a CFO at a multinational corporation implementing a comprehensive compliance programme to manage the differing tax and reporting requirements across various countries.

Technology plays an increasingly important role in simplifying and improving financial reporting and compliance. Automated systems can reduce the risk of human error, streamline data collection, and ensure consistency across reports. For instance, enterprise resource planning (ERP) software can integrate financial data from different departments, enabling CFOs to produce consolidated reports with greater efficiency. Additionally, data analytics tools can help identify anomalies or trends, assisting in the early detection of potential compliance risks.

However, technology alone cannot guarantee compliance. CFOs must also cultivate a culture of accountability within their organisation. This involves training staff on regulatory requirements, encouraging ethical behaviour, and establishing clear policies and procedures. Regular internal audits can further strengthen compliance efforts by identifying weaknesses and ensuring continuous improvement.

An illustrative case is that of Sarah, the CFO of a rapidly growing tech company. When the company decided to go public, Sarah faced the daunting task of ensuring compliance with new regulatory requirements, including SOX. By investing in automated systems, hiring specialised compliance staff, and working closely with external auditors, Sarah successfully navigated the transition, earning the trust of investors and positioning the company for long-term success.

In conclusion, financial reporting and compliance are indispensable responsibilities for CFOs, underpinning the organisation's reputation and operational success. By combining technical expertise, strategic oversight, and a commitment to ethical practices, CFOs can ensure their organisation meets its obligations while building trust with stakeholders. In a world of increasing scrutiny and complexity, this aspect of the CFO's role is more critical than ever.

1.6 - Ethics and Integrity in Finance

Ethics and integrity are at the heart of the CFO's role, underpinning every decision and action they take. As stewards of an organisation's financial health, CFOs are entrusted with safeguarding not only the company's resources but also its reputation. In an era of heightened scrutiny and public accountability, a strong ethical foundation is essential for maintaining stakeholder trust and ensuring long-term sustainability.

The importance of ethics in finance cannot be overstated. CFOs are often faced with decisions that test their moral compass, from choosing whether to disclose unfavourable financial results to navigating conflicts of interest. Ethical lapses, such as manipulating earnings or engaging in insider trading, can have devastating consequences for both the organisation and its leaders. The collapse of companies like Enron and Lehman Brothers serves as a stark reminder of what can happen when ethical standards are compromised.

Integrity in finance begins with transparency. CFOs must ensure that financial reports accurately reflect the organisation's performance without omissions or distortions. This transparency builds trust with investors, employees, and regulators, creating a foundation for sustainable success. For instance, a CFO who discovers an accounting error in a previous financial report must prioritise correcting the mistake and disclosing it to stakeholders, even if it leads to short-term reputational challenges.

Ethical leadership also involves fostering a culture of accountability within the organisation. CFOs must lead by example, demonstrating a commitment to ethical principles in their own behaviour. This includes setting clear expectations for their teams, providing training on ethical practices, and encouraging employees to speak up when they encounter unethical conduct. Whistleblower protections are particularly important in this regard, as they empower employees to report concerns without fear of retaliation.

One of the most challenging aspects of maintaining integrity in finance is navigating grey areas where ethical guidelines are not clearly defined. For example, a CFO may face pressure from executives or board members to take aggressive tax positions that, while legal, may be viewed as ethically questionable. In such situations, CFOs must weigh the potential benefits against the risks to the organisation's reputation and stakeholder trust. Engaging in open dialogue with other leaders and seeking external advice can help ensure balanced decision-making.

Technology has introduced new ethical considerations for CFOs, particularly in areas like data privacy and cybersecurity. As organisations collect and store increasing amounts of financial and personal data, CFOs must ensure that this information is handled responsibly and securely. Failure to protect sensitive data can result in significant legal and reputational repercussions, as demonstrated by high-profile breaches in recent years.

A compelling example of ethical leadership is John, the CFO of a global manufacturing company. When John discovered that a subsidiary had been inflating sales figures to meet performance targets, he took swift action. Despite resistance from local management, John reported the issue to the board and initiated an internal investigation. His decision not only resolved the immediate problem but also reinforced the company's commitment to integrity, earning the respect of stakeholders.

In conclusion, ethics and integrity are central to the CFO's role, shaping how they approach decisions and interact with stakeholders. By prioritising transparency, accountability, and ethical leadership, CFOs can build trust, navigate challenges, and ensure their organisation's long-term success. In an increasingly complex and interconnected world, these qualities are more important than ever.

1.7 - Relationship Management with the C-Suite

The role of the CFO extends far beyond managing financial data and ensuring compliance; it is also deeply rooted in fostering collaborative relationships with other members of the C-suite. The effectiveness of a CFO often hinges on their ability to build trust, communicate clearly, and align financial strategies with the organisation's overarching goals. Relationship management within the C-suite is not just a professional necessity; it is a cornerstone of effective leadership and organisational success.

At the heart of these relationships is the CFO's partnership with the Chief Executive Officer (CEO). The CEO relies on the CFO to provide a clear and accurate picture of the company's financial health, enabling informed decision-making. This relationship must be built on mutual trust, as the CFO often acts as the CEO's strategic advisor, offering insights into the financial implications of business decisions. For example, when a CEO is considering expanding into a new market, the CFO's role is to evaluate the financial risks and opportunities, ensuring that the decision aligns with the organisation's long-term strategy.

However, trust does not develop overnight. It requires consistent communication, transparency, and a shared vision for the organisation. A CFO who can articulate complex financial data in a way that resonates with the CEO and the rest of the executive team can bridge the gap between strategy and execution. For instance, when presenting financial projections for a new product line, a CFO might use visual aids, such as charts and graphs, to make the data more accessible and compelling.

The CFO's relationship with the Chief Operating Officer (COO) is equally critical, as these two roles often intersect in areas like cost management, resource allocation, and operational efficiency. A strong partnership between the CFO and COO ensures that financial strategies are grounded in operational realities. Consider the example of a CFO and COO at a manufacturing firm working together to optimise supply chain costs. While the COO identifies process inefficiencies, the CFO evaluates the financial impact of potential improvements, creating a synergy that drives both efficiency and profitability.

Another key relationship is with the Chief Marketing Officer (CMO). While finance and marketing may seem like disparate functions, they are closely intertwined when it comes to resource allocation and measuring return on investment (ROI). A CFO who collaborates effectively with the CMO can ensure that marketing budgets are aligned with the organisation's financial goals. For instance, by analysing the ROI of different marketing campaigns, the CFO can provide data-driven recommendations on where to focus future efforts, enhancing the effectiveness of marketing spend.

The Chief Information Officer (CIO) is also a critical ally for the CFO, especially in today's technology-driven business environment. As organisations increasingly rely on data analytics, cybersecurity, and digital transformation, the CFO and CIO must work together to ensure that technology investments deliver value. For example, a CFO and CIO might collaborate to implement an enterprise resource planning (ERP) system, balancing the initial investment against the long-term benefits of improved data accuracy and operational efficiency.

Building strong relationships within the C-suite requires a combination of technical expertise and interpersonal skills. CFOs must be able to listen actively, understand the priorities of their colleagues, and adapt their communication style to different audiences. For instance, while a CEO may appreciate high-level financial summaries, a COO might prefer detailed breakdowns of operational costs.

Challenges in relationship management often arise from misaligned goals or communication gaps. A CFO who prioritises cost-cutting, for example, may clash with a CMO focused on increasing brand visibility through significant marketing spend. To navigate these conflicts, CFOs must adopt a collaborative mindset, seeking common ground and emphasising shared objectives. Regular C-suite meetings, where leaders openly discuss priorities and challenges, can foster alignment and minimise misunderstandings.

A compelling example of effective relationship management is Sarah, the CFO of a fast-growing e-commerce company. When the company faced liquidity challenges during a period of rapid expansion, Sarah worked closely with the CEO, COO, and CIO to develop a comprehensive plan. She collaborated with the COO to streamline logistics, with the CIO to implement cost-saving technologies, and with the CEO to secure additional funding. By leveraging her relationships across the C-suite, Sarah not only resolved the immediate crisis but also positioned the company for sustained growth.

In conclusion, relationship management with the C-suite is a vital aspect of the CFO's role, enabling collaboration, alignment, and shared success. By building trust, communicating effectively, and understanding the priorities of their colleagues, CFOs can bridge functional silos and drive organisational performance. In today's complex and interconnected business environment, these relationships are more important than ever.

1.8 - The CFO's Role in Corporate Governance

Corporate governance is the system by which organisations are directed and controlled, encompassing the processes, policies, and structures that ensure accountability, transparency, and ethical behaviour. As a key member of the executive team, the CFO plays a central role in upholding these principles, ensuring that financial practices align with the organisation's values and objectives. The CFO's responsibilities in corporate governance extend beyond compliance; they include shaping the organisation's culture, managing risks, and fostering trust with stakeholders.

One of the CFO's primary contributions to corporate governance is financial oversight. By ensuring the accuracy and integrity of financial reporting, the CFO provides stakeholders with a clear and reliable picture of the organisation's performance. This transparency is critical for building trust with investors, regulators, and the board of directors. For example, a CFO who oversees the preparation of annual financial statements must ensure that they comply with relevant accounting standards and reflect the organisation's true financial position.

Another key aspect of corporate governance is risk management, an area where the CFO plays a pivotal role. From financial risks like currency fluctuations and credit exposure to broader operational risks, the CFO is responsible for identifying, assessing, and mitigating potential threats to the organisation. For instance, a CFO at a multinational corporation might implement hedging strategies to minimise the impact of currency volatility on earnings.

The CFO is also a critical link between the board of directors and the executive team. As the primary financial spokesperson, the CFO must present financial information to the board in a way that supports informed decision-making. This requires not only technical expertise but also the ability to communicate complex data clearly and concisely. A CFO who can articulate the financial implications of strategic decisions, such as acquiring a competitor or entering a new market, helps the board fulfil its governance responsibilities effectively.

Ethical leadership is another cornerstone of the CFO's role in corporate governance. By setting the tone at the top, the CFO influences the organisation's culture and ensures that ethical considerations are embedded in decision-making processes.

For instance, a CFO who discovers irregularities in financial reporting must act swiftly to address the issue, demonstrating a commitment to integrity and accountability.

Corporate governance also involves balancing the interests of various stakeholders, including shareholders, employees, customers, and the broader community. The CFO must navigate these sometimes-competing interests, ensuring that the organisation's financial strategies align with its long-term goals and societal responsibilities. This is particularly relevant in the context of environmental, social, and governance (ESG) initiatives, where CFOs are increasingly called upon to demonstrate how financial practices support sustainable growth.

In conclusion, the CFO's role in corporate governance is multifaceted, encompassing financial oversight, risk management, ethical leadership, and stakeholder engagement. By upholding the principles of accountability and transparency, CFOs not only protect the organisation's reputation but also contribute to its long-term success. As expectations around governance continue to evolve, the CFO's role in this area will only grow in importance.

1.9 - Setting Financial Goals for the Organisation

Setting financial goals is one of the most strategic responsibilities of a CFO. These goals provide a roadmap for the organisation, guiding decision-making, resource allocation, and performance measurement. Effective financial goal-setting requires a deep understanding of the company's overall strategy, its current financial position, and the external factors that influence its operations. By aligning financial objectives with broader organisational aims, the CFO ensures that the company is well-positioned for both short-term stability and long-term growth.

Financial goals can take various forms, including revenue targets, profitability benchmarks, cash flow objectives, and investment priorities. While these goals may differ depending on the organisation's size, industry, and growth stage, they all serve a common purpose: to provide clarity and focus for the organisation's financial efforts. For example, a startup in the technology sector might prioritise securing funding and achieving rapid revenue growth, while an established manufacturing firm might focus on improving operational efficiency and maintaining consistent profit margins.

The process of setting financial goals begins with a thorough assessment of the organisation's financial health. This involves analysing key financial metrics, such as liquidity ratios, debt levels, and profit margins, to identify strengths and weaknesses. For instance, if an analysis reveals that the company has a high debt-to-equity ratio, the CFO might set a goal to reduce debt by reallocating resources or increasing revenue. Conversely, if the company has excess cash reserves, the CFO might explore opportunities for investment or expansion.

Once the organisation's financial position has been assessed, the CFO must consider external factors that could impact goal-setting. These include market trends, economic conditions, and competitive dynamics. For example, a CFO in the retail sector might set sales targets based on projected consumer spending patterns while also accounting for potential disruptions, such as supply chain delays or changes in consumer behaviour.

Collaboration is a critical element of financial goal-setting. The CFO must work closely with other members of the executive team to ensure that financial objectives are aligned with departmental priorities and the company's overall mission. For instance, the CFO might collaborate with the Chief Marketing Officer to set a budget for advertising campaigns, ensuring that marketing spending aligns with revenue targets. Similarly, the CFO might partner with the Chief Operating Officer to identify cost-saving opportunities within the supply chain.

Communication is equally important. Once financial goals have been established, the CFO must clearly articulate these objectives to stakeholders, including employees, investors, and board members. This involves not only outlining the goals themselves but also explaining the rationale behind them and the strategies for achieving them. For example, a CFO might present a plan to increase profitability by optimising pricing strategies, providing data to support their recommendations and addressing potential challenges.

One of the challenges of setting financial goals is balancing short-term and long-term priorities. While short-term goals, such as meeting quarterly earnings targets, are essential for maintaining stakeholder confidence, long-term goals, such as investing in research and development, are crucial for ensuring sustainable growth. The CFO must navigate this tension, making decisions that strike an appropriate balance between immediate needs and future aspirations.

Another challenge is managing uncertainty. Financial goals are often influenced by factors beyond the organisation's control, such as economic downturns or regulatory changes. To address this, CFOs must build flexibility into their goal-setting process, allowing for adjustments as circumstances evolve. For example, during the COVID-19 pandemic, many CFOs revised their financial goals to prioritise liquidity and cost management, enabling their organisations to weather the crisis.

A compelling example of effective financial goal-setting is that of Tom, the CFO of a mid-sized technology company. When Tom joined the organisation, he conducted a comprehensive financial analysis that revealed high customer acquisition costs and declining margins. Based on this assessment, he set three key goals: reduce acquisition costs by 20% over the next year, improve gross margins by optimising the pricing structure, and achieve 15% revenue growth through expansion into new markets. By collaborating with the marketing and sales teams, Tom developed a detailed action plan that included targeted advertising campaigns and product bundling strategies. Within 18 months, the company had exceeded its goals, achieving sustainable growth and improved profitability.

In conclusion, setting financial goals is a vital function of the CFO, providing direction and focus for the organisation's financial efforts. By combining rigorous analysis, strategic collaboration, and effective communication, CFOs can establish objectives that drive both short-term success and long-term growth. While the process is not without its challenges, a well-executed goal-setting strategy can position the organisation for lasting success.

1.10 - Overview of the CFO Career Path

The journey to becoming a CFO is one of dedication, learning, and strategic career progression. While there is no single path to this coveted position, most CFOs share a common trajectory that includes a blend of education, professional experience, and leadership development. Understanding the typical career path of a CFO can help aspiring finance professionals map out their own journey and identify the skills and experiences they need to succeed.

The foundation of a CFO's career often begins with formal education in finance, accounting, or business. Many CFOs hold degrees in fields such as economics, accounting, or business administration, which provide a strong grounding in financial principles and analytical skills. Advanced qualifications, such as a Chartered Accountant (CA), Certified Public Accountant (CPA), or Chartered Financial Analyst (CFA) certification, are also common, as they demonstrate technical expertise and a commitment to professional development. Additionally, many CFOs pursue an MBA to enhance their strategic thinking and leadership capabilities.

After completing their education, aspiring CFOs typically gain experience in entry-level roles within finance or accounting, such as financial analyst, auditor, or management accountant. These positions provide opportunities to develop technical skills, such as financial reporting, budgeting, and forecasting, while also offering insights into the inner workings of an organisation. For example, a financial analyst might work on creating detailed reports that help senior leaders make data-driven decisions, gaining exposure to the strategic aspects of financial management.

As they progress in their careers, finance professionals often take on mid-level roles, such as finance manager, controller, or head of financial planning and analysis (FP&A). These positions involve greater responsibility, including overseeing teams, managing budgets, and contributing to strategic planning. For instance, a controller might be responsible for ensuring the accuracy of the organisation's financial statements while also working closely with senior leaders to identify opportunities for cost savings or revenue growth.

Leadership experience is a critical component of the CFO's career path. Many aspiring CFOs seek opportunities to lead cross-functional teams, collaborate with other departments, and contribute to major organisational initiatives. These experiences not only demonstrate leadership potential but also provide a broader perspective on the business, which is essential for the CFO role. For example, a finance director who leads a company-wide digital transformation project gains valuable insights into technology implementation, change management, and stakeholder engagement.

Cross-functional experience is another important aspect of the CFO career path. CFOs must understand how finance interacts with other areas of the business, such as operations, marketing, and technology. Aspiring CFOs who take on roles that involve working closely with these functions are better prepared to provide strategic advice and drive organisational success. For example, a finance professional who collaborates with the marketing team on a product pricing strategy develops a deeper understanding of customer behaviour and market dynamics.

The final step on the path to becoming a CFO is often a senior leadership role, such as vice president of finance or chief operating officer (COO). These positions provide the opportunity to refine leadership skills, gain exposure to the board of directors, and develop a strategic vision for the organisation. By the time they step into the CFO role, these professionals have a well-rounded skill set that encompasses technical expertise, strategic thinking, and leadership ability.

While the path to becoming a CFO is demanding, it is also highly rewarding. CFOs have the opportunity to shape the direction of their organisations, drive innovation, and make a lasting impact. For aspiring CFOs, the key to success lies in continuous learning, building strong relationships, and seeking out opportunities to develop both technical and leadership skills. By taking a proactive and strategic approach to their career development, finance professionals can position themselves to achieve their goals and excel in this critical role.

Chapter 2

Mastering Financial Planning and Analysis (FP&A)

"The true power of FP&A lies not in the numbers it generates, but in the decisions it enables."
Robert N. Jacobs

In today's dynamic business environment, mastering Financial Planning and Analysis (FP&A) is no longer a supplemental skill for CFOs; it is an essential discipline that shapes strategic decisions, drives operational excellence, and ensures financial resilience. This chapter delves into the tools, techniques, and best practices that enable financial leaders to go beyond managing numbers to forecasting the future, aligning plans with business goals, and empowering data-driven decision-making. This chapter equips readers with a comprehensive understanding of FP&A's role as the connective tissue between strategy and execution, highlighting its transformative impact on organisational success.

2.1 - Introduction to FP&A

Financial Planning and Analysis (FP&A) is a cornerstone of modern financial management, providing organisations with the tools to align their financial strategies with broader business goals. FP&A goes beyond traditional accounting and reporting by focusing on forward-looking activities such as forecasting, budgeting, and strategic decision support. For CFOs, mastering FP&A is essential, as it enables them to drive financial discipline, inform decision-making, and support long-term growth.

The origins of FP&A can be traced to the increasing complexity of global business environments. As organisations expanded into new markets and faced growing competition, they needed more sophisticated methods to manage their resources and anticipate challenges. Unlike traditional financial reporting, which focuses on historical data, FP&A takes a proactive approach, analysing trends and creating predictive models to guide decision-making.

A key feature of FP&A is its dynamic nature. While a static budget might serve as a financial plan for the year, FP&A processes are continuous, allowing organisations to adapt to changing circumstances. For example, if a company's revenue projections fall short due to an unexpected market downturn, the FP&A team can revise forecasts, identify areas for cost reduction, and recommend strategies to mitigate the impact.

The FP&A function also serves as a bridge between finance and other departments. By working closely with teams such as marketing, operations, and sales, FP&A professionals ensure that financial plans are informed by operational realities and aligned with organisational goals. This collaborative approach fosters a culture of accountability, as all departments understand how their activities contribute to the organisation's financial success.

One of the defining characteristics of FP&A is its reliance on data. Modern FP&A teams use advanced analytics tools to process vast amounts of information, identify trends, and generate insights. For instance, an FP&A team at a retail company might analyse customer purchasing patterns to predict future demand, enabling the organisation to optimise inventory levels and pricing strategies. This data-driven approach not only improves accuracy but also enhances the organisation's ability to respond to market changes.

Technology has played a transformative role in FP&A, enabling greater efficiency and accuracy. Tools such as Tableau, Power BI, and dedicated FP&A platforms allow finance teams to visualise data, model scenarios, and track performance in real-time. These tools empower CFOs to make informed decisions based on up-to-date information rather than relying on outdated reports.

However, the effectiveness of FP&A depends on more than just technology. Successful FP&A requires strong leadership, analytical skills, and an understanding of both financial and operational dynamics. CFOs must ensure that their FP&A teams are equipped with the right skills and resources, fostering a culture of continuous improvement.

In conclusion, FP&A is a vital function that enables organisations to navigate complexity, anticipate challenges, and achieve their financial goals. For CFOs, mastering FP&A is not just a technical requirement, it is a strategic imperative. By leveraging data, fostering collaboration, and embracing technology, CFOs can use FP&A to drive financial performance and support sustainable growth.

2.2 - Budgeting Techniques and Best Practices

Budgeting is the financial cornerstone of any organisation, providing a structured plan for managing resources, controlling costs, and aligning spending with strategic objectives. While it is a fundamental process in financial management, effective budgeting is far more than a routine exercise, it is a dynamic tool that helps organisations navigate uncertainty, seize opportunities, and achieve their goals. For CFOs, mastering advanced budgeting techniques and best practices is critical to ensuring the organisation remains financially disciplined while fostering growth.

Budgeting serves multiple purposes within an organisation. First, it establishes financial boundaries, ensuring that resources are allocated efficiently and effectively. It also provides a mechanism for monitoring performance, enabling leaders to compare actual results against planned objectives and make adjustments as needed. Perhaps most importantly, budgeting fosters accountability across departments, creating a shared understanding of financial priorities and responsibilities.

There are several approaches to budgeting, each suited to different organisational needs. One of the most widely used methods is incremental budgeting, which involves adjusting the previous year's budget to reflect changes in revenue, expenses, or strategic priorities. While this approach is simple and efficient, it can perpetuate inefficiencies by assuming that past spending patterns are the best predictor of future needs.

In contrast, zero-based budgeting (ZBB) starts from a blank slate, requiring each department to justify every expense for each budget cycle. This method can uncover hidden inefficiencies and eliminate unnecessary spending, making it particularly valuable for organisations seeking to optimise costs. For instance, a CFO at a manufacturing company might use ZBB to identify overlapping software subscriptions across departments, consolidating them to reduce expenses without sacrificing functionality. However, ZBB is also resource-intensive, requiring significant time and effort to implement effectively.

Another advanced approach is activity-based budgeting (ABB), which links spending to specific activities and their associated costs. ABB provides greater transparency into how funds are used and helps organisations align spending with strategic goals. For example, a retail company might use ABB to allocate funds for marketing campaigns based on projected revenue generation, ensuring that resources are focused on high-impact activities.

The effectiveness of any budgeting approach depends on the organisation's ability to integrate it into a broader strategic framework. Collaboration is key; successful budgeting requires input from all departments to ensure that financial plans are realistic, comprehensive, and aligned with operational realities.

For instance, a CFO might work closely with the Chief Marketing Officer to set a marketing budget that balances brand-building initiatives with revenue generation. Similarly, the CFO might partner with the Chief Operating Officer to identify cost-saving opportunities within the supply chain.

One of the most significant challenges in budgeting is managing uncertainty. Economic conditions, market dynamics, and organisational changes can all disrupt financial plans. To address this, many CFOs incorporate scenario planning into the budgeting process, developing multiple budgets based on different assumptions. For example, a CFO at a logistics company might create "best-case," "worst-case," and "base-case" budgets, allowing the organisation to adjust its spending quickly if fuel prices rise unexpectedly or demand fluctuates.

Technology plays a vital role in modern budgeting, enabling greater accuracy, efficiency, and flexibility. Software tools such as Adaptive Insights, Anaplan, and Workday provide CFOs with powerful platforms for automating calculations, tracking spending in real-time, and identifying variances in the budget. These tools also enhance collaboration by providing a centralised platform where stakeholders can contribute data, review plans, and monitor progress.

Despite its technical nature, budgeting is as much about communication as it is about numbers. CFOs must ensure that their teams understand the rationale behind the budget, fostering a sense of shared ownership over financial goals.

Transparent communication also helps manage expectations, particularly during periods of financial constraint. For instance, a CFO might hold regular meetings with department heads to explain budgetary decisions, address concerns, and reinforce the organisation's commitment to achieving its objectives.

A compelling example of effective budgeting is Amanda, the CFO of a mid-sized technology company. Facing declining profitability, Amanda implemented a zero-based budgeting approach to identify inefficiencies across the organisation. By closely examining every expense, she discovered opportunities to streamline operations, reduce overhead costs, and reinvest savings into high-growth areas such as product development. Within two years, the company not only returned to profitability but also gained a competitive edge in the market.

In conclusion, budgeting is both a science and an art, requiring technical expertise, strategic insight, and effective communication. By mastering advanced techniques and adopting best practices, CFOs can create budgets that serve as powerful tools for driving organisational success. Whether managing day-to-day expenses or planning for long-term growth, a well-constructed budget is an indispensable asset in navigating the complexities of modern business.

2.3 - Forecasting Fundamentals

Forecasting is a cornerstone of financial planning, enabling organisations to anticipate future conditions, align resources with objectives, and navigate uncertainty with confidence. Unlike budgeting, which sets a fixed plan for a specific period, forecasting is a dynamic process that provides ongoing insights into the organisation's financial trajectory. For CFOs, mastering the fundamentals of forecasting is essential, as it forms the basis for informed decision-making and strategic agility.

At its core, forecasting involves projecting key financial metrics, such as revenue, expenses, and cash flow, over a defined time frame. These projections are based on a combination of historical data, current trends, and forward-looking assumptions. While forecasting may seem straightforward, its accuracy and value depend on the quality of the underlying data, the validity of the assumptions, and the methodologies used.

There are several types of financial forecasts, each serving a distinct purpose within the organisation. Short-term forecasts, typically covering one to three months, focus on immediate operational needs, such as cash flow management or inventory planning. For instance, a CFO at a retail company might use a short-term forecast to ensure sufficient liquidity during the holiday season, when sales and expenses are expected to spike.

Medium-term forecasts, spanning six to twelve months, align closely with the organisation's annual financial goals. These forecasts provide a framework for monitoring progress, identifying variances, and making adjustments as needed. For example, a CFO at a pharmaceutical company might use a medium-term forecast to track the performance of a newly launched drug, adjusting marketing spend or production levels based on early sales data.

Long-term forecasts, covering periods of three to five years or more, are inherently strategic. These forecasts guide high-level decisions, such as market expansion, capital investments, or mergers and acquisitions. For example, a CFO in the renewable energy sector might develop a long-term forecast to evaluate the financial feasibility of building a new solar farm, incorporating assumptions about energy prices, government incentives, and technological advancements.

The process of forecasting requires a careful balance of art and science. On the one hand, forecasts must be grounded in data, using quantitative methods to analyse trends and predict outcomes. On the other hand, they must account for qualitative factors, such as market dynamics, regulatory changes, and competitive pressures. For instance, a CFO projecting revenue growth for a luxury goods retailer might consider not only historical sales data but also emerging trends in consumer behaviour and economic conditions.

One of the key challenges in forecasting is managing uncertainty. External factors such as economic downturns, geopolitical events, and technological disruptions can significantly impact financial performance, making accurate forecasting difficult. To address this, many CFOs employ scenario analysis, creating multiple forecasts based on different assumptions. For example, a CFO at an automotive manufacturer might develop separate forecasts for scenarios where raw material prices increase, decrease, or remain stable.

Technology has revolutionised the forecasting process, enabling CFOs to leverage advanced analytics and machine learning to enhance accuracy and efficiency. Tools such as Tableau, Power BI, and specialised forecasting software allow finance teams to process vast amounts of data, identify patterns, and generate actionable insights. For instance, a CFO using predictive analytics might identify early signs of a slowdown in customer demand, enabling the organisation to adjust its strategy proactively.

Collaboration is another critical element of effective forecasting. CFOs must engage with leaders across departments to gather accurate data, understand operational priorities, and ensure alignment with strategic goals. For example, a CFO might collaborate with the Chief Sales Officer to refine revenue projections, incorporating insights from the sales pipeline into the forecast.

In conclusion, forecasting is an indispensable tool for driving organisational success, providing the insights needed to anticipate challenges, capitalise on opportunities, and make informed decisions. By mastering the fundamentals of forecasting, leveraging technology, and fostering collaboration, CFOs can ensure their organisations remain agile and resilient in an ever-changing business environment.

2.4 - Financial Modelling 101

Financial modelling is a powerful tool in the arsenal of modern CFOs, enabling them to evaluate decisions, anticipate challenges, and map out the potential outcomes of various strategies. At its core, financial modelling involves constructing a numerical representation of an organisation's financial performance, allowing for scenario analysis, risk assessment, and value projection. For CFOs, understanding and leveraging financial models is essential for making data-driven decisions that align with the organisation's strategic objectives.

A financial model is essentially a mathematical framework that integrates historical data, key assumptions, and projected performance metrics. These models are commonly used to assess investments, evaluate new business opportunities, and determine the financial feasibility of strategic initiatives. For example, a CFO considering the acquisition of a competitor might use a financial model to estimate the potential impact on revenue, costs, and cash flow over a five-year period.

There are several types of financial models, each tailored to specific purposes. The most foundational model is the three-statement model, which integrates the income statement, balance sheet, and cash flow statement into a single framework. This model provides a comprehensive view of the organisation's financial health and is often used for budgeting and forecasting. For instance, a CFO might use a three-statement model to project the company's performance over the next fiscal year, identifying areas where adjustments are needed to meet financial goals.

Another widely used model is the discounted cash flow (DCF) model, which estimates the value of an investment or business based on projected future cash flows. This model is particularly useful for evaluating long-term projects or acquisitions. For example, a CFO at a renewable energy company might use a DCF model to assess the financial viability of building a new solar farm, incorporating assumptions about construction costs, energy prices, and regulatory incentives.

Scenario and sensitivity analysis models are also critical for CFOs, as they allow organisations to test the impact of different variables on financial outcomes. For instance, a CFO at a manufacturing company might use these models to evaluate how changes in raw material prices, labour costs, or currency exchange rates would affect profitability. By understanding these sensitivities, the CFO can develop strategies to mitigate risks and capitalise on opportunities.

Creating a robust financial model requires careful attention to detail and a deep understanding of the organisation's operations. The first step is gathering accurate and reliable data, as the quality of the model depends on the inputs. This includes historical financial statements, market research, and operational metrics. For example, a retail CFO developing a sales forecast model would need data on past sales trends, customer demographics, and seasonal patterns.

Assumptions play a central role in financial modelling, as they form the basis for projections. These assumptions must be grounded in reality and supported by credible evidence. For instance, a CFO projecting revenue growth for an e-commerce business might assume a specific rate of customer acquisition based on historical performance and industry benchmarks. Unrealistic assumptions can lead to flawed models and misguided decisions.

A well-designed financial model should also be flexible and transparent, allowing users to adjust inputs and assumptions easily. This is particularly important for scenario analysis, as it enables CFOs to test different outcomes and identify the most favourable course of action. For example, a CFO might create high, medium, and low scenarios for a new product launch, helping the executive team make informed decisions about pricing, marketing, and production.

Despite its benefits, financial modelling is not without challenges. One common issue is overcomplication, as overly complex models can be difficult to understand, use, and maintain. To address this, CFOs should prioritise simplicity and clarity, focusing on the most critical variables and ensuring that calculations are logically structured.

Another challenge is managing uncertainty, as even the most carefully constructed models are subject to external factors beyond the organisation's control. To mitigate this, CFOs should incorporate buffers and contingencies into their models, preparing for unexpected changes in market conditions, regulations, or customer behaviour.

In conclusion, financial modelling is an essential skill for CFOs, enabling them to navigate complexity, assess risks, and guide their organisations toward strategic goals. By mastering the principles of financial modelling and adhering to best practices, CFOs can create tools that provide valuable insights, inform decision-making, and drive long-term success. In today's fast-paced business environment, the ability to build and interpret financial models is not just a technical skill, it is a strategic advantage.

2.5 - Scenario Analysis and Stress Testing

Scenario analysis and stress testing are critical tools in the CFO's toolkit, enabling organisations to prepare for uncertainty and make resilient financial plans. These methods involve evaluating the potential impact of various hypothetical situations on an organisation's financial performance, providing insights that help leaders anticipate challenges and identify opportunities. For CFOs, mastering these techniques is essential for navigating volatility and ensuring the organisation's long-term stability.

Scenario analysis involves creating multiple "what-if" scenarios to test the impact of different variables on financial outcomes. This approach is particularly valuable for assessing the feasibility of strategic initiatives, such as entering a new market or launching a new product. For example, a CFO at a consumer goods company might use scenario analysis to evaluate the potential impact of a new product line on revenue and profitability, considering variables such as production costs, pricing strategies, and market demand.

In contrast, stress testing focuses on evaluating the organisation's ability to withstand extreme or adverse conditions. This method is often used to assess financial resilience during economic downturns, industry disruptions, or other crises. For instance, a CFO at a bank might conduct stress tests to determine how the organisation would perform under scenarios such as a sharp increase in interest rates or a sudden drop in loan repayments.

The effectiveness of scenario analysis and stress testing lies in their ability to provide actionable insights. By identifying potential risks and vulnerabilities, these methods enable CFOs to develop contingency plans and make proactive adjustments to financial strategies. For example, if a stress test reveals that a manufacturing company would face liquidity challenges during a prolonged supply chain disruption, the CFO might recommend diversifying suppliers or securing additional lines of credit.

Steps to Conduct Effective Scenario Analysis and Stress Testing:

- **Define Objectives:** The first step is to determine the purpose of the analysis, whether it is to evaluate a strategic decision, assess financial resilience, or prepare for a specific risk. For example, a CFO planning a major capital investment might focus on scenarios related to market demand and financing costs.

- **Identify Key Variables:** Next, the CFO must identify the variables that are most likely to influence financial outcomes. These could include revenue growth rates, cost structures, exchange rates, or regulatory changes. For instance, a CFO at a multinational corporation might focus on currency fluctuations and trade tariffs.

- **Develop Scenarios:** The CFO should create multiple scenarios that reflect different assumptions about the key variables. These scenarios should include both likely outcomes (base-case scenarios) and extreme conditions (worst-case scenarios). For example, a CFO at an airline might develop scenarios based on fuel price volatility and changes in passenger demand.

- **Analyse Results:** Once the scenarios are developed, the CFO must evaluate their impact on financial performance using tools such as financial models or sensitivity analysis. This step provides insights into the organisation's strengths, weaknesses, and potential vulnerabilities.

- **Develop Action Plans:** The final step is to translate the insights into actionable strategies. This might involve adjusting budgets, reallocating resources, or implementing risk mitigation measures.

One of the primary challenges in scenario analysis and stress testing is the inherent uncertainty of external factors. To address this, CFOs should focus on creating a range of plausible scenarios rather than attempting to predict exact outcomes. Another challenge is the complexity of integrating these methods into existing financial processes. Leveraging advanced tools and technologies, such as Monte Carlo simulations or predictive analytics, can streamline the process and enhance accuracy.

In conclusion, scenario analysis and stress testing are indispensable tools for CFOs, providing the insights needed to navigate uncertainty and build resilient financial plans. By anticipating potential risks and preparing for a range of outcomes, CFOs can position their organisations to thrive in both favourable and challenging conditions. In an increasingly volatile business environment, these techniques are not just valuable, they are essential.

2.6 - Leveraging Data for Decision-Making

In the modern business landscape, data is one of the most valuable assets an organisation possesses. For CFOs, leveraging data effectively is no longer a competitive advantage, it is a necessity. Data-driven decision-making allows CFOs to move beyond intuition and assumptions, enabling them to base financial strategies on accurate, real-time information. By utilising data effectively, CFOs can uncover insights, anticipate trends, and make informed decisions that drive growth and stability.

The sheer volume of data available today, often referred to as "big data," presents both opportunities and challenges for CFOs. On the one hand, the proliferation of financial, operational, and market data provides unprecedented visibility into every aspect of an organisation's performance. On the other hand, extracting meaningful insights from this data requires sophisticated tools, analytical skills, and a structured approach to data management.

Data plays a pivotal role in various FP&A activities, from forecasting and budgeting to scenario analysis and risk management. For instance, a retail CFO might use point-of-sale data to identify purchasing patterns, enabling the company to optimise inventory levels and improve supply chain efficiency. Similarly, an FP&A team at a software company might analyse customer usage data to refine pricing strategies and identify opportunities for upselling or cross-selling.

One of the key benefits of leveraging data is the ability to identify trends and patterns that might not be immediately apparent through traditional analysis. For example, a CFO analysing historical sales data might notice that certain product lines perform better during specific seasons or in particular geographic regions. By using this insight to adjust marketing strategies or inventory allocations, the organisation can maximise revenue and minimise waste.

While raw data is valuable, its true power lies in the ability to communicate insights effectively. Data visualisation tools, such as Tableau, Power BI, and Qlik, enable CFOs to transform complex datasets into clear, actionable visuals. For example, a CFO presenting revenue projections to the board might use a combination of charts and graphs to highlight key trends and illustrate the potential impact of strategic initiatives.

Storytelling is another critical component of data-driven decision-making. By framing data within a narrative, CFOs can make insights more relatable and persuasive. For instance, instead of simply presenting a decline in profit margins, a CFO might explain how rising raw material costs are impacting profitability and outline specific actions to address the issue, such as renegotiating supplier contracts or exploring alternative materials.

Despite its potential, leveraging data effectively comes with challenges. One common issue is data quality. Inaccurate, incomplete, or inconsistent data can undermine the reliability of insights and lead to poor decision-making. To address this, CFOs must prioritise data governance, implementing processes and tools to ensure that data is accurate, consistent, and up-to-date.

Another challenge is managing the sheer volume and variety of data available. CFOs must strike a balance between collecting comprehensive datasets and focusing on the metrics that truly matter. For example, a CFO at a healthcare organisation might prioritise data related to patient outcomes and cost efficiency rather than attempting to analyse every available dataset.

The integration of data across departments is also critical. Siloed data can hinder collaboration and prevent organisations from gaining a holistic view of their performance. CFOs should work closely with IT and other departments to implement systems that facilitate data sharing and integration. For instance, an enterprise resource planning (ERP) system can provide a centralised platform for collecting and analysing data from finance, operations, sales, and marketing.

When Emily became CFO of a fast-growing e-commerce startup, she recognised the need to improve the company's decision-making processes. By implementing advanced analytics tools, Emily enabled the FP&A team to analyse customer behaviour in real time, identifying trends such as peak shopping times and popular product categories. Armed with this data, Emily worked with the marketing and operations teams to adjust promotional strategies and optimise inventory levels. As a result, the company increased revenue by 20% while reducing excess inventory costs.

Leveraging data is a critical capability for CFOs, enabling them to transform information into actionable insights that drive strategic decision-making. By embracing advanced analytics, prioritising data quality, and fostering collaboration across departments, CFOs can unlock the full potential of data to enhance performance and achieve organisational goals. In a world where data is increasingly abundant and complex, the ability to harness its power is an indispensable skill for today's financial leaders.

2.7 - Aligning Financial Plans with Business Goals

The alignment of financial plans with business goals is a cornerstone of effective financial management. For CFOs, this alignment ensures that every financial decision supports the organisation's broader objectives, creating a cohesive strategy that drives sustainable growth. Without this connection, financial plans risk becoming siloed exercises, disconnected from the realities of the business and its strategic priorities.

Financial plans serve as the roadmap for an organisation, outlining how resources will be allocated to achieve specific objectives. These plans typically include budgets, forecasts, and investment strategies, all designed to support key initiatives such as product development, market expansion, or operational efficiency. For example, a CFO at a manufacturing company might develop a financial plan that prioritises investments in automation technology, aligning with the organisation's goal of improving productivity and reducing costs.

Achieving alignment between financial plans and business goals requires close collaboration between the finance department and other parts of the organisation. CFOs must work closely with the CEO and other members of the C-suite to understand the company's strategic vision and translate it into actionable financial plans. For instance, if the CEO's primary goal is to expand into international markets, the CFO might allocate resources for market research, logistics, and compliance with foreign regulations.

Collaboration with operational leaders is equally important. Financial plans must reflect the realities of day-to-day operations, ensuring that resources are allocated to the areas that will deliver the greatest impact. For example, a CFO at a logistics company might work with the Chief Operating Officer to identify cost-saving opportunities in the supply chain, using these savings to fund investments in customer service or technology.

One of the key challenges in aligning financial plans with business goals is ensuring that financial metrics are integrated with operational metrics. While financial metrics such as revenue, profit margins, and return on investment are critical, they must be complemented by operational metrics that reflect the organisation's core activities. For instance, a CFO at a healthcare provider might track metrics such as patient outcomes and service delivery times alongside traditional financial metrics, ensuring that the organisation's financial plans support its mission to deliver high-quality care.

Technology plays a crucial role in achieving this integration. Advanced planning tools enable CFOs to link financial and operational data, creating a unified view of the organisation's performance. For example, an enterprise performance management (EPM) system can provide dashboards that combine financial metrics with key performance indicators (KPIs) from other departments, facilitating data-driven decision-making.

Another critical aspect of alignment is communication. CFOs must clearly articulate how financial plans support the organisation's goals, ensuring that employees at all levels understand the rationale behind budgetary decisions. This transparency fosters a sense of shared purpose and accountability, encouraging teams to work together to achieve common objectives. For instance, a CFO might hold workshops with department heads to explain how their budgets align with the company's strategic priorities, addressing any concerns and building consensus.

In conclusion, aligning financial plans with business goals is a vital responsibility for CFOs, ensuring that financial strategies are both effective and purposeful. By fostering collaboration, integrating financial and operational metrics, and communicating clearly, CFOs can create plans that drive organisational success and support long-term objectives. In an increasingly complex business environment, this alignment is essential for achieving sustainable growth and resilience.

2.8 - Communication of Financial Insights

Effective communication of financial insights is a critical skill for CFOs, bridging the gap between complex financial data and actionable business strategies. In their role as financial stewards and strategic advisors, CFOs must not only generate accurate and meaningful insights but also convey them in a way that resonates with a diverse range of stakeholders, including board members, executives, employees, and external partners. Mastering the art of financial communication is essential for driving alignment, fostering transparency, and empowering informed decision-making across the organisation.

The financial landscape is inherently complex, filled with technical jargon, intricate calculations, and nuanced metrics. For many stakeholders, these complexities can be intimidating or confusing, especially if they lack a financial background. As the organisation's chief financial communicator, the CFO serves as a translator, converting raw data into clear, concise, and accessible narratives that stakeholders can understand and act upon.

For example, when presenting quarterly earnings to the board, a CFO might summarise key performance indicators (KPIs), such as revenue growth, profit margins, and cash flow, while also contextualising these figures within the broader business strategy. Instead of overwhelming the board with granular details, the CFO focuses on the most relevant insights, such as the reasons behind a rise in operating expenses or the impact of a recent product launch on revenue.

One of the hallmarks of effective financial communication is the ability to tailor the message to the audience. Different stakeholders have different levels of financial literacy and unique priorities, requiring CFOs to adapt their approach accordingly. For instance:

- **The Board of Directors:** Board members are often focused on high-level performance metrics, strategic risks, and long-term growth. A CFO might use visual aids, such as graphs and dashboards, to present a concise overview of financial performance, emphasising trends and strategic implications.

- **The Executive Team:** Executives from departments like marketing, operations, and IT need insights that directly relate to their functional areas. For example, a CFO presenting to the Chief Marketing Officer might highlight the ROI of recent campaigns or provide recommendations for reallocating budgets to maximise impact.

- **Investors and Analysts:** External stakeholders require transparent and credible communication that builds confidence in the organisation's financial health. This might involve detailed explanations of quarterly results, forecasts, and plans for managing risks or seizing opportunities.

- **Employees:** Communicating financial insights to employees fosters a sense of ownership and alignment. For instance, a CFO might use simplified language and relatable examples to explain how individual contributions affect overall financial performance, helping employees understand the "why" behind organisational decisions.

Numbers alone rarely inspire action or buy-in. By incorporating storytelling into their communication, CFOs can bring financial data to life, demonstrating its relevance and significance. A compelling financial story connects the dots between past performance, current strategies, and future goals, making the data more engaging and relatable.

For example, instead of merely reporting a drop in profit margins, a CFO might explain how increased raw material costs have affected production expenses and outline a plan to negotiate better supplier contracts or explore alternative materials. This narrative approach not only informs stakeholders but also instils confidence in the CFO's ability to address challenges effectively.

Data visualisation is another powerful tool for enhancing financial communication. Charts, graphs, and dashboards can simplify complex data sets, making trends and patterns easier to understand. Tools like Tableau, Power BI, and Google Data Studio enable CFOs to create dynamic and interactive visuals that cater to different audiences.

For example, a CFO presenting revenue trends over the past year might use a line graph to highlight seasonality, accompanied by a heat map to illustrate regional variations in sales performance. These visuals make it easier for stakeholders to grasp key insights at a glance, reducing the risk of misinterpretation.

Despite its importance, communicating financial insights is not without challenges. One common issue is information overload, where too much data overwhelms the audience and obscures the key message. To overcome this, CFOs must prioritise clarity and focus, emphasising the most critical insights and avoiding unnecessary details.

Another challenge is bridging the gap between financial and non-financial stakeholders. While CFOs may be comfortable discussing complex metrics like EBITDA, working capital, or return on equity, these terms may be unfamiliar to others. Using plain language, analogies, and real-world examples can help demystify these concepts and make them more accessible.

In conclusion, effective communication of financial insights is a critical skill for CFOs, enabling them to bridge the gap between data and decision-making. By tailoring their approach to different audiences, incorporating storytelling, leveraging visualisation tools, and fostering transparency, CFOs can ensure that their messages resonate and inspire action. In a world where financial data drives strategy, the ability to communicate insights effectively is as important as the insights themselves.

2.9 - Tools and Software for FP&A

Modern Financial Planning and Analysis (FP&A) relies heavily on technology to streamline processes, enhance accuracy, and provide real-time insights. The days of manually updating spreadsheets and consolidating data from disparate sources are long gone; today's FP&A teams leverage sophisticated tools and software to analyse complex datasets, model scenarios, and support decision-making. For CFOs, understanding and implementing the right tools is essential for maximising the efficiency and effectiveness of the FP&A function.

Technology plays a transformative role in FP&A by automating routine tasks, enabling dynamic forecasting, and improving collaboration. Advanced tools allow FP&A teams to process large volumes of data quickly, freeing up time for high-value activities such as strategic analysis and decision support. For example, a cloud-based FP&A platform can automate the collection and consolidation of financial data, reducing the risk of errors and ensuring consistency across reports.

Key Categories of FP&A Tools

1. **Budgeting and Forecasting Software:** Tools like Adaptive Insights, Anaplan, and Workday enable organisations to create detailed budgets and forecasts, update them in real-time, and perform scenario analysis. For instance, a CFO at a retail company might use Anaplan to model the impact of different pricing strategies on revenue and margins.

2. **Data Visualisation and Business Intelligence (BI) Tools:** Platforms such as Tableau, Power BI, and Qlik allow CFOs to create interactive dashboards and visualisations that make financial data more accessible and actionable. For example, a CFO might use Tableau to track KPIs like revenue growth and customer acquisition costs, presenting insights to the board in a visually engaging format.

3. **Enterprise Resource Planning (ERP) Systems:** ERP platforms like SAP, Oracle NetSuite, and Microsoft Dynamics provide an integrated view of financial and operational data, enabling better coordination across departments. For instance, a CFO might use an ERP system to link sales forecasts with production schedules, ensuring alignment between demand and supply.

4. **Predictive Analytics and Machine Learning Tools:** Advanced analytics platforms leverage AI and machine learning to identify patterns, predict trends, and optimise decision-making. For example, a CFO at an e-

commerce company might use predictive analytics to forecast customer demand during peak shopping seasons, enabling better inventory planning.

While these tools offer significant benefits, their implementation can be challenging. One common issue is resistance to change, as employees may be reluctant to adopt new technologies or workflows. To address this, CFOs must lead by example, demonstrating the value of these tools and providing adequate training.

Another challenge is ensuring data quality and integration. Disparate systems and inconsistent data formats can hinder the effectiveness of FP&A tools. CFOs should prioritise data governance and work closely with IT teams to establish a unified data infrastructure.

In conclusion, the right tools and software are essential for modern FP&A, providing the efficiency, accuracy, and insights needed to navigate complexity and drive success. By investing in advanced technologies, CFOs can empower their teams to focus on strategic priorities and make data-driven decisions that support the organisation's goals. In an era where technology is reshaping finance, embracing these tools is not just an option, it is a necessity.

2.10 - Case Study: Successful Budgeting in a Crisis

Budgeting during a crisis is one of the most challenging tasks a CFO can face. When uncertainty reigns, financial plans must be both flexible and robust, balancing the immediate need for stability with the organisation's long-term goals. This case study explores how a CFO successfully navigated a crisis by implementing strategic budgeting practices, leveraging technology, and fostering cross-departmental collaboration.

In early 2020, Global Goods Inc., a mid-sized manufacturing company, was hit hard by the COVID-19 pandemic. The company, which relied heavily on international suppliers, faced unprecedented challenges as supply chains were disrupted, raw material costs soared, and demand for certain product lines plummeted. At the same time, cash flow was under significant pressure due to delayed payments from key clients.

The CFO, Angela, quickly recognised that the company's traditional budgeting approach, which was static and relied heavily on historical data, was inadequate for the rapidly changing circumstances. To steer the company through the crisis, Angela needed to implement a more dynamic and responsive budgeting process.

Step 1: Assessing the Financial Landscape

Angela's first step was to conduct a comprehensive assessment of the company's financial position. Working closely with the finance team, she analysed cash flow projections, identified critical cost drivers, and reviewed the profitability of each product line. This exercise revealed that while demand for certain products had declined, others, such as essential goods, were experiencing a surge in sales.

Armed with this information, Angela prioritised securing liquidity. She renegotiated payment terms with suppliers, delayed non-essential capital expenditures, and worked with the sales team to expedite collections from clients. These measures provided the company with the cash it needed to weather the initial shock.

Step 2: Implementing a Flexible Budgeting Framework

Recognising the need for adaptability, Angela replaced the company's static budget with a rolling budget. This approach allowed the finance team to update forecasts monthly based on the latest data and market conditions. For example, if raw material costs rose unexpectedly, the budget could be adjusted to reflect the higher expenses, enabling more accurate decision-making.

Angela also introduced scenario planning to prepare for a range of potential outcomes. The finance team developed best-case, worst-case, and base-case scenarios, each with its own set of assumptions about revenue, costs, and external factors. These scenarios allowed the company to anticipate challenges and plan responses in advance. For instance, the worst-case scenario highlighted the need to secure additional credit lines, which Angela proactively arranged.

Step 3: Leveraging Technology

To streamline the budgeting process and improve accuracy, Angela invested in a cloud-based FP&A platform. The platform integrated data from across the organisation, enabling real-time tracking of key metrics such as sales, expenses, and cash flow. This technology not only reduced the time spent on manual data entry but also provided Angela and her team with the insights they needed to make informed decisions quickly.

For example, when a key supplier announced a price increase, the platform allowed Angela to simulate the impact on the company's margins instantly. Armed with this information, she was able to negotiate more favourable terms with the supplier and adjust the budget accordingly.

Step 4: Engaging Stakeholders

Angela understood that successful budgeting during a crisis required buy-in from all departments. She held weekly cross-departmental meetings to review the budget, share updates on the company's financial performance, and discuss potential adjustments. This collaborative approach ensured that everyone, from operations to marketing, understood the organisation's priorities and worked together to achieve them.

For instance, the operations team contributed by identifying cost-saving opportunities in the production process, while the marketing team reallocated its budget to focus on promoting high-demand products. This alignment not only improved efficiency but also fostered a sense of shared responsibility for navigating the crisis.

Step 5: Monitoring and Adjusting

As the situation evolved, Angela and her team continuously monitored the company's financial performance and adjusted the budget as needed. This iterative approach allowed the organisation to respond quickly to new challenges, such as additional lockdowns and changing customer preferences. For example, when demand for non-essential goods began to recover in late 2020, the budget was updated to support increased production and marketing efforts.

The Outcome: Resilience and Recovery

Thanks to Angela's leadership and the company's agile budgeting process, Global Goods Inc. not only survived the crisis but emerged stronger. By the end of 2021, the company had restored its cash reserves, improved its profit margins, and regained market share in key product categories. The rolling budget and scenario planning framework became permanent fixtures of the organisation's financial strategy, ensuring that it was better prepared for future challenges.

Lessons Learned

Angela's success highlights several key lessons for CFOs managing budgets during a crisis:

5. **Flexibility is Essential:** A static budget is insufficient in a volatile environment. Rolling budgets and scenario planning provide the adaptability needed to respond to rapid changes.

6. **Data-Driven Decision-Making:** Leveraging technology to track real-time data and simulate scenarios allows CFOs to make informed decisions with confidence.

7. **Collaboration is Key:** Engaging stakeholders from across the organisation ensures alignment and fosters a culture of shared responsibility.
8. **Proactive Liquidity Management:** Securing cash flow early in the crisis provides the financial stability needed to navigate uncertainty.

Conclusion

Budgeting during a crisis is one of the most demanding aspects of a CFO's role, requiring a blend of strategic foresight, adaptability, and collaboration. Angela's story demonstrates how dynamic budgeting, combined with technology and cross-functional teamwork, can turn a crisis into an opportunity for resilience and growth. For CFOs, the ability to navigate uncertainty and lead with clarity is a defining characteristic of successful financial leadership.

Chapter 3

Corporate Finance Essentials

> *"Decisions in corporate finance echo through the future, choose wisely, align strategically, and lead confidently."*
> **Robert N. Jacobs**

Corporate finance is the backbone of an organisation's financial strategy, encompassing key decisions that influence its stability, growth, and overall success. Whether it's managing capital structure, appraising investments, or navigating mergers and acquisitions, corporate finance requires a nuanced approach that combines financial acumen with strategic foresight. For CFOs, mastering the essentials of corporate finance is not just about technical expertise but also about making decisions that align with the organisation's long-term objectives. This chapter delves deeply into the critical components of corporate finance, equipping CFOs with the tools and insights to excel in this vital domain.

3.1 - Capital Structure Fundamentals

The capital structure of a company, the mix of debt and equity financing used to fund its operations, is a cornerstone of corporate finance. It determines not only how an organisation secures the resources it needs but also how it manages risk, maximises profitability, and positions itself for long-term growth. For CFOs, understanding and optimising the capital structure is essential, as it directly impacts financial health and strategic flexibility.

Debt financing involves borrowing money, typically through loans or bonds, which must be repaid over time with interest. This approach has several advantages, particularly its tax benefits; interest payments are tax deductible, which lowers the overall cost of borrowing. Additionally, debt allows existing shareholders to retain full control over the company, as lenders do not have voting rights or equity stakes. However, debt financing also comes with inherent risks. Excessive debt, or over-leveraging, can strain cash flow and increase the likelihood of default, particularly during economic downturns or periods of declining revenue. For example, a hospitality company that takes on significant debt to expand its operations may struggle to meet repayment obligations if tourist demand declines unexpectedly.

Equity financing, on the other hand, involves raising capital by issuing shares to investors. Unlike debt, equity does not require repayment, making it a more flexible option for companies with unpredictable cash flows or those in growth phases. Startups, for instance, often rely on equity financing to fund research and development or market expansion without the immediate burden of debt repayments. However, issuing equity comes with trade-offs, including ownership dilution. As more shares are issued, existing shareholders see their stake, and potentially their influence, reduced. Additionally, equity investors often expect higher returns, placing pressure on the company to achieve strong performance metrics.

The optimal capital structure varies depending on several factors, including the company's industry, growth stage, and risk appetite. For instance, utility companies with stable cash flows and predictable revenue often rely more heavily on debt, while technology firms in rapidly changing markets may favour equity to maintain flexibility. Market conditions also play a significant role. During periods of low interest rates, debt becomes a more attractive option, while strong equity markets may make issuing shares a better choice.

CFOs must carefully balance these considerations to create a capital structure that supports both immediate needs and long-term goals. Financial metrics such as the debt-to-equity ratio, interest coverage ratio, and return on equity provide valuable insights for evaluating the health of the capital structure. Regular reassessments are essential, as changes in market conditions, business strategy, or operational needs can necessitate adjustments.

A real-world example highlights the importance of strategic capital structuring. When Emily became CFO of a mid-sized manufacturing company, she realised that its reliance on equity financing was limiting its growth potential. By introducing moderate levels of debt, she reduced the company's weighted average cost of capital (WACC) and freed up resources to invest in new production technologies. This not only improved profitability but also restored investor confidence.

In conclusion, the capital structure is more than just a financial framework; it is a strategic tool that shapes an organisation's ability to grow, innovate, and compete. For CFOs, mastering the fundamentals of capital structure and tailoring decisions to the company's unique circumstances is essential for achieving sustainable success.

3.2 - Equity vs. Debt Financing

The decision between equity and debt financing is one of the most fundamental in corporate finance, with far-reaching implications for a company's operations, risk profile, and shareholder value. Each approach has distinct advantages and drawbacks, and the optimal choice depends on a variety of factors, including the organisation's financial health, market conditions, and strategic objectives. For CFOs, navigating this decision-making process requires a thorough understanding of both options and the ability to align financial strategies with the company's overarching goals.

Equity financing involves raising capital by selling shares of the company, which provides investors with ownership stakes. This approach is particularly advantageous for organisations that require significant funds but wish to avoid the repayment obligations associated with debt. For example, a biotechnology startup might rely on equity financing to fund the development of a new drug, given the uncertain timeline for regulatory approval and commercialisation. Equity financing offers flexibility, allowing the company to allocate resources toward long-term initiatives without the immediate pressure of debt repayments. Additionally, equity investors often bring more than just capital to the table; they may offer strategic guidance, industry expertise, and valuable networks.

However, equity financing is not without its challenges. Issuing new shares dilutes the ownership stakes of existing shareholders, potentially reducing their influence and share of future profits. Furthermore, equity investors typically expect higher returns than debt holders, which can create pressure to prioritise growth and profitability. Companies that fail to meet these expectations risk losing investor confidence, which can negatively impact share prices and future fundraising efforts.

Debt financing, in contrast, involves borrowing funds from lenders, such as banks or bondholders, with the obligation to repay the principal amount along with interest. This approach is often favoured by companies with steady cash flows and a desire to retain full ownership. For instance, a retail chain planning to open new locations might take out a loan, confident that revenue from existing stores will cover interest payments and principal repayment.

Debt financing offers several advantages, including its cost-effectiveness. Interest payments are tax-deductible, reducing the overall cost of borrowing. Additionally, debt does not dilute ownership, allowing existing shareholders to maintain control over the company. However, the risks associated with debt financing are significant. High levels of leverage increase financial vulnerability, particularly during economic downturns or periods of declining revenue. Companies that cannot meet their debt obligations may face default, bankruptcy, or forced asset sales.

The choice between equity and debt financing is rarely a binary decision. Most organisations use a combination of both, tailoring the mix to their specific circumstances and strategic goals. Market conditions also influence the decision. For example, during periods of low interest rates, debt financing becomes more attractive, while robust equity markets may provide favourable conditions for issuing shares. CFOs must continuously assess these factors and adapt their strategies to ensure the company remains financially resilient.

Consider the case of Global Goods Inc., a consumer products company that sought to expand into new markets. The CFO opted for a hybrid approach, using equity financing to fund brand-building initiatives and debt to finance the construction of a new manufacturing facility. This balanced strategy allowed the company to achieve its growth objectives while maintaining a manageable risk profile.

In conclusion, equity and debt financing each play vital roles in corporate finance, offering unique benefits and challenges. For CFOs, understanding the nuances of these funding options and aligning them with the company's strategic objectives is essential for achieving financial stability and long-term success.

3.3 - Managing Working Capital

Working capital management is a critical function in corporate finance, essential for ensuring that an organisation has the resources it needs to meet its day-to-day operational requirements. Defined as the difference between current assets and current liabilities, working capital serves as a measure of liquidity and short-term financial health. For CFOs, managing working capital effectively is not just about maintaining financial stability; it is also about improving operational efficiency and creating opportunities for growth.

Working capital is the lifeblood of an organisation, ensuring that funds are available to cover essential expenses such as salaries, supplier payments, and utility bills. A company with positive working capital has more current assets than current liabilities, signalling its ability to meet short-term obligations. Conversely, negative working capital can indicate financial stress, potentially leading to cash flow problems and even insolvency.

For example, a manufacturing company with slow-moving inventory and delayed receivables collection may struggle to pay its suppliers on time, jeopardising operations. On the other hand, a retailer that efficiently manages inventory turnover and receivables collection can free up cash for investment in new stores or marketing campaigns.

Effective working capital management involves optimising three main components: receivables, inventory, and payables.

1. **Accounts Receivable:** Collecting payments from customers promptly is vital for maintaining healthy cash flow. CFOs must ensure that credit terms are aligned with industry norms and that overdue accounts are minimised. For instance, implementing automated

invoicing systems and offering early payment discounts can encourage timely payments. Additionally, credit risk assessments help prevent extending credit to customers who may default.

2. **Inventory:** Inventory management is a delicate balance. Holding too much inventory ties up capital and increases storage costs, while holding too little risks stockouts and lost sales. CFOs should collaborate with supply chain and operations teams to implement demand forecasting tools and just-in-time inventory practices. For example, a food and beverage company might use historical sales data to optimise stock levels during seasonal peaks, avoiding waste while meeting customer demand.

3. **Accounts Payable:** Managing payables involves negotiating favourable payment terms with suppliers without compromising relationships. Delaying payments can conserve cash, but excessive delays may damage supplier trust. CFOs must strike a balance, ensuring that payments are aligned with cash flow while maintaining good supplier relationships. For instance, extending payment terms from 30 to 60 days can improve liquidity, but only if suppliers are amenable to the change.

One of the central challenges in working capital management is balancing liquidity and profitability. While maintaining high levels of liquidity reduces financial risk, it also comes with opportunity costs. Excess cash tied up in working capital could be invested in growth initiatives, such as new product development or market expansion. Conversely, overly aggressive working capital strategies, such as minimal inventory levels or stringent receivables policies, can disrupt operations or strain customer relationships.

CFOs must take a holistic approach, considering both short-term needs and long-term goals. For example, a CFO at a construction company might focus on aligning receivables and payables to ensure liquidity during project delays while also investing surplus cash in short-term securities to generate returns.

Modern tools and technologies play a crucial role in optimising working capital. Enterprise resource planning (ERP) systems provide real-time insights into cash flow, inventory levels, and payment schedules, enabling CFOs to make informed decisions. For example, an ERP system might highlight trends in receivables ageing, prompting the CFO to adjust credit terms or implement stricter collection policies.

Advanced analytics and artificial intelligence (AI) can further enhance working capital management. AI-powered tools can predict demand patterns, optimise inventory levels, and automate payment processes, improving efficiency and accuracy. For instance, a CFO at a retail company might use AI to forecast seasonal demand and ensure optimal stock levels without overcommitting resources.

In conclusion, managing working capital effectively is a vital responsibility for CFOs, directly impacting an organisation's liquidity, operational efficiency, and growth potential. By optimising receivables, inventory, and payables, CFOs can ensure that their organisations maintain the financial flexibility needed to navigate challenges and seize opportunities. In today's competitive business environment, mastering the art of working capital management is essential for driving long-term success.

3.4 - Investment Appraisal Techniques

Investment appraisal is a cornerstone of corporate finance, enabling CFOs to evaluate the financial viability of projects, acquisitions, and other capital expenditures. Whether assessing the profitability of a new product line or determining the value of a potential acquisition, investment appraisal provides the analytical framework needed to allocate resources effectively and achieve strategic goals.

Every organisation faces resource constraints, making it impossible to pursue every potential opportunity. Investment appraisal ensures that decisions are guided by data and analysis rather than intuition or guesswork. By quantifying costs, benefits, and risks, CFOs can prioritise projects that offer the greatest returns while aligning with the organisation's broader objectives.

For example, a CFO at a renewable energy company may need to choose between investing in a new solar farm or expanding an existing wind energy project. Through detailed financial analysis, the CFO can compare the projected returns, risks, and alignment with the company's sustainability goals, ensuring that resources are allocated wisely.

Several methods are commonly used in investment appraisal, each offering unique insights into a project's feasibility:

1. **Net Present Value (NPV):** NPV calculates the difference between the present value of cash inflows and outflows over the life of a project. A positive NPV indicates that the investment is expected to generate value, while a negative NPV suggests it may result in a net loss. For instance, a CFO analysing a factory expansion might calculate NPV to ensure that projected cost savings and revenue increases outweigh the initial capital expenditure.

2. **Internal Rate of Return (IRR):** IRR represents the discount rate at which NPV equals zero. It provides a percentage measure of a project's profitability, allowing CFOs to compare it against the organisation's required rate of return. For example, a CFO at a software company might use IRR to evaluate the financial attractiveness of developing a new application.

3. **Payback Period:** This method calculates how long it will take for an investment to recover its initial costs. While it does not account for cash flows beyond the breakeven point or the time value of money, it is useful for assessing liquidity risks. For instance, a CFO in the hospitality industry might use the payback period to evaluate the feasibility of refurbishing a hotel.

4. **Profitability Index (PI):** PI measures the ratio of the present value of cash inflows to the initial investment,

providing a relative measure of profitability. A PI greater than 1 indicates a worthwhile investment. For example, a CFO evaluating two competing projects might use PI to determine which offers the greatest value per pound invested.

Investment appraisal is not just about identifying potential returns; it is also about managing risk. Sensitivity analysis, scenario planning, and Monte Carlo simulations can help CFOs evaluate how changes in key variables, such as costs or market conditions, impact project outcomes. For instance, a CFO at a pharmaceutical company might use sensitivity analysis to assess how variations in regulatory approval timelines could affect the profitability of a new drug.

In conclusion, investment appraisal is a vital tool for CFOs, enabling them to evaluate opportunities, allocate resources wisely, and balance financial and strategic priorities. By mastering techniques such as NPV, IRR, and sensitivity analysis, CFOs can make informed decisions that drive organisational success and create sustainable value. In an increasingly complex business environment, the ability to assess investments rigorously is a defining characteristic of effective financial leadership.

3.5 - The CFO's Role in Mergers and Acquisitions

Mergers and acquisitions (M&A) are transformative events that can redefine an organisation's trajectory, offering opportunities for growth, innovation, and increased market share. However, they are inherently complex and carry significant risks. For

CFOs, overseeing M&A transactions requires a blend of strategic insight, financial acumen, and operational expertise. From evaluating potential targets to managing post-merger integration, the CFO's role is central to ensuring the success of these high-stakes initiatives.

Organisations pursue M&A for various strategic reasons, including entering new markets, acquiring innovative technologies, achieving economies of scale, or diversifying revenue streams. For example, a pharmaceutical company might acquire a smaller biotech firm to gain access to its proprietary drug pipeline, accelerating the time to market for life-saving treatments. Alternatively, a retail chain may merge with a competitor to consolidate market share and reduce competition.

For CFOs, understanding the strategic rationale behind an M&A deal is the first step in evaluating its feasibility. They must ensure that the transaction aligns with the organisation's long-term objectives and delivers tangible value to shareholders. This requires a thorough assessment of the potential synergies, risks, and costs associated with the deal.

The CFO's involvement in M&A spans three critical phases: target evaluation and due diligence, deal structuring and negotiation, and post-merger integration.

1. **Target Evaluation and Due Diligence:** During this phase, the CFO works closely with the CEO and other executives to identify potential acquisition targets or merger partners. This involves analysing industry

trends, assessing competitive dynamics, and identifying organisations that complement the acquiring company's strengths. For instance, a CFO at a technology firm might look for targets with complementary software solutions or access to new customer segments.

Once potential targets are identified, the CFO leads a rigorous due diligence process to evaluate their financial health, operational performance, and strategic fit. This includes analysing financial statements, revenue streams, cost structures, and liabilities. Advanced financial modelling is often used to project the impact of the transaction on the acquiring company's performance. For example, a CFO might model how an acquisition will affect earnings per share (EPS) and return on investment (ROI) over a five-year horizon.

2. **Deal Structuring and Negotiation:** Structuring the deal is one of the most critical aspects of the CFO's role in M&A. The CFO must decide on the appropriate mix of cash, debt, and equity to finance the transaction, balancing the need to preserve financial flexibility with the desire to minimise dilution or leverage. For example, a CFO might propose a combination of cash payments and stock issuance to fund an acquisition while maintaining a healthy debt-to-equity ratio.

The CFO also plays a key role in negotiating the terms of the deal. This includes finalising the purchase price, representations and warranties, and earnout provisions. Effective negotiation ensures that the terms of the deal are favourable and protect the acquiring company's interests.

3. **Post-Merger Integration:** The success of an M&A transaction ultimately depends on how effectively the two organisations are integrated. The CFO oversees the alignment of financial systems, reporting structures, and operational processes. This includes harmonising accounting standards, consolidating ERP systems, and implementing unified budgeting practices.

Cultural integration is equally important. Misalignment between organisational cultures can undermine the benefits of the transaction. For example, if the acquired company's culture prioritises innovation while the acquiring company values efficiency, the CFO must work closely with HR and other departments to bridge these gaps and foster collaboration.

M&A transactions are inherently risky, with a significant percentage failing to achieve their intended objectives. Common challenges include overestimating synergies, underestimating integration complexities, and encountering unexpected regulatory hurdles. For CFOs, mitigating these risks requires a combination of rigorous analysis, proactive planning, and effective communication.

Another challenge is managing stakeholder expectations. Shareholders often have high hopes for M&A deals, expecting immediate improvements in financial performance or share price. The CFO must set realistic expectations, providing transparent updates on the progress of the transaction and its expected timeline for delivering results.

In conclusion, the CFO's role in M&A is multifaceted and requires a blend of strategic vision, financial expertise, and leadership skills. By carefully evaluating targets, structuring deals effectively, and managing integration challenges, CFOs can unlock significant value and drive long-term growth. In a competitive and dynamic business environment, M&A remains a powerful tool for transformation, and the CFO's guidance is critical to its success.

3.6 - Raising Capital in Private vs. Public Markets

Raising capital is one of the most fundamental responsibilities of a CFO, as it ensures that an organisation has the resources needed to fund operations, pursue growth initiatives, and achieve strategic goals. Companies can access capital through private or public markets, each of which offers unique advantages, challenges, and implications. For CFOs, understanding these differences and determining the right approach for their organisation is critical.

Private Markets: Flexibility and Confidentiality

Private markets involve raising capital from non-public sources, such as venture capital firms, private equity investors, or institutional lenders. This approach is often favoured by startups, early-stage companies, or businesses with innovative projects that require customised funding solutions. One of the key benefits of private markets is their flexibility. Investors in private markets are often willing to tailor their terms to the specific needs of the organisation, providing both funding and strategic guidance.

Confidentiality is another significant advantage. Unlike public offerings, which require extensive disclosure of financial and operational information, private fundraising allows companies to maintain greater control over sensitive data. For example, a CFO at a healthcare startup might seek funding from venture capitalists to develop a new medical device, avoiding the regulatory complexities and public scrutiny associated with a public offering.

However, private markets also present challenges. Access to private capital can be competitive, requiring companies to demonstrate strong business plans, financial projections, and clear exit strategies. Additionally, private funding often comes with restrictions, such as board representation or performance-based milestones, which can limit managerial autonomy.

Public Markets: Scale and Liquidity

Public markets involve raising capital by issuing shares or bonds that are traded on stock exchanges. This approach is best suited for established companies with strong financial performance and broad investor appeal. The primary advantage of public markets is their scale. By going public, companies can raise substantial amounts of capital to fund large-scale projects, acquisitions, or international expansion.

Public offerings also enhance liquidity, as shares can be freely traded, providing investors with an easy exit mechanism. This liquidity often attracts a wider pool of investors, including institutional and retail participants. For example, a CFO at a manufacturing firm might opt for an initial public offering (IPO) to fund the construction of a new production facility and diversify the company's investor base.

However, public markets come with challenges. The process of going public is time-consuming and costly, involving regulatory approvals, legal compliance, and underwriting fees. Public companies are also subject to ongoing reporting requirements, which can increase administrative burdens and expose the organisation to market volatility.

Balancing Private and Public Options

Many organisations use a combination of private and public funding to meet their capital needs. For instance, a technology startup might raise early-stage funding from venture capitalists before pursuing an IPO once it achieves profitability. The decision to transition from private to public markets often depends on factors such as growth trajectory, funding requirements, and market conditions.

In conclusion, the choice between private and public markets is one of the most critical decisions CFOs make when raising capital. By understanding the advantages and challenges of each option and aligning the decision with the organisation's strategic goals, CFOs can secure the resources needed to drive growth and create value. In a dynamic financial landscape, the ability to navigate these funding options is a hallmark of effective financial leadership.

3.7 - Treasury Management Basics

Treasury management is one of the most crucial yet often overlooked functions in corporate finance. It ensures that an organisation has the liquidity to meet its short-term obligations while maximising the returns on its financial resources. For CFOs, effective treasury management is about much more than managing cash; it's about creating a financial framework that supports the organisation's strategic goals and safeguards against potential risks. Whether dealing with cash flow forecasting, managing debt, or mitigating financial risks, the treasury function is integral to the organisation's financial health.

The primary objective of treasury management is ensuring liquidity, making sure the organisation can meet its financial obligations as they come due. This might include paying suppliers, meeting payroll, or servicing debt. Liquidity management becomes especially critical during periods of financial uncertainty, such as economic downturns or industry-specific disruptions.

Another key objective is optimising cash flow. For CFOs, this involves not only managing inflows and outflows efficiently but also identifying opportunities to improve operational efficiency. For example, a CFO might streamline accounts payable processes to improve payment accuracy while negotiating extended payment terms with suppliers to preserve cash.

Finally, treasury management plays a central role in financial risk mitigation. Whether it's managing interest rate fluctuations, foreign exchange volatility, or credit risk, the treasury function ensures that the organisation is well-protected against adverse financial events. Tools such as hedging instruments, credit risk assessments, and insurance policies are commonly used in this area.

Effective treasury management starts with accurate cash flow forecasting. By predicting inflows from sales, receivables, and investments alongside outflows for expenses, loan repayments, and capital expenditures, CFOs can ensure that the organisation has the cash it needs when it needs it. A robust cash flow forecast also helps identify potential cash shortages or surpluses, allowing CFOs to take proactive steps to address them.

For example, a CFO at a seasonal business, such as a holiday-themed retail chain, might use cash flow forecasting to anticipate low-revenue months and secure a short-term line of credit to cover operational expenses. Conversely, a company experiencing a surplus might invest idle cash in short-term, low-risk financial instruments to generate returns without jeopardising liquidity.

Treasury management also encompasses debt management, including negotiating favourable loan terms, ensuring timely repayments, and maintaining an optimal balance between short-term and long-term liabilities. CFOs must carefully evaluate the cost of debt relative to its benefits, ensuring that leverage is used effectively to support growth initiatives without overextending the organisation's financial capacity.

For instance, a CFO at a real estate development firm might choose to refinance high-interest short-term loans with lower-interest long-term debt, freeing up cash flow for new projects. Alternatively, a company seeking to minimise its debt burden might prioritise repaying high-interest loans while maintaining sufficient reserves for operational needs.

Idle cash represents an opportunity cost, as it could be earning returns elsewhere. Treasury management involves identifying the best use of surplus funds, often by investing in short-term, low-risk instruments such as money market funds, government securities, or certificates of deposit. The goal is to generate returns while preserving capital and ensuring funds remain accessible when needed.

For example, a CFO at a technology company might invest surplus cash from a successful product launch in short-term treasury bonds, earning a modest return while ensuring liquidity for future research and development initiatives.

Modern treasury management relies heavily on technology to improve efficiency, accuracy, and decision-making. Treasury management systems (TMS) provide real-time visibility into cash positions, automate routine processes, and integrate financial data from across the organisation. For example, a TMS might consolidate global cash balances, track payment statuses, and generate detailed liquidity reports, enabling CFOs to make informed decisions quickly.

Artificial intelligence (AI) and machine learning are also transforming treasury management. These technologies can analyse historical data to predict cash flow patterns, identify anomalies, and optimise investment decisions. For instance, an AI-powered tool might alert a CFO to an unexpected drop in receivables collections, prompting immediate corrective action.

In conclusion, treasury management is a vital component of corporate finance, ensuring liquidity, optimising cash flow, and mitigating financial risks. For CFOs, mastering this function requires a combination of technical expertise, strategic vision, and the ability to leverage modern technologies. By implementing robust treasury management practices, CFOs can strengthen their organisation's financial foundation, enabling it to thrive in both favourable and challenging conditions.

3.8 - Foreign Exchange and Risk Management

As globalisation continues to expand, managing foreign exchange (FX) risk has become a critical responsibility for CFOs. Organisations that operate across borders face exposure to currency fluctuations, which can significantly impact revenues, costs, and profitability. Effective FX and risk management strategies enable CFOs to protect the organisation from these uncertainties, ensuring financial stability and supporting long-term success.

FX risk arises when an organisation conducts transactions, holds assets, or incurs liabilities in multiple currencies. There are three primary types of FX risk:

1. Transaction Risk: This occurs when future cash flows, such as payments to suppliers or receipts from customers, are denominated in foreign currencies. For example, a UK-based importer that pays in US dollars is exposed to transaction risk if the pound weakens against the dollar, increasing the cost of goods.
2. Translation Risk: Companies with international operations face translation risk when consolidating their financial statements. Fluctuations in exchange rates can affect the reported value of foreign revenues, assets, and liabilities. For instance, a multinational company with significant operations in Europe might see a decline in reported earnings if the euro depreciates against the pound.
3. Economic Risk: This long-term risk relates to the impact of exchange rate movements on a company's market position and competitiveness. For example, a UK-based exporter may lose market share if the pound appreciates, making its products more expensive for foreign customers.

CFOs use a variety of tools and strategies to mitigate FX risk, including:

- **Natural Hedging:** Aligning revenues and expenses in the same currency reduces exposure to exchange rate fluctuations. For instance, a UK-based manufacturer with US customers might source raw materials from US suppliers, ensuring that both revenues and costs are in dollars.
  - **Forward Contracts:** These agreements lock in an exchange rate for a future transaction, providing certainty about the cost or value of foreign currency cash

flows. For example, a CFO might use forward contracts to secure the exchange rate for an upcoming payment to a supplier.

- **Options Contracts:** Currency options provide the right, but not the obligation, to exchange currencies at a predetermined rate. This flexibility allows CFOs to benefit from favourable exchange rate movements while limiting downside risk.

- **Swaps:** Currency swaps involve exchanging cash flows in one currency for cash flows in another, often used to manage longer-term exposures. For instance, a company with foreign currency debt might use a swap to convert its obligations into its home currency.

Technology has revolutionised FX risk management. Treasury management systems and FX platforms provide real-time visibility into currency exposures, enabling CFOs to make informed decisions. Advanced analytics and AI can also identify patterns and correlations between currencies and economic indicators, enhancing risk mitigation strategies.

In conclusion, foreign exchange and risk management are essential for organisations operating in a global environment. By leveraging advanced tools and strategies, CFOs can mitigate the impact of currency fluctuations, ensuring financial stability and protecting shareholder value. In an increasingly interconnected world, mastering FX risk management is a vital skill for today's financial leaders.

3.9 - Dividend Policy and Shareholder Returns

A company's dividend policy is a critical component of its financial strategy, reflecting how it balances rewarding shareholders with retaining capital for growth. For CFOs, crafting and maintaining an effective dividend policy involves considering the organisation's financial health, market conditions, and long-term strategic objectives. An optimised dividend policy not only enhances shareholder value but also signals financial stability and strategic intent, influencing investor confidence and market perceptions.

Dividends are payments made to shareholders from a company's profits. They represent a tangible return on investment and are often viewed as a sign of financial health and managerial confidence in the organisation's future prospects. However, dividends are not just about distributing profits; they are a strategic tool that can attract specific types of investors. For instance, income-focused investors, such as pension funds, often prioritise companies with consistent and predictable dividend payouts.

There are three main types of dividend policies:

- **Stable Dividend Policy:** Under this approach, companies pay a consistent dividend regardless of fluctuations in earnings. For example, a utility company with steady cash flows might adopt a stable policy to attract conservative investors seeking reliability. This approach signals financial strength and provides shareholders with a predictable income stream.
- **Target Payout Ratio:** This policy ties dividends to a fixed percentage of earnings, allowing payments to rise

or fall in line with profitability. Companies in cyclical industries, such as automotive or construction, often adopt this approach to align payouts with financial performance.

- **Residual Dividend Policy:** In this case, dividends are paid only after meeting all operational and investment needs. This policy is more common among growth-oriented companies that prioritise reinvesting profits to fund expansion or innovation.

Several factors influence a company's dividend policy, including:

- **Financial Stability:** Companies must ensure they have sufficient cash flow to sustain dividend payments without jeopardising operational needs. For example, a CFO at a manufacturing firm facing declining demand might reduce dividends to preserve cash for restructuring efforts.

- **Growth Opportunities:** Organisations in high-growth industries may prefer to reinvest profits into research and development or market expansion rather than distributing them to shareholders. For instance, a technology firm developing a new product line might suspend dividends temporarily to allocate resources toward innovation.

- **Market Expectations:** Publicly traded companies often face pressure from shareholders and analysts to maintain or increase dividends. Reducing dividends can negatively impact investor sentiment, even if the decision aligns with long-term strategic goals.

- **Industry Norms:** Dividend practices vary by industry. Real estate investment trusts (REITs), for example, are required by law to distribute a significant portion of their earnings as dividends, while tech startups often retain all profits to fuel growth.

- **Tax Implications:** Dividends are often taxed at a higher rate than capital gains, influencing shareholder preferences. CFOs must consider the tax efficiency of their dividend policies when making decisions.

The CFO plays a pivotal role in shaping and implementing dividend policy. This involves conducting thorough financial analyses to determine the company's capacity to pay dividends while balancing other priorities. CFOs must also communicate the rationale behind dividend decisions to stakeholders, ensuring transparency and maintaining trust.

For example, if a company decides to reduce dividends to fund a strategic acquisition, the CFO must clearly articulate how the acquisition will create long-term value for shareholders. Conversely, if the company increases dividends, the CFO should highlight the financial metrics, such as strong cash flow or reduced debt, that justify the decision.

In addition to dividends, companies can return value to shareholders through share buybacks. Buybacks reduce the number of outstanding shares, increasing earnings per share (EPS) and potentially boosting share prices. CFOs must weigh the merits of dividends versus buybacks based on the organisation's financial position, investor preferences, and market conditions. For instance, a CFO at a company with undervalued shares might prioritise buybacks to enhance shareholder returns while signalling confidence in the company's prospects.

In conclusion, dividend policy is a powerful tool for balancing shareholder expectations with organisational priorities. For CFOs, setting and managing dividends involves not only financial analysis but also strategic foresight and effective communication. By aligning dividend decisions with the company's long-term objectives, CFOs can enhance shareholder value, support sustainable growth, and build investor confidence.

3.10 - Case Study: Navigating a Complex M&A

Mergers and acquisitions (M&A) represent some of the most complex and impactful decisions an organisation can undertake. While they offer the potential for significant growth, innovation, and market expansion, they also involve substantial risks and challenges. This case study illustrates how a CFO successfully navigated a complex M&A transaction, balancing strategic objectives with financial discipline to deliver long-term value.

The Context: Expanding into a New Sector

TechWorld, a mid-sized technology company specialising in enterprise software, identified the healthcare sector as a strategic growth opportunity. The industry was experiencing rapid digital transformation, and TechWorld's leadership believed that entering this market could drive significant revenue growth. After extensive research, the company identified MediSoft, a healthcare IT firm with proprietary patient management software, as an ideal acquisition target.

The CFO, Mark, was tasked with leading the transaction. MediSoft's valuation was heavily influenced by its intellectual property and market position, making the deal both high-stakes and complex.

Phase 1: Target Evaluation and Due Diligence

Mark began by conducting comprehensive due diligence, working closely with external advisors to evaluate MediSoft's financial health, intellectual property, and operational capabilities. This included analysing revenue streams, customer contracts, and regulatory compliance. Mark also conducted scenario analyses to assess potential risks, such as changes in healthcare regulations or shifts in customer demand.

To ensure the acquisition would create value, Mark developed detailed financial models projecting the impact of the deal on TechWorld's earnings, cash flow, and market share. His analysis revealed significant synergies, including the ability to integrate MediSoft's software into TechWorld's existing platform and expand its customer base.

Phase 2: Structuring the Deal

Mark structured the deal as a combination of cash and equity, minimising the financial strain on TechWorld while incentivising MediSoft's management team to stay on board. He also negotiated an earnout provision tied to the performance of

MediSoft's software over the next three years, aligning the interests of both companies.

To fund the acquisition, Mark secured a credit facility with favourable terms and worked with the investor relations team to reassure shareholders about the strategic rationale behind the transaction.

Phase 3: Post-Merger Integration

Post-merger integration was critical to the success of the acquisition. Mark established a dedicated integration team to oversee the alignment of financial systems, reporting processes, and operational workflows. He prioritised open communication, holding regular meetings with stakeholders to address challenges and ensure alignment.

One of Mark's key initiatives was leveraging MediSoft's software to enhance TechWorld's product offerings. By integrating the software into its existing platform, TechWorld was able to differentiate itself in the competitive healthcare IT market, attracting new clients and increasing revenue.

The Outcome

Within two years, the acquisition delivered significant value. TechWorld's revenue in the healthcare sector grew by 40%, and operational efficiencies reduced costs by 15%. The company's share price rose by 25%, reflecting investor confidence in its strategic direction. Mark's leadership and meticulous planning were widely credited as key factors in the transaction's success.

Lessons Learned

This case highlights several important lessons for CFOs navigating complex M&A transactions:

1. **Thorough Due Diligence**: A rigorous evaluation of the target's financials, operations, and strategic fit is essential for identifying risks and opportunities.

2. **Strategic Deal Structuring**: Tailoring the deal structure to balance risk, cost, and incentives ensures financial sustainability.

3. **Effective Integration Planning**: Proactive planning and stakeholder engagement are critical for realising synergies and minimising disruption.

Conclusion

M&A transactions offer immense potential for growth and transformation, but their complexity requires careful planning and execution. For CFOs, the ability to navigate these challenges is a defining skill, enabling organisations to capitalise on strategic opportunities while managing risks. By combining financial expertise with strategic vision, CFOs can drive successful M&A outcomes that deliver long-term value.

Chapter 4

Cost Management and Optimisation

> *"Every Pound saved through smart cost management is a step closer to reinvestment in innovation and future success."*
> **Robert N. Jacobs**

Effective cost management is the foundation of financial resilience and strategic agility for any organisation. For CFOs, mastering cost management is about more than reducing expenses; it involves understanding the underlying factors driving costs, identifying inefficiencies, and implementing strategies that ensure resources are used optimally. This chapter explores key principles of cost management, offering practical insights for CFOs to optimise costs without compromising growth or operational integrity.

4.1 - Understanding Cost Drivers

Understanding cost drivers is an essential first step in effective cost management. Cost drivers are the underlying factors that influence the expenses incurred by an organisation. Identifying and analysing these drivers enables CFOs to allocate resources more efficiently, reduce unnecessary costs, and create strategies that align with business objectives.

Cost drivers vary significantly across industries and operational models. In manufacturing, for example, key cost drivers often include raw material prices, labour costs, energy consumption, and production volume. Meanwhile, in service-based industries, salaries, client acquisition expenses, and project delivery timelines may dominate the cost structure. Regardless of the sector, understanding what causes costs to rise or fall is vital for maintaining financial stability and competitiveness.

To identify cost drivers, CFOs need to conduct a detailed analysis of the organisation's operations. This often involves mapping processes, analysing spending patterns, and examining historical financial data. For instance, a CFO at a logistics company might discover that rising transportation costs are driven primarily by inefficient routing rather than fuel prices. Similarly, a retailer might find that higher inventory holding costs stem from overstocking seasonal products.

Quantifying cost drivers is equally important. Advanced tools such as data analytics and cost allocation models can help CFOs determine the extent to which each driver impacts overall expenses. For example, in a construction firm, analysing project costs might reveal that labour inefficiencies account for a significant portion of budget overruns. Armed with this knowledge, the CFO can develop targeted strategies to address the issue, such as investing in workforce training or adopting automated scheduling tools.

In addition to addressing inefficiencies, understanding cost drivers can support strategic decision-making. For instance, if labour costs are identified as a primary cost driver in a manufacturing business, the CFO might consider automating certain processes to reduce reliance on human resources.

Alternatively, a company heavily reliant on imported raw materials might explore opportunities to diversify its supplier base or source locally to mitigate the impact of fluctuating exchange rates.

Moreover, cost drivers often serve as indicators of broader organisational health. Rising maintenance costs, for example, might signal ageing equipment or inadequate preventive maintenance schedules, while increasing overtime expenses could point to workforce management challenges. By addressing these root causes, CFOs can achieve cost savings while improving overall efficiency and productivity.

The relationship between cost drivers and revenue generation should also be considered. In many cases, cost drivers are closely tied to business performance metrics. For instance, higher marketing expenses might initially appear as a cost burden but could drive long-term revenue growth through increased customer acquisition. CFOs must balance short-term cost control with long-term value creation, ensuring that cost-cutting measures do not undermine strategic goals.

To illustrate the importance of understanding cost drivers, consider the example of a CFO at a mid-sized healthcare organisation. Upon analysing the company's financial data, she discovered that administrative inefficiencies, particularly in billing and claims processing, were driving up operational costs. By implementing a new software system to streamline these processes, she reduced administrative expenses by 20% while improving patient satisfaction and staff productivity.

In conclusion, understanding cost drivers is foundational to effective cost management. For CFOs, this involves not only identifying and quantifying the factors that influence expenses but also using this insight to guide strategic decisions and address inefficiencies. By focusing on the most impactful cost drivers, organisations can achieve meaningful cost savings, improve operational efficiency, and build a foundation for sustainable growth.

4.2 - Fixed vs. Variable Costs

The distinction between fixed and variable costs is one of the most fundamental concepts in cost management. Fixed costs remain constant regardless of production levels or business activity, while variable costs fluctuate in direct proportion to operational output. For CFOs, understanding how these cost types behave and interact is critical for effective budgeting, forecasting, and strategic planning.

Fixed costs provide stability but also represent a significant financial commitment. Examples include rent, salaries of permanent staff, depreciation of machinery, and insurance premiums. These expenses do not change even if business activity declines, which can pose challenges during economic downturns. For instance, a retail chain that pays fixed rent for its stores must continue to meet these obligations even during periods of low foot traffic or seasonal slumps. While fixed costs are predictable, they can become a burden if revenue falls below expectations.

In contrast, variable costs are directly tied to operational activity. Common examples include raw materials, direct labour, and transportation costs. For example, a bakery's cost of flour and sugar will increase as production ramps up to meet higher customer demand. Variable costs offer flexibility, as they naturally adjust with changes in business activity. However, they also require close monitoring to avoid inefficiencies or wastage.

The balance between fixed and variable costs has profound implications for an organisation's risk profile and profitability. Companies with a high proportion of fixed costs, such as airlines or manufacturers, face greater financial risk during periods of low demand but benefit significantly from economies of scale during high production. Conversely, businesses with predominantly variable costs, such as consulting firms, have greater flexibility to adapt to market fluctuations but may struggle to achieve significant cost savings as activity levels rise.

CFOs play a critical role in managing this balance. In industries with high fixed costs, they must ensure that revenue streams are sufficient to cover these expenses. This might involve diversifying revenue sources, optimising pricing strategies, or implementing cost-sharing arrangements. For instance, a hotel chain with high fixed costs for property maintenance might partner with event organisers to generate additional income during off-peak seasons.

Alternatively, CFOs can explore opportunities to convert fixed costs into variable costs. This approach, known as cost transformation, can enhance flexibility and reduce financial risk. For example, a technology company might switch from owning servers to using cloud-based infrastructure, paying only for the storage and processing power it actually uses. Similarly, a logistics firm might outsource certain transportation activities, transforming fixed costs such as vehicle depreciation into variable costs tied to service usage.

Another important consideration is the interplay between fixed and variable costs in decision-making. For example, when evaluating a proposal to expand production capacity, the CFO must consider not only the additional variable costs but also the impact on fixed costs, such as the need for new equipment or facilities. Similarly, pricing decisions should account for both cost types to ensure that products or services remain profitable at different volume levels.

To illustrate these principles, consider the example of a CFO at a growing e-commerce company. Faced with rising fulfilment costs, she analysed the business's cost structure and identified opportunities to reduce fixed costs. By outsourcing warehousing to a third-party logistics provider, she converted a significant portion of fixed costs into variable costs, improving the company's ability to scale operations during peak shopping seasons. This strategy not only reduced financial risk but also enhanced customer satisfaction through faster delivery times.

In conclusion, understanding and managing fixed and variable costs is essential for effective cost management and strategic planning. For CFOs, this involves analysing cost behaviour, optimising spending, and aligning cost structures with the organisation's goals and risk tolerance. By striking the right balance between stability and flexibility, organisations can improve profitability, enhance resilience, and position themselves for sustainable growth.

4.3 - Activity-Based Costing (ABC)

Activity-Based Costing (ABC) is a modern approach to cost management that provides a more accurate method of assigning costs to products, services, or activities. Traditional cost accounting often allocates overhead costs based on simplistic factors such as labour hours or machine usage, which can result in distorted cost information. ABC, by contrast, identifies the true drivers of overhead and assigns costs accordingly. For CFOs, mastering ABC offers an opportunity to gain deeper insights into operational efficiency, pricing strategies, and profitability.

ABC starts with the premise that costs are driven by activities. Each activity within an organisation consumes resources, and these activities exist to support products, services, or customers. For example, activities in a manufacturing business might include machine setups, quality inspections, and inventory management. In a professional services firm, activities might include client meetings, proposal writing, and project reviews.

Under ABC, costs are allocated to activities based on their use of resources and then assigned to products or services based on their consumption of those activities. This multi-step process allows for a more precise understanding of cost behaviour.

Consider the example of a furniture manufacturer. Traditional costing might allocate factory overhead evenly across all products based on production hours. However, ABC would account for the fact that a custom-designed piece of furniture requires more design work, special tooling, and quality checks compared to a standard item. These additional activities and the resources they consume would result in higher costs being allocated to the custom product, providing a clearer picture of its true profitability.

Implementing ABC requires a systematic approach:

1. **Identify Activities**: The first step is to identify all significant activities within the organisation that consume resources. This might include production processes, customer service tasks, or administrative functions.

2. **Assign Costs to Activities**: Next, costs are allocated to these activities based on their resource consumption. For example, the cost of machine maintenance might be assigned to the "equipment setup" activity, while employee training expenses might be allocated to the "workforce development" activity.

3. **Determine Cost Drivers**: Each activity is linked to a cost driver, a measurable factor that reflects the consumption of resources. For instance, the number of setups might be the cost driver for the equipment setup activity, while

the number of customer interactions might drive customer service costs.

4. **Assign Costs to Products or Services**: Finally, costs are traced to specific products, services, or customers based on their use of activities. This step reveals the true cost of delivering each output.

The primary advantage of ABC is its ability to provide more accurate cost information. By recognising the diversity of activities and their resource requirements, ABC allows organisations to identify which products or services are truly profitable. This insight is particularly valuable in industries with high levels of customisation, complex operations, or significant overhead.

For example, a CFO at a technology company using ABC might discover that certain high-volume products, while generating substantial revenue, are less profitable due to their high consumption of support services. This realisation could prompt the company to adjust pricing, streamline operations, or reconsider its product mix.

ABC also supports better decision-making by highlighting opportunities for cost optimisation. For instance, if ABC analysis reveals that quality inspections are a major cost driver, the CFO might explore ways to reduce defects or streamline inspection processes.

While ABC offers significant benefits, its implementation can be challenging. The process requires detailed data collection, robust accounting systems, and collaboration across departments. Resistance to change is another common obstacle, as employees may be reluctant to adopt new methodologies or share the detailed information needed for ABC analysis.

Additionally, the complexity of ABC can make it resource-intensive, particularly for smaller organisations with limited capacity. However, advances in technology, such as enterprise resource planning (ERP) systems and data analytics tools, have made ABC more accessible and efficient to implement.

In conclusion, Activity-Based Costing is a powerful tool for understanding the true cost of operations, products, and services. For CFOs, implementing ABC provides a clearer picture of profitability, supports more informed decision-making, and reveals opportunities for cost optimisation. While the process requires effort and commitment, the long-term benefits in terms of accuracy, efficiency, and strategic alignment make it a worthwhile investment for organisations seeking to thrive in competitive markets.

4.4 - Lean Finance Principles

Lean finance is an approach to cost management that focuses on maximising value while minimising waste. Borrowed from lean manufacturing principles, lean finance emphasises efficiency, agility, and continuous improvement. For CFOs, adopting lean finance principles offers a framework for streamlining financial operations, enhancing decision-making, and fostering a culture of accountability.

Lean finance is built on several key principles:

1. **Value Focus:** The primary goal of lean finance is to deliver maximum value to stakeholders, whether shareholders, customers, or employees. This involves identifying financial processes that directly contribute to organisational goals and eliminating those that do not.

2. **Waste Reduction:** Lean finance seeks to eliminate waste in all its forms, including inefficiencies, redundancies, and errors. For example, automating repetitive tasks like invoice processing or expense reporting can save time and reduce costs.

3. **Empowerment:** Lean finance encourages collaboration and accountability across teams. By involving employees in identifying inefficiencies and suggesting improvements, organisations can create a culture of ownership and innovation.

4. **Agility:** In today's dynamic business environment, lean finance prioritises flexibility and adaptability. This might involve implementing rolling forecasts instead of static budgets or using real-time data to make faster, more informed decisions.

Adopting lean finance requires a strategic and incremental approach:

- **Map Financial Processes**: The first step is to map out all key financial processes, such as budgeting, forecasting, reporting, and compliance. This provides a clear picture of current workflows and identifies areas for improvement.

- **Identify Bottlenecks**: Next, CFOs should analyse these processes to identify bottlenecks, redundancies, or inefficiencies. For example, a lengthy approval process for capital expenditures might delay critical investments and create frustration among employees.

- **Implement Technology**: Technology plays a crucial role in lean finance. Tools such as cloud-based accounting software, robotic process automation (RPA), and data visualisation platforms can streamline workflows, enhance accuracy, and provide actionable insights.

- **Measure and Monitor**: Continuous improvement is a cornerstone of lean finance. CFOs should establish metrics to track progress, such as cycle times, error rates, or cost savings, and use this data to drive further refinements.

Lean finance delivers several benefits, including cost savings, improved efficiency, and enhanced decision-making. By eliminating waste, organisations can redirect resources toward strategic priorities, such as innovation or market expansion. Lean finance also fosters greater transparency and accountability, creating a stronger foundation for long-term success.

For example, a CFO at a multinational corporation might implement lean finance principles to streamline the annual budgeting process. By replacing traditional, time-consuming methods with rolling forecasts and collaborative planning tools, the company could reduce cycle times by 50% and improve the accuracy of its financial projections.

In conclusion, lean finance is a transformative approach to cost management that prioritises value, efficiency, and adaptability. For CFOs, implementing lean finance principles provides a roadmap for optimising financial processes, reducing costs, and fostering a culture of continuous improvement. In an increasingly competitive and fast-paced business environment, lean finance offers a strategic advantage that can drive sustained success.

4.5 - Identifying Inefficiencies

In cost management, identifying inefficiencies is often the first step toward meaningful optimisation. Inefficiencies, whether in processes, resource allocation, or decision-making, can significantly drain an organisation's profitability and operational effectiveness. For CFOs, uncovering these inefficiencies is about more than cutting costs; it's about building a sustainable framework that maximises value and enhances organisational agility.

Inefficiencies arise when resources are not used optimally to achieve the desired outcomes. They can manifest in various ways, such as redundant processes, excessive resource consumption, or delays that disrupt workflows. For example, a manufacturing firm with an outdated inventory management system may face inefficiencies in tracking stock levels, leading to overproduction or stockouts. Similarly, a service-based organisation with a high employee turnover rate may incur additional costs in recruitment, onboarding, and training without addressing the underlying issues.

Identifying inefficiencies requires a comprehensive understanding of how resources are allocated and utilised across the organisation. This often involves examining processes from end to end, analysing data for trends and anomalies, and engaging with employees at all levels to uncover bottlenecks or pain points. For instance, in a retail chain, the CFO might analyse discrepancies between sales forecasts and actual inventory levels to pinpoint inefficiencies in demand planning.

Several areas are particularly prone to inefficiencies, making them critical focal points for CFOs:

1. **Processes:** Inefficient workflows, whether caused by redundant steps, manual interventions, or poor coordination, are a common source of wasted time and resources. For example, a multi-step approval process for supplier payments might delay critical orders and frustrate employees.

2. **Technology:** Outdated or poorly integrated technology systems can hinder productivity and increase operational costs. For instance, a company relying on disconnected accounting and payroll systems may spend excessive time reconciling data manually.

3. **Resource Allocation:** Inefficient use of resources, such as labour, equipment, or office space, can lead to higher operational costs. For example, a consultancy firm assigning highly skilled professionals to routine administrative tasks may inadvertently drive up labour costs without adding value.

4. **Supply Chain:** Inefficiencies in procurement, logistics, or vendor management can significantly impact costs and service levels. For instance, a company with a fragmented supplier base might face higher shipping costs and longer lead times.

5. **Energy Consumption:** For organisations with significant physical infrastructure, inefficiencies in energy use can lead to substantial expenses. For example, a manufacturing plant operating machinery during peak electricity hours may incur higher energy bills unnecessarily.

CFOs have access to a range of tools and techniques to identify inefficiencies effectively:

1. **Process Mapping:** Visualising workflows helps identify redundant steps, delays, or bottlenecks. For example, mapping the procurement process might reveal excessive back-and-forth between departments, causing delays in supplier approvals.

2. **Benchmarking:** Comparing performance metrics against industry standards or competitors provides insights into areas for improvement. For instance, a CFO at a logistics company might benchmark delivery times and costs against industry leaders to identify gaps.

3. **Data Analytics:** Advanced analytics tools can uncover inefficiencies by identifying patterns, trends, or anomalies in operational data. For example, a retail chain might use analytics to detect stores with unusually high shrinkage rates and address underlying issues.

4. **Employee Feedback:** Engaging with employees at all levels can uncover inefficiencies that may not be immediately apparent in data. For example, frontline workers in a warehouse might identify outdated processes that slow down order fulfilment.

5. **Cost Variance Analysis:** Examining variances between budgeted and actual costs helps pinpoint areas where inefficiencies are driving overspending. For example, a CFO might investigate why a particular department consistently exceeds its travel budget.

Once inefficiencies are identified, the next step is to address them. This often involves streamlining processes, upgrading technology, or reallocating resources. For example, a company with redundant approval steps in its procurement process might implement an automated system to reduce delays and improve efficiency.

In some cases, addressing inefficiencies requires cultural or organisational changes. For instance, a company with siloed departments might need to foster greater collaboration and communication to improve workflow integration. Similarly, an organisation with high employee turnover may need to invest in training and employee engagement initiatives to retain talent and reduce recruitment costs.

In conclusion, identifying inefficiencies is a critical aspect of cost management and a key responsibility for CFOs. By using tools such as process mapping, benchmarking, and data analytics, CFOs can uncover areas where resources are being wasted and implement targeted solutions to address them. Beyond cost savings, tackling inefficiencies enhances organisational performance, builds resilience, and creates a foundation for sustainable growth. In a competitive business environment, the ability to identify and eliminate inefficiencies is a hallmark of effective financial leadership.

4.6 - Strategies for Cost Reduction

Cost reduction is a cornerstone of financial management, but it requires more than simply slashing budgets. Effective cost reduction strategies focus on optimising expenses without compromising quality, growth potential, or organisational culture. For CFOs, this delicate balancing act demands a nuanced understanding of the organisation's operations, goals, and market conditions.

Proactive vs. Reactive Cost Reduction

Cost reduction strategies can be either proactive or reactive. Proactive strategies are implemented as part of long-term financial planning, with a focus on improving efficiency and aligning costs with strategic objectives. For example, a CFO might renegotiate supplier contracts to secure better terms or invest in energy-efficient equipment to lower utility bills over time.

Reactive cost reduction, on the other hand, is often driven by external pressures, such as economic downturns, declining revenue, or sudden increases in costs. While necessary in certain situations, reactive measures, such as across-the-board budget cuts or layoffs, can have unintended consequences, such as reduced employee morale or diminished customer satisfaction.

Holistic Cost Reduction Strategies

Effective cost reduction requires a holistic approach that considers the organisation's entire cost structure. Key strategies include:

1. **Process Optimisation:** Streamlining workflows and eliminating redundancies can reduce operational costs significantly. For example, a manufacturing company might implement lean principles to minimise waste and improve production efficiency.

2. **Technology Integration:** Investing in technology can lower costs by automating manual processes, improving accuracy, and enhancing productivity. For instance, a retail chain might adopt inventory management software to reduce stockouts and overstocking.

3. **Strategic Outsourcing:** Outsourcing non-core functions, such as IT support or payroll processing, allows organisations to focus on their core competencies while reducing overhead. For example, a CFO might outsource data entry tasks to a specialised provider, freeing up internal resources for more strategic initiatives.

4. **Supplier Negotiations:** Renegotiating contracts with suppliers can yield significant savings. For instance, a restaurant chain might secure bulk discounts or flexible payment terms from food distributors.

5. **Energy Efficiency:** Reducing energy consumption not only lowers costs but also supports sustainability goals. For example, installing LED lighting or upgrading HVAC systems can result in substantial savings over time.

6. **Employee Engagement:** Engaging employees in cost-saving initiatives often uncovers innovative ideas. For example, a company might launch a suggestion programme where employees propose cost-saving measures, rewarding those that are successfully implemented.

While cost reduction is essential, it must be approached carefully to avoid unintended consequences. Overzealous cuts can harm the organisation's ability to grow or maintain quality. For example, cutting marketing budgets too deeply might reduce brand visibility, impacting sales and market share. Similarly, excessive layoffs can lead to a loss of institutional knowledge and reduced employee morale.

CFOs must ensure that cost reduction initiatives align with the organisation's strategic priorities and long-term goals. This often involves communicating the rationale behind cost-saving measures to employees and stakeholders, building consensus, and maintaining transparency.

In conclusion, cost reduction is a vital aspect of financial management, but it requires a strategic and balanced approach. For CFOs, the key is to implement measures that optimise expenses without undermining growth or quality. By focusing on process efficiency, technology integration, and strategic partnerships, organisations can achieve sustainable savings that support long-term success. In today's competitive landscape, effective cost reduction is not just a necessity; it is a competitive advantage.

4.7 - Balancing Cost-Cutting with Growth

Balancing cost-cutting initiatives with growth objectives is one of the most critical challenges for CFOs. While cost reduction can enhance profitability and improve operational efficiency, excessive or poorly executed cost-cutting measures can stifle innovation, hinder employee morale, and undermine long-term growth. The art of balancing these competing priorities lies in developing strategies that achieve financial savings without compromising the organisation's ability to innovate, expand, and adapt.

Cost-cutting and growth often seem at odds. On the one hand, reducing expenses is essential for improving margins, especially during periods of financial stress or economic uncertainty. On the other hand, growth requires investment, whether in talent, technology, marketing, or research and development (R&D). CFOs must navigate this tension by identifying areas where costs can be optimised without hindering the organisation's strategic goals.

For instance, a CFO at a pharmaceutical company may need to cut operating expenses to improve cash flow but must carefully protect investments in R&D, which are essential for future revenue generation. Similarly, a retail chain facing declining sales might reduce non-essential expenses such as administrative overhead but continue investing in digital transformation to enhance the customer experience and drive growth.

Strategic Approaches to Balancing Cost-Cutting with Growth

1. **Prioritising Value-Driven Investments**

   A key principle in balancing cost-cutting with growth is to focus on value-driven investments, initiatives that deliver the highest return on investment (ROI) or align most closely with the organisation's strategic objectives. For example, a technology company may choose to scale back spending on non-core activities while increasing its investment in artificial intelligence (AI) research to maintain a competitive edge in the market.

CFOs can use tools such as cost-benefit analysis and ROI modelling to evaluate the trade-offs between cost savings and growth opportunities. By quantifying the potential impact of each decision, they can allocate resources more effectively.

1. **Emphasising Operational Efficiency**: Cost-cutting does not always mean sacrificing growth. In many cases, improving operational efficiency can achieve both objectives. For example, streamlining supply chain processes, adopting automation technologies, or renegotiating vendor contracts can reduce costs while enhancing productivity and scalability.

Consider a logistics company that invests in route optimisation software. This initiative not only reduces fuel costs but also enables faster deliveries, improving customer satisfaction and driving business growth.

1. **Fostering a Culture of Innovation**: Cost-cutting initiatives should not come at the expense of creativity and innovation. CFOs must ensure that employees remain motivated and empowered to contribute ideas for improving efficiency and driving growth. For instance, implementing a company-wide suggestion programme can encourage employees to identify cost-saving opportunities while fostering a culture of continuous improvement.

2. **Adopting a Long-Term Perspective**: While short-term cost reductions may be necessary in some cases, CFOs must also consider the long-term implications of their decisions. For example, cutting training budgets may save money in the short term but could lead to skill gaps and lower productivity over time. Similarly, scaling back on marketing during a downturn might harm brand visibility and market share, making recovery more difficult when conditions improve.

A balanced approach involves maintaining or even increasing spending in areas that directly support growth, such as employee development, technology adoption, and customer acquisition while identifying non-essential areas for cost reduction.

3. **Leveraging Data and Analytics**: Data-driven decision-making is essential for balancing cost-cutting with growth. Advanced analytics tools can provide CFOs with insights into cost behaviour, customer trends, and market opportunities, enabling them to make informed decisions about where to allocate resources. For instance, a retailer might use predictive analytics to

identify high-growth product categories and focus its marketing and inventory efforts on those areas.

In conclusion, cost-cutting with growth is a complex but essential responsibility for CFOs. By prioritising value-driven investments, improving operational efficiency, and maintaining a long-term perspective, organisations can achieve financial savings without jeopardising their ability to innovate and expand. In a rapidly changing business environment, the ability to balance these priorities effectively is a hallmark of strong financial leadership.

4.8 - Managing Overhead Costs

Overhead costs, expenses that are not directly tied to production or service delivery, can significantly impact an organisation's profitability. These include costs such as office rent, utilities, administrative salaries, and IT infrastructure. While overhead costs are essential for supporting operations, they can also become a burden if not managed effectively. For CFOs, optimising overhead costs requires a strategic approach that balances cost control with the need to maintain organisational capabilities and employee morale.

Overhead costs are often classified into three categories:

1. **Fixed Overheads:** These remain constant regardless of business activity, such as office rent or insurance premiums. For example, a law firm pays the same lease amount for its office space, whether it serves 10 clients or 100 clients.

2. **Variable Overheads:** These fluctuate with business activity, such as utilities or office supplies. For instance,

an e-commerce company's electricity bill may increase during peak shopping seasons due to higher server usage.

3. **Semi-Variable Overheads:** These include costs that have both fixed and variable components, such as employee salaries with performance-based bonuses.

Understanding these categories helps CFOs identify which costs can be controlled and where flexibility exists.

Strategies for Managing Overhead Costs

1. **Conducting an Overhead Audit**: The first step in managing overhead costs is to conduct a thorough audit to identify areas of inefficiency or unnecessary spending. For example, a company might discover that it is paying for unused office space or underutilised software subscriptions. By eliminating or renegotiating these expenses, the organisation can achieve immediate cost savings.

2. **Embracing Technology**: Technology can play a significant role in reducing overhead costs. For instance, implementing cloud-based software can lower IT infrastructure expenses, while automating administrative tasks can reduce labour costs. A finance department that uses robotic process automation (RPA) to handle data entry tasks can reallocate staff to higher-value activities, improving overall efficiency.

3. **Optimising Facilities Management**: Office space and utilities are major components of overhead costs. CFOs can reduce these expenses by adopting flexible working arrangements, consolidating office locations, or

implementing energy-efficient practices. For example, a hybrid work model might allow a company to downsize its office footprint, resulting in substantial savings.

4. **Negotiating Vendor Contracts**: Many overhead costs, such as maintenance services or office supplies, involve third-party vendors. CFOs can achieve savings by renegotiating contracts, consolidating suppliers, or leveraging economies of scale. For instance, a multinational corporation might centralise its procurement function to negotiate better terms with global vendors.

5. **Monitoring and Controlling Discretionary Spending**: Overhead costs often include discretionary spending, such as travel, entertainment, and employee perks. While these expenses contribute to employee satisfaction and business development, they must be managed carefully. For example, introducing travel policies or approval processes for discretionary expenses can prevent overspending without compromising employee morale.

In conclusion, managing overhead costs is a critical component of cost optimisation. For CFOs, this involves identifying inefficiencies, leveraging technology, and adopting innovative strategies to reduce expenses without compromising organisational capabilities. By taking a strategic approach, organisations can achieve sustainable savings and build a leaner, more agile operational model that supports long-term success.

4.9 - Vendor and Supply Chain Cost Optimisation

The costs associated with vendors and supply chains represent a significant portion of many organisations' operational expenses. Managing these costs effectively is not just about reducing expenses but also about ensuring reliability, quality, and resilience in supply chain operations. For CFOs, vendor and supply chain cost optimisation is a critical area that requires strategic thinking, strong negotiation skills, and the ability to align cost-saving measures with broader organisational goals.

Vendors and supply chains form the backbone of operational efficiency. From sourcing raw materials to delivering finished goods, every step in the supply chain incurs costs. Inefficiencies or disruptions in this system can lead to escalating expenses, delayed production, or even lost revenue. For example, a manufacturing company dependent on a single supplier for critical components might face skyrocketing costs if the supplier experiences a shortage or increases prices unexpectedly.

Optimising vendor and supply chain costs can yield significant benefits, including improved profitability, enhanced operational agility, and reduced financial risk. However, achieving these benefits requires a careful balance between cost reduction and maintaining strong relationships with vendors and suppliers.

Strategies for Vendor and Supply Chain Cost Optimisation

1. **Consolidating Vendors**: One of the most effective ways to reduce supply chain costs is to consolidate vendors. By working with fewer suppliers, organisations can

leverage their purchasing power to negotiate better terms, such as bulk discounts or extended payment periods. For instance, a food processing company might consolidate its packaging vendors to secure volume-based pricing and reduce administrative overhead.

However, vendor consolidation must be approached carefully to avoid over-reliance on a single supplier, which could increase risk in the event of disruptions. CFOs must evaluate supplier reliability, financial stability, and contingency plans before making decisions.

2. **Enhancing Supplier Relationships**: Building strong, collaborative relationships with suppliers can lead to mutually beneficial cost-saving opportunities. For example, a CFO might engage suppliers in joint planning sessions to identify inefficiencies or explore ways to reduce costs through process improvements. A logistics company, for instance, could work with its carriers to optimise shipping routes, lowering fuel consumption and transportation costs.

3. **Implementing Just-in-Time (JIT) Inventory Management**: JIT inventory management reduces carrying costs by aligning inventory levels with actual demand. By sourcing materials or products only as needed, organisations can minimise storage costs and reduce the risk of inventory obsolescence. For example, a retailer implementing JIT practices might work closely with suppliers to ensure timely deliveries based on real-time sales data.

While JIT offers significant cost savings, it requires robust coordination and reliable suppliers to avoid stockouts or production delays. CFOs must assess whether their supply chains are resilient enough to support this approach.

4. **Leveraging Technology and Data Analytics**: Advanced technologies such as supply chain management software, predictive analytics, and artificial intelligence (AI) can provide valuable insights into cost drivers and inefficiencies. For example, an e-commerce company might use AI to analyse shipping patterns and identify cost-saving opportunities, such as consolidating shipments or selecting more efficient delivery routes.

Technology can also improve visibility across the supply chain, enabling CFOs to monitor vendor performance, track costs, and identify potential risks. For instance, blockchain technology can enhance transparency by providing a secure, immutable record of transactions across the supply chain.

5. **Diversifying the Supplier Base**: While consolidating vendors can lead to cost savings, it's equally important to diversify the supplier base to reduce risk. A diversified supply chain can protect organisations from price increases, shortages, or geopolitical disruptions. For example, a pharmaceutical company sourcing active ingredients from multiple countries might avoid production delays caused by regulatory changes in one region.

6. **Negotiating Flexible Terms**: Negotiating favourable terms with vendors is a core responsibility of CFOs. This

might include securing volume discounts, extending payment terms, or incorporating price adjustment clauses into contracts. For example, a manufacturing firm might negotiate a fixed price for raw materials over a specified period to protect against market volatility.

In conclusion, vendor and supply chain cost optimisation is a critical area of focus for CFOs seeking to enhance operational efficiency and profitability. By consolidating vendors, leveraging technology, and building strong supplier relationships, organisations can achieve substantial cost savings while maintaining reliability and quality. In an increasingly complex and interconnected business environment, effective supply chain management is a vital component of financial leadership.

4.10 - Case Study: Implementing Cost Controls

Cost control is a cornerstone of financial management, yet it requires a nuanced approach to achieve meaningful and sustainable results. This case study explores how a mid-sized manufacturing company successfully implemented cost controls under the leadership of its CFO, demonstrating the impact of strategic planning, collaboration, and continuous monitoring.

The Context: Rising Operational Costs

When Mark joined the company as CFO, he faced a significant challenge: rising operational costs were eroding profit margins despite steady revenue growth. The company's cost structure was bloated by inefficiencies in production, high overhead expenses, and escalating supply chain costs. Mark recognised that addressing these issues would require a comprehensive and strategic cost control initiative.

The Approach

Mark began by conducting a detailed cost analysis to identify key inefficiencies and cost drivers. Using data analytics tools, he categorised costs into direct, indirect, and overhead expenses, allowing him to pinpoint areas with the greatest potential for savings.

> **Step 1: Streamlining Production Processes:** Mark worked closely with the operations team to implement lean manufacturing principles. By optimising workflows, reducing waste, and improving equipment maintenance schedules, the company achieved a 15% reduction in production costs. For example, introducing preventive maintenance eliminated costly equipment breakdowns while standardising processes reduced variability in output.
>
> **Step 2: Optimising Overhead Costs:** Mark identified opportunities to reduce overhead costs by renegotiating vendor contracts, consolidating office spaces, and adopting energy-efficient technologies. For instance, the company installed LED lighting and upgraded HVAC systems, resulting in annual energy savings of £250,000. Additionally, Mark introduced a hybrid work model, allowing the company to downsize its headquarters and save on rent.
>
> **Step 3: Enhancing Supply Chain Efficiency:** Supply chain inefficiencies were another significant cost driver. Mark

collaborated with suppliers to implement just-in-time inventory practices, reducing carrying costs and minimising waste. He also introduced predictive analytics to improve demand forecasting, ensuring that the company maintained optimal inventory levels without overstocking or understocking.

Step 4: Engaging Employees in Cost Control: Recognising that cost control required buy-in across the organisation, Mark launched a cost-saving initiative that encouraged employees to propose ideas for reducing expenses. The programme generated over 100 suggestions, ranging from process improvements to energy-saving measures, many of which were implemented with measurable results.

The Results

Within two years, Mark's cost control initiatives delivered impressive results. The company reduced total operating expenses by 18%, improving profit margins significantly. These savings were reinvested into R&D and marketing, enabling the company to launch new products and expand into international markets. Employee engagement also improved, as the collaborative approach fostered a sense of ownership and accountability.

Lessons Learned

This case highlights several key lessons for CFOs implementing cost controls:

1. **Data-Driven Decisions**: A thorough cost analysis is essential for identifying inefficiencies and prioritising initiatives.

2. **Cross-functional collaboration**: Engaging employees and working closely with departments ensures buy-in and maximises the impact of cost control measures.
3. **Continuous Improvement**: Cost control is an ongoing process that requires regular monitoring, adaptation, and innovation.

Conclusion

Implementing cost controls is a complex but rewarding endeavour that can significantly enhance organisational performance and profitability. For CFOs, the key to success lies in taking a strategic, data-driven approach that balances short-term savings with long-term goals. By fostering collaboration, leveraging technology, and prioritising continuous improvement, organisations can achieve sustainable cost control and build a foundation for growth.

Chapter 5

Strategic Decision-Making

"The essence of strategy lies in choosing what to sacrifice today to secure tomorrow's success."
Robert N. Jacobs

In the dynamic world of modern business, the ability to make strategic decisions is a cornerstone of effective financial leadership. For CFOs, strategic decision-making extends far beyond balancing spreadsheets; it involves aligning financial insights with organisational goals, anticipating market changes, and navigating competitive landscapes. This chapter explores the principles, tools, and frameworks that empower CFOs to make decisions that drive sustainable growth and resilience. By mastering the art of balancing short-term priorities with long-term aspirations, CFOs can lead their organisations through uncertainty, seize opportunities, and create value for stakeholders in an increasingly complex global economy.

5.1 - Strategic vs. Tactical Financial Decisions

In the realm of financial leadership, one of the most critical distinctions a CFO must understand is the difference between strategic and tactical financial decisions. While both are essential to the organisation's success, they serve distinct purposes and operate on different timelines. Strategic decisions focus on long-term goals and the broader vision of the organisation, while tactical decisions address immediate operational needs and short-term objectives. A CFO's ability to navigate and balance these dimensions can significantly impact organisational performance.

Strategic financial decisions are future-oriented and designed to shape the organisation's trajectory over an extended period. These decisions often involve significant resource allocation, such as entering a new market, acquiring a competitor, or investing in innovative technology. For example, a CFO at a pharmaceutical company might decide to allocate a substantial portion of the budget to research and development for breakthrough treatments expected to generate revenue in five to ten years. Such decisions are complex, requiring thorough market analysis, scenario planning, and alignment with the company's overarching goals. Strategic decisions are inherently high-stakes, as their outcomes can redefine the organisation's position within its industry.

In contrast, tactical financial decisions are short-term actions that address specific, immediate needs. These decisions are often operational in nature, focusing on cash flow management, cost containment, or resource reallocation. For instance, a CFO at a retail company experiencing a temporary liquidity challenge might decide to renegotiate payment terms with suppliers or secure a short-term credit facility. Tactical decisions are generally less risky than strategic ones but require quick thinking and precise execution to ensure operational continuity.

While strategic and tactical decisions operate on different timelines, they are deeply interconnected. Tactical decisions often serve as the foundation for achieving strategic objectives. For instance, a company aiming to expand its presence in emerging markets might implement tactical measures such as reallocating marketing budgets or establishing partnerships with local distributors. These short-term actions enable the organisation to make gradual progress toward its long-term goals. Conversely, strategic decisions set the framework within which tactical decisions are made. Without a clear strategic vision, tactical actions can become disjointed, leading to inefficiencies and missed opportunities.

Balancing these two dimensions requires a holistic perspective and robust analytical tools. CFOs must assess the potential trade-offs between short-term gains and long-term objectives. For example, cutting discretionary spending might improve the organisation's cash position in the short term but could hinder innovation or customer satisfaction in the long run. The ability to evaluate such trade-offs is particularly crucial during periods of economic uncertainty or market disruption, where both immediate action and long-term resilience are essential.

The tools available to CFOs for managing strategic and tactical decisions are increasingly sophisticated. Scenario planning, for instance, allows decision-makers to evaluate the potential outcomes of various courses of action under different market conditions. Financial modelling provides a detailed understanding of how decisions will impact key metrics such as revenue, profitability, and cash flow. By leveraging these tools,

CFOs can make informed decisions that align with the organisation's goals while mitigating risks.

A compelling example of this balance comes from a CFO in the renewable energy sector. Facing regulatory changes that incentivised green energy adoption, the CFO developed a strategic plan to invest in solar and wind energy projects. To support this long-term initiative, the CFO implemented tactical measures such as renegotiating supplier contracts and streamlining operational costs to free up capital. This dual approach ensured the organisation could respond to immediate financial challenges while positioning itself for sustainable growth in a rapidly evolving market.

In conclusion, the distinction between strategic and tactical financial decisions is fundamental to effective financial leadership. While strategic decisions shape the organisation's future, tactical decisions ensure its immediate operational success. The ability to balance these dimensions, aligning short-term actions with long-term goals, is a hallmark of a successful CFO. By leveraging their expertise and using advanced tools, CFOs can navigate the complexities of modern business environments, driving both resilience and growth.

5.2 - Role of CFO in Business Strategy

The role of the Chief Financial Officer in business strategy has evolved significantly over the past decade. Today, CFOs are no longer confined to managing budgets, overseeing financial reports, or ensuring compliance. Instead, they are strategic leaders who play a pivotal role in shaping the organisation's vision, driving innovation, and steering it toward long-term success. This evolution reflects the increasing complexity of modern business environments, where financial insights are integral to navigating challenges, seizing opportunities, and maintaining competitive advantage.

At the heart of the CFO's strategic role is their ability to connect financial performance with broader business goals. This requires a deep understanding of the organisation's mission, industry trends, and market dynamics. For instance, a CFO in the automotive sector might analyse the financial implications of transitioning from internal combustion engines to electric vehicles. This analysis would include assessing the costs of R&D, forecasting revenue from new product lines, and evaluating potential government incentives for clean energy adoption. By translating financial data into actionable insights, the CFO ensures that strategic decisions are grounded in economic reality.

The CFO's influence on business strategy extends beyond numbers. They are often the voice of reason, challenging assumptions and advocating for data-driven decisions. For example, during a board discussion on launching a new product, the CFO might highlight risks such as market saturation or high production costs, ensuring that the organisation fully understands the financial implications before proceeding. This ability to combine analytical rigour with strategic vision makes the CFO an indispensable member of the executive team.

Collaboration is another cornerstone of the CFO's strategic role. Business strategy is inherently cross-functional, requiring input from departments such as marketing, operations, and R&D. The CFO acts as a bridge, aligning financial resources with the needs of these functions. For example, when planning an international expansion, the CFO might work with the marketing team to allocate budgets for localised campaigns, with the operations team to establish supply chain infrastructure, and with HR to recruit talent in the target region. This collaborative approach ensures that the organisation's strategy is cohesive and well-supported.

In addition to collaboration, the CFO must also drive organisational alignment. This involves translating high-level strategic objectives into actionable plans and ensuring that all departments are working toward common goals. For instance, a CFO in the retail industry might develop a financial plan that prioritises investment in e-commerce capabilities, reflecting the company's strategy to capitalise on shifting consumer behaviour. By aligning budgets, forecasts, and KPIs with strategic priorities, the CFO creates a framework for effective execution and accountability.

Risk management is another critical aspect of the CFO's strategic role. Every business strategy involves a degree of uncertainty, whether it's entering a new market, adopting a disruptive technology, or responding to regulatory changes. The CFO is responsible for identifying these risks, quantifying their potential impact, and developing mitigation strategies. For example, a CFO at a pharmaceutical company considering an acquisition might conduct due diligence to uncover hidden liabilities or operational challenges. By addressing these risks proactively, the CFO protects the organisation's financial health and reputation.

A compelling illustration of the CFO's strategic role comes from the technology sector. When a mid-sized software company faced declining market share due to outdated products, its CFO led a strategic transformation. By reallocating budgets to R&D, streamlining operational costs, and securing investment for cloud-based services, the CFO positioned the company to compete in the growing SaaS market. Within three years, the company's revenue had doubled, and its market position was significantly strengthened.

In conclusion, the modern CFO is a strategic leader whose role extends far beyond financial management. By connecting financial insights with business objectives, fostering cross-functional collaboration, and driving organisational alignment, CFOs play a central role in shaping their companies' futures. In an era of rapid change and increasing complexity, their ability to balance analytical precision with visionary leadership is more important than ever.

5.3 - Evaluating Market Opportunities

For CFOs, evaluating market opportunities is a cornerstone of strategic decision-making. In an era of constant change, where industries are shaped by technological advancements, shifting consumer behaviours, and global economic trends, identifying and assessing growth opportunities is critical to maintaining a competitive edge. This process requires a balance of analytical expertise, strategic foresight, and a deep understanding of the organisation's goals and capabilities.

Market opportunities arise from unmet needs, emerging trends, or gaps in existing markets that an organisation can address profitably. They may include expanding into new geographic regions, launching innovative products or services, targeting under-served customer segments, or capitalising on disruptive technologies. For instance, during the rapid adoption of e-commerce, many traditional retailers recognised opportunities to establish digital sales channels, reaching customers beyond their physical locations.

Evaluating these opportunities begins with understanding their potential impact on the organisation's growth and profitability. CFOs must ensure that market opportunities align with the company's strategic objectives, financial capacity, and risk tolerance. This involves answering key questions: Is this market aligned with our core competencies? Do we have the resources to execute effectively? What are the potential risks and rewards?

The evaluation process relies heavily on data. CFOs must analyse quantitative and qualitative information to assess the feasibility and attractiveness of a given opportunity. Market research provides insights into demand dynamics, customer preferences, and competitive positioning. For example, a CFO exploring expansion into a new region might examine data on population demographics, purchasing power, and local competitors to determine whether the market has sufficient potential.

Additionally, financial modelling plays a crucial role in evaluating market opportunities. By projecting potential revenue, costs, and profit margins, CFOs can estimate the return on investment (ROI) and break-even timelines. Sensitivity analyses further enhance this process by assessing how changes in key variables, such as pricing, costs, or market share, could impact outcomes. For instance, a CFO evaluating a new product launch might model scenarios where raw material prices fluctuate due to supply chain disruptions.

While financial metrics are vital, market evaluation should also consider non-financial factors that could influence success. These include cultural differences, regulatory environments, and technological readiness. For example, a global food and beverage company entering a new region might need to adapt its product offerings to local tastes and comply with stringent health and safety regulations. Ignoring these factors could result in costly missteps.

Another critical consideration is the organisation's internal readiness. Entering a new market or launching a new product often requires significant operational adjustments, from scaling production capacity to hiring local talent. CFOs must assess whether the organisation has the capabilities and resources to execute effectively or whether additional investment is required.

Market opportunities inherently involve risk, and the CFO's role is to balance these risks against potential rewards. This requires a comprehensive risk assessment, identifying potential challenges such as market saturation, economic volatility, or technological obsolescence. For instance, a CFO considering an acquisition in a fast-growing industry might evaluate whether the target company's growth is sustainable or driven by short-term trends.

Diversification is another important risk management strategy. Rather than relying heavily on a single market or product line, CFOs can explore opportunities that complement the organisation's existing portfolio. For example, a technology company focused on hardware might expand into software development, creating a more balanced and resilient revenue stream.

In conclusion, evaluating market opportunities is a complex but essential process for CFOs. By combining data-driven analysis with strategic insight and a clear understanding of organisational capabilities, CFOs can identify opportunities that align with long-term goals while managing risks effectively. In a competitive and fast-changing world, this ability to assess and seize opportunities is a defining characteristic of successful financial leadership.

5.4 - Resource Allocation Strategies

Resource allocation is a critical aspect of strategic decision-making, involving the distribution of an organisation's finite resources, capital, personnel, and time, toward initiatives that maximise value and support long-term goals. For CFOs, mastering resource allocation means ensuring that investments are not only aligned with strategic priorities but also optimised for efficiency and impact. Effective resource allocation can make the difference between an organisation that thrives and one that falters in a competitive marketplace.

At its core, resource allocation is about alignment. CFOs must ensure that every pound spent contributes directly or indirectly to the organisation's strategic objectives. This requires a deep understanding of the company's goals, such as entering new markets, driving innovation, or enhancing customer experience. For example, a retail chain pursuing digital transformation might prioritise investments in e-commerce platforms and data analytics while scaling back on traditional advertising channels.

Strategic alignment also involves balancing competing priorities. Organisations often face multiple, equally compelling opportunities but limited resources. The CFO's role is to evaluate these opportunities and allocate resources where they will generate the greatest impact. This might involve prioritising high-growth markets, funding R&D for innovative products, or addressing operational inefficiencies that constrain profitability.

Effective resource allocation is underpinned by robust data and analysis. CFOs use tools such as cost-benefit analysis, ROI modelling, and scenario planning to assess the potential outcomes of different investment options. For instance, when deciding between upgrading manufacturing equipment or expanding into a new market, a CFO might compare the projected returns, payback periods, and risks associated with each option.

In addition to financial metrics, non-financial factors play a crucial role in resource allocation. These include organisational capabilities, market trends, and competitive dynamics. For example, investing in employee training might not yield immediate financial returns but could enhance productivity and innovation over time, supporting long-term growth.

In today's fast-paced business environment, static resource allocation models are no longer sufficient. CFOs must adopt a dynamic approach, continuously reassessing and reallocating resources in response to changing circumstances. For example, during the COVID-19 pandemic, many organisations shifted resources toward digital initiatives and supply chain resilience to adapt to disruptions.

Dynamic resource allocation also involves identifying and addressing resource bottlenecks. For instance, a technology company experiencing delays in product development might reallocate funding from marketing to R&D to accelerate progress. By maintaining flexibility, CFOs can ensure that resources are deployed where they are needed most.

One of the greatest challenges in resource allocation is balancing efficiency with innovation. While cost-cutting measures can free up resources for growth, excessive focus on efficiency can stifle creativity and limit the organisation's ability to innovate. CFOs must find a balance that supports both operational excellence and strategic experimentation.

For example, a pharmaceutical company might allocate a portion of its R&D budget to high-risk, high-reward projects while ensuring that core operations remain well-funded. This dual approach enables the organisation to pursue breakthrough innovations without compromising its financial stability.

In conclusion, resource allocation is a fundamental responsibility of the CFO, requiring a strategic and dynamic approach. By aligning resources with organisational priorities, leveraging data-driven insights, and balancing efficiency with innovation, CFOs can ensure that every investment drives value and supports long-term success. In an increasingly competitive world, effective resource allocation is not just a financial discipline; it is a strategic imperative.

5.5 - Navigating Competitive Landscapes

In today's rapidly evolving business environment, navigating competitive landscapes has become an essential skill for CFOs. The ability to understand and adapt to competition not only ensures survival but also creates opportunities for growth and differentiation. This requires a strategic approach that blends financial analysis, market intelligence, and a deep understanding of the organisation's strengths and weaknesses. By effectively navigating competitive pressures, CFOs can position their organisations for sustained success.

Every industry is shaped by unique competitive dynamics, including market saturation, customer expectations, and technological advancements. For CFOs, the first step in navigating these landscapes is gaining a comprehensive understanding of the competitive environment. This involves analysing competitors' strategies, identifying emerging trends, and assessing the organisation's position in the market.

Tools such as **SWOT analysis** (Strengths, Weaknesses, Opportunities, and Threats) and Porter's Five Forces can provide valuable insights into competitive pressures. For example, a CFO in the retail sector might evaluate how bargaining power among suppliers and buyers impacts profitability, while also identifying opportunities to differentiate through customer experience or product innovation.

Competitive analysis should also include benchmarking against industry peers. By comparing key financial metrics, such as profit margins, revenue growth, and cost structures, CFOs can identify areas where the organisation lags behind or excels. For instance, discovering that a competitor has achieved lower production costs through automation could prompt the CFO to explore similar technologies.

Disruption is a defining feature of modern competitive landscapes. Whether driven by technological innovation, regulatory changes, or shifting consumer preferences, disruption can rapidly alter the rules of competition. For CFOs, the ability to anticipate and adapt to these changes is critical.

Consider the impact of digital transformation on traditional industries. Media companies, for instance, have faced significant disruption as audiences shift from print to digital platforms. CFOs in this sector must allocate resources toward developing digital capabilities while managing the decline of legacy revenue streams. Similarly, in the automotive industry, the rise of electric vehicles and autonomous technology has forced CFOs to reevaluate investment priorities and strategic partnerships.

Adapting to disruption often involves a willingness to take calculated risks. For example, a CFO at a manufacturing firm might decide to invest in 3D printing technology, recognising its potential to reduce costs and improve customisation capabilities. While the technology may require significant upfront investment, its long-term benefits could position the company as a leader in its field.

In highly competitive markets, differentiation is key to gaining an edge. CFOs play a central role in identifying and supporting initiatives that set the organisation apart from its competitors. This might involve investing in innovation, enhancing customer experience, or building a strong brand.

For instance, a CFO at a hospitality company might allocate resources to developing a loyalty programme that rewards repeat customers and fosters brand loyalty. By analysing customer data and identifying preferences, the CFO can tailor the programme to meet customer expectations, creating a competitive advantage.

Differentiation can also be achieved through strategic partnerships. For example, a healthcare company might collaborate with technology firms to develop telemedicine solutions, addressing a growing demand for remote healthcare services. CFOs must assess the financial implications of such partnerships, ensuring that they deliver value while mitigating risks.

Navigating competitive landscapes requires a balance between offensive and defensive strategies. Offensive strategies focus on capturing market share, such as launching new products, entering untapped markets, or underpricing competitors. Defensive strategies, on the other hand, aim to protect the organisation's existing position by retaining customers, improving operational efficiency, or addressing competitive threats.

For example, a CFO at an e-commerce company facing competition from new market entrants might implement defensive strategies such as optimising logistics to reduce delivery times or offering personalised promotions to retain customers. Simultaneously, the CFO could pursue offensive strategies such as expanding into niche markets or introducing exclusive product lines.

In conclusion, navigating competitive landscapes is a multifaceted challenge that requires strategic insight, adaptability, and a deep understanding of market dynamics. For CFOs, success lies in combining financial expertise with a forward-looking perspective, identifying opportunities to differentiate, and balancing offensive and defensive strategies.

In an increasingly complex and disruptive world, the ability to navigate competition effectively is a defining trait of strong financial leadership.

5.6 - Creating Value for Stakeholders

Creating value for stakeholders is at the core of a CFO's responsibilities. Stakeholders, including shareholders, employees, customers, suppliers, and communities, expect organisations to deliver not only financial performance but also social, environmental, and ethical benefits. Balancing these diverse expectations requires a holistic approach that integrates financial strategy with broader organisational goals. For CFOs, creating value means going beyond short-term profitability to drive sustainable growth and build trust with all stakeholders.

Stakeholders have varying and sometimes conflicting interests. Shareholders typically prioritise financial returns, such as dividends and share price appreciation. Employees value fair wages, career development opportunities, and job security. Customers seek high-quality products and services at competitive prices, while suppliers depend on reliable contracts and timely payments. Communities and regulators increasingly demand that organisations operate sustainably and ethically.

CFOs must understand these expectations and ensure that the organisation's strategies address them effectively. For instance, a CFO in the energy sector might focus on balancing shareholder returns with investments in renewable energy to meet societal expectations for sustainability. This involves not only allocating resources wisely but also communicating the organisation's efforts transparently to build trust.

Financial performance remains a key pillar of value creation. By maintaining profitability, managing costs, and ensuring liquidity, CFOs provide the organisation with the stability needed to support other stakeholder priorities. For example, a retail chain with strong financial performance can invest in employee training, enhance customer experience, and support community initiatives.

Value creation also involves optimising capital allocation. CFOs must ensure that investments deliver measurable benefits, whether through revenue growth, cost savings, or improved operational efficiency. For instance, a CFO at a logistics company might allocate capital toward automation technologies that enhance productivity and reduce environmental impact.

Creating stakeholder value requires balancing short-term results with long-term sustainability. While quarterly earnings reports are important for shareholders, long-term investments in innovation, infrastructure, or talent development are equally critical. CFOs must articulate this balance to stakeholders, ensuring they understand the strategic rationale behind investment decisions.

For example, a CFO at a technology firm might explain to shareholders why prioritising R&D over immediate dividend payouts is necessary to maintain competitiveness in a fast-evolving industry. This transparency helps build trust and aligns stakeholder expectations with the organisation's vision.

Environmental, Social, and Governance (ESG) factors have become central to stakeholder value creation. Organisations are increasingly judged not only on financial performance but also on their impact on society and the environment. CFOs play a critical role in integrating ESG considerations into financial strategy.

For instance, a CFO in the manufacturing sector might invest in energy-efficient equipment to reduce the company's carbon footprint, aligning with regulatory requirements and consumer preferences. By demonstrating a commitment to ESG principles, the organisation can enhance its reputation, attract socially conscious investors, and differentiate itself in the market.

In conclusion, creating value for stakeholders is a multifaceted challenge that requires CFOs to balance financial performance with social and environmental impact. By understanding stakeholder expectations, optimising resource allocation, and integrating ESG considerations, CFOs can drive sustainable growth and build trust. In an era where stakeholder expectations are higher than ever, the ability to create value across multiple dimensions is a hallmark of effective financial leadership.

5.7 - Long-Term vs. Short-Term Decision-Making

The balance between long-term and short-term decision-making is one of the most challenging aspects of a CFO's role.

Both perspectives are crucial for organisational success: short-term decisions ensure operational continuity and financial stability, while long-term strategies focus on growth, innovation, and resilience. Striking the right balance requires a nuanced understanding of organisational priorities, stakeholder expectations, and market dynamics.

Short-term decisions are tactical in nature and focus on addressing immediate needs. These could include managing liquidity, optimising working capital, or implementing quick cost-saving measures. For instance, during a period of declining sales, a CFO might decide to reduce discretionary spending or renegotiate supplier terms to maintain cash flow. Such decisions are often reactive, driven by current market conditions, operational challenges, or financial constraints.

Short-term decisions are essential for maintaining stability and ensuring the organisation can meet its obligations, such as payroll, debt repayments, or supplier payments. However, they can also carry risks if not aligned with the organisation's long-term goals. Excessive focus on short-term performance, such as prioritising quarterly earnings at the expense of innovation, can undermine the organisation's future competitiveness.

Long-term decision-making is strategic, focusing on the future trajectory of the organisation. These decisions involve significant investments in areas such as research and development, infrastructure, talent acquisition, or market expansion. For example, a CFO at a renewable energy company might allocate resources toward developing new solar panel technologies, recognising their potential to drive revenue growth over the next decade.

Long-term decisions are inherently complex and involve greater uncertainty than short-term actions. They require CFOs to anticipate market trends, technological advancements, and regulatory changes. For instance, a CFO in the automotive industry considering a shift to electric vehicles must evaluate not only the financial implications but also the evolving competitive landscape and environmental regulations.

While long-term strategies often take time to deliver results, they are critical for ensuring the organisation remains competitive and resilient. They reflect the organisation's commitment to innovation, sustainability, and stakeholder value, building trust and credibility over time.

The tension between short-term and long-term priorities is a constant challenge for CFOs. Shareholders and analysts often focus on immediate financial performance, while employees, customers, and communities expect organisations to invest in sustainable growth and innovation. CFOs must navigate these competing demands by aligning short-term actions with long-term goals.

One effective approach is to adopt a portfolio mindset, treating short-term and long-term initiatives as complementary rather than conflicting. For instance, a CFO at a technology firm might maintain a strong focus on operational efficiency to free up resources for long-term investments in artificial intelligence and machine learning. By optimising the use of current resources, the organisation can achieve both immediate financial stability and future growth.

Another key strategy is transparency. CFOs must communicate the rationale behind their decisions clearly to stakeholders, highlighting how short-term measures support long-term objectives. For example, during a period of cost-cutting, the CFO might explain how the savings will be reinvested in strategic initiatives such as market expansion or product innovation.

Advanced financial tools and frameworks can help CFOs balance short-term and long-term decision-making effectively. Scenario analysis allows organisations to explore the potential outcomes of different strategies under various conditions, helping CFOs assess trade-offs between immediate and future benefits. Key performance indicators (KPIs) that track both short-term and long-term metrics, such as cash flow, market share, and R&D spending, can provide a balanced view of organisational performance.

In conclusion, balancing long-term and short-term decision-making is a defining challenge for CFOs. While short-term decisions ensure operational stability, long-term strategies are essential for sustainable growth and competitiveness. By aligning these perspectives, leveraging advanced tools, and communicating effectively with stakeholders, CFOs can navigate this complexity and drive value across multiple time horizons. In an increasingly dynamic and competitive world, mastering this balance is a hallmark of effective financial leadership.

5.8 - Crisis Management and Recovery

Crisis management is an unavoidable aspect of leadership, and CFOs play a central role in guiding organisations through periods of uncertainty and disruption. Whether caused by economic downturns, natural disasters, technological failures, or global pandemics, crises test the resilience and adaptability of organisations. The CFO's ability to manage financial risks, stabilise operations, and plan for recovery is critical to ensuring organisational survival and long-term success.

In a crisis, the CFO is often at the forefront of decision-making, responsible for safeguarding the organisation's financial health while addressing immediate challenges. This involves assessing the organisation's liquidity, managing cash flow, and identifying areas where costs can be reduced without jeopardising critical functions. For instance, during the COVID-19 pandemic, many CFOs implemented measures such as renegotiating payment terms, deferring non-essential capital expenditures, and securing emergency funding to maintain liquidity.

Equally important is the CFO's role in risk assessment and mitigation. Crises often expose vulnerabilities in supply chains, operational processes, or financial systems. CFOs must identify these risks quickly and develop strategies to address them. For example, a CFO at a manufacturing company facing supply chain disruptions might diversify suppliers or invest in inventory management systems to reduce dependence on a single source.

The first priority in any crisis is stabilising the organisation. This requires a clear understanding of the organisation's financial position, including cash reserves, debt obligations, and revenue streams. CFOs must work closely with other executives to prioritise expenditures, ensuring that critical operations, such as production, customer support, or IT infrastructure, are maintained.

Effective communication is essential during this phase. CFOs must keep stakeholders informed about the organisation's financial status and the steps being taken to address the crisis. This transparency builds trust and ensures that employees, investors, and customers remain engaged and supportive.

Once the immediate crisis is under control, the focus shifts to recovery. CFOs must develop a roadmap for rebuilding financial stability, restoring operations, and positioning the organisation for growth. This often involves re-evaluating budgets, reallocating resources, and identifying new opportunities that have emerged as a result of the crisis.

For instance, a CFO in the retail industry might shift investments from physical stores to e-commerce platforms in response to changes in consumer behaviour. Similarly, a CFO at a travel company recovering from a downturn might prioritise partnerships with local tourism providers to rebuild revenue streams.

Every crisis presents an opportunity for learning and improvement. CFOs must conduct a thorough post-crisis analysis to identify what worked, what didn't, and what can be done differently in the future. This might involve revising risk management frameworks, investing in business continuity planning, or enhancing data analytics capabilities to improve decision-making.

In conclusion, crisis management and recovery are defining tests of a CFO's leadership. By acting swiftly to stabilise the organisation, planning strategically for recovery, and learning from the experience, CFOs can turn challenges into opportunities for growth and resilience. In an unpredictable world, the ability to navigate crises effectively is an essential skill for financial leaders.

5.9 - Aligning Strategy Across Teams

Alignment is one of the most critical aspects of effective strategy execution. A well-crafted strategy is only as good as its implementation, and that requires every team and department in an organisation to work toward shared goals. For CFOs, ensuring alignment across teams goes beyond financial oversight; it involves fostering collaboration, breaking down silos, and creating a cohesive framework where all efforts are directed toward common objectives.

Strategic alignment ensures that all parts of the organisation are working harmoniously to achieve the broader vision and objectives. Misalignment, on the other hand, can lead to inefficiencies, conflicting priorities, and wasted resources. For example, while the executive team might prioritise innovation, a misaligned operations team could focus solely on cost-cutting, inadvertently stifling creativity and progress.

The CFO plays a pivotal role in maintaining alignment by connecting financial resources to strategic priorities. Through budgeting, performance measurement, and resource allocation, the CFO ensures that every department understands its role in supporting the organisation's goals. For instance, if the company's strategy focuses on market expansion, the CFO might work closely with the marketing and sales teams to ensure they have the financial backing needed to execute campaigns in new regions.

One of the greatest barriers to alignment is organisational silos. Departments often operate independently, with limited visibility into each other's objectives and challenges. This can create inefficiencies and undermine strategic initiatives. CFOs are uniquely positioned to address this issue, as their role requires cross-functional collaboration and a comprehensive understanding of the organisation's operations.

To break down silos, CFOs must foster a culture of transparency and collaboration. Regular cross-departmental meetings, joint planning sessions, and shared performance metrics can help create a unified approach to strategy execution. For example, during the rollout of a new product, the CFO might facilitate collaboration between R&D, marketing, and supply chain teams to ensure that the project remains on budget, on schedule, and aligned with market needs.

Clear objectives are the foundation of strategic alignment. Every team must understand not only what the organisation is trying to achieve but also how their specific roles contribute to these goals. CFOs can support this process by translating high-level strategic objectives into actionable financial plans and KPIs.

For instance, if a company aims to increase its market share by 15% over the next year, the CFO might develop departmental budgets and targets that reflect this goal. The sales team could be tasked with achieving a 20% increase in new customer acquisition while the operations team focuses on scaling production capacity to meet anticipated demand.

Modern technology offers powerful tools for driving alignment across teams. Enterprise resource planning (ERP) systems, for example, provide a single platform for tracking budgets, resources, and performance metrics, ensuring that all departments have access to the same data. Similarly, collaborative tools like project management software and dashboards allow teams to monitor progress in real time, identify bottlenecks, and make informed decisions.

CFOs can champion the adoption of these technologies, ensuring that they are integrated seamlessly into the organisation's processes. For example, a CFO at a construction firm might implement a cloud-based project management system that enables the finance, operations, and procurement teams to collaborate on large-scale projects, reducing delays and cost overruns.

Effective communication is essential for maintaining alignment. CFOs must work closely with the executive team to articulate the strategic vision clearly and consistently across all levels of the organisation. This includes explaining the rationale behind key decisions, addressing concerns, and ensuring that employees understand how their work contributes to the organisation's success.

For example, during a major restructuring initiative, the CFO might hold town hall meetings to discuss the financial implications of the changes, answer employee questions, and highlight the long-term benefits of the strategy. By fostering transparency and trust, the CFO can build support for the organisation's goals and ensure that teams remain engaged and motivated.

In conclusion, aligning strategy across teams is a critical responsibility for CFOs and a key factor in successful strategy execution. By breaking down silos, establishing clear objectives, leveraging technology, and fostering effective communication, CFOs can ensure that all departments work toward shared goals. In an increasingly complex and competitive business environment, the ability to drive alignment is a hallmark of strong financial leadership.

5.10 - Case Study: Leading Through Uncertainty

Uncertainty is an inherent part of the business landscape, and the ability to lead effectively during turbulent times is a defining characteristic of a successful CFO. This case study explores how a CFO navigated a period of significant uncertainty, demonstrating the importance of strategic decision-making, adaptability, and resilience in ensuring organisational stability and growth.

The Context: A Sudden Market Disruption

When Elena became CFO of a global manufacturing company, she faced an unprecedented challenge: a geopolitical crisis disrupted supply chains, causing delays in raw material deliveries and escalating costs. Compounding this issue was a sharp decline in customer demand as economic uncertainty led to reduced spending across the company's key markets. Elena's immediate priority was to stabilise the organisation's financial position while laying the groundwork for recovery.

Stabilising the Organisation

Elena began by conducting a comprehensive assessment of the company's financial health. She analysed cash flow projections, reviewed debt obligations, and identified areas where expenses could be reduced without compromising critical operations. Through these efforts, she implemented a series of tactical measures, including deferring non-essential capital expenditures, renegotiating supplier contracts, and securing a short-term credit facility to maintain liquidity.

At the same time, Elena worked closely with the operations team to address supply chain disruptions. She facilitated partnerships with alternative suppliers and introduced inventory management practices to optimise resource allocation. These measures helped the company navigate the immediate challenges and ensure continued production.

Planning for Recovery

With the organisation stabilised, Elena shifted her focus to recovery. Recognising that the crisis had fundamentally altered market dynamics, she worked with the executive team to reassess the company's strategic priorities. This included identifying new opportunities, such as expanding into markets less affected by the disruption and diversifying the product portfolio to meet changing customer needs.

Elena also prioritised investments in digital transformation, recognising that increased automation and data-driven decision-making would enhance the company's agility and resilience. By reallocating resources toward technology adoption, she positioned the organisation to respond more effectively to future disruptions.

Learning and Adaptation

One of Elena's key takeaways from the crisis was the importance of proactive risk management. She spearheaded the development of a comprehensive risk management framework that included scenario planning, real-time monitoring of market conditions, and enhanced communication channels across departments. These initiatives not only improved the company's preparedness but also strengthened its ability to adapt to future challenges.

The Outcome

Elena's leadership through uncertainty delivered remarkable results. Within two years, the company had recovered its financial stability, expanded its market presence, and achieved a 15% increase in revenue. Her ability to balance immediate tactical decisions with long-term strategic planning earned widespread recognition, both within the organisation and across the industry.

Conclusion

Leading through uncertainty requires a combination of strategic vision, operational focus, and the ability to adapt to changing circumstances. As this case study illustrates, CFOs play a critical role in navigating crises, stabilising organisations, and positioning them for future success. In a world where uncertainty is the norm, the ability to lead with resilience and foresight is a defining trait of effective financial leadership.

Chapter 6

Technology and Digital Transformation

> *"In a world driven by technology, the most powerful asset a CFO can leverage is the ability to transform data into decisions and insights into impact."*
> **Robert N. Jacobs**

In an era defined by rapid technological advancements, the finance function has undergone a profound transformation, shifting from traditional roles to becoming a strategic enabler of innovation and growth. This chapter explores how CFOs can leverage cutting-edge tools and digital strategies to revolutionise financial operations, enhance decision-making, and position their organisations for success in an increasingly complex business landscape. From harnessing the power of AI and blockchain to mitigating cybersecurity risks and driving cultural change, this chapter provides a roadmap for financial leaders to navigate and lead in the digital age.

6.1 - Role of Technology in Modern Finance

The integration of technology into modern finance has redefined the role of the finance function, transforming it from a support activity into a strategic driver of organisational success. For CFOs, technology has become a catalyst for innovation, enabling real-time insights, enhanced operational efficiency, and data-driven decision-making. It is no longer a question of whether to adopt technology but rather how to maximise its potential in creating sustainable value.

One of the most immediate benefits of technology in finance is its ability to streamline processes. Repetitive tasks such as invoice processing, payroll management, and bank reconciliation have traditionally been labour-intensive and prone to errors. With advancements like robotic process automation (RPA), these processes are now executed with unparalleled speed and precision. For instance, an RPA system can process thousands of invoices per day, automatically flagging discrepancies for review and reducing processing time by over 70%. This not only minimises errors but also frees up finance teams to focus on more strategic responsibilities, such as forecasting and risk management.

Beyond efficiency, technology plays a critical role in improving the accuracy and accessibility of financial data. Legacy systems often fragment data across multiple platforms, making it difficult for organisations to gain a clear picture of their financial health. Modern enterprise resource planning (ERP) systems address this challenge by integrating data into a single, unified platform. CFOs can now access real-time insights into cash flow, revenue trends, and expense patterns, enabling faster and more informed decision-making. Tools such as data visualisation dashboards further enhance this capability, presenting complex financial metrics in a digestible format that resonates with stakeholders.

The impact of technology extends beyond operational improvements to strategic decision-making. Advanced tools such as predictive analytics allow CFOs to identify trends, model outcomes, and assess risks with unparalleled accuracy. For example, a CFO evaluating an international expansion might use predictive analytics to analyse potential revenue growth, currency fluctuations, and tax implications in target markets. By providing data-backed insights, technology enables CFOs to make confident decisions that align with the organisation's long-term goals.

However, adopting technology comes with challenges. Implementation often requires significant investment in infrastructure and employee training. Resistance to change can also be a barrier, particularly in organisations reliant on legacy systems. CFOs must address these challenges by crafting a clear digital transformation strategy, securing leadership buy-in, and demonstrating the long-term value of the investment. Effective change management and communication are essential to ensure successful adoption.

A compelling example of technology's transformative power can be seen in a global retail company that struggled with fragmented financial systems across its subsidiaries. By implementing a cloud-based ERP system, the CFO centralised data management, reducing month-end closing times by 50%. This improved visibility into financial performance allowed the company to optimise working capital and fund expansion into new markets.

In conclusion, the role of technology in modern finance is multifaceted and transformative. From enhancing operational efficiency to enabling data-driven strategy, technology equips CFOs with the tools needed to navigate complexity and drive growth. While the journey to digital transformation requires investment and effort, the benefits, ranging from improved accuracy to strategic agility, make it an essential endeavour for any forward-thinking organisation.

6.2 - AI and Machine Learning in Financial Analytics

Artificial intelligence (AI) and machine learning (ML) are revolutionising the way organisations approach financial analytics, offering CFOs unprecedented capabilities to process data, uncover insights, and make predictions. These technologies, once considered futuristic, have now become integral to modern finance, enabling faster and more accurate decision-making while driving innovation in how data is used.

One of the most transformative applications of AI and ML in finance is their ability to process large volumes of data at incredible speed. Traditional financial analysis often involved manual processes, requiring teams to sift through spreadsheets to identify patterns and generate reports. In contrast, AI-driven systems can analyse millions of data points in real time, identifying trends and correlations that might otherwise go unnoticed. For example, an AI-powered analytics platform could examine sales data across multiple regions, highlighting seasonal trends and recommending adjustments to inventory levels or pricing strategies based on those insights.

Machine learning takes this capability further by enabling systems to adapt and improve over time. Unlike traditional software that operates based on pre-defined rules, ML algorithms learn from new data, refining their predictions with each iteration. This feature is particularly valuable in areas like revenue forecasting and risk management. For instance, a CFO at a logistics firm might use ML tools to forecast demand fluctuations based on historical data, economic indicators, and market trends. As the system learns from additional data, its predictions become increasingly accurate, allowing the CFO to make better-informed decisions about fleet utilisation and resource allocation.

Another significant application of AI in finance is fraud detection. Fraudulent activities can have devastating financial and reputational consequences, and traditional detection methods often fall short of identifying subtle anomalies. AI-driven systems excel at recognising irregular patterns in real-time, flagging potentially fraudulent transactions for review. For example, a financial institution employing AI for fraud detection might prevent millions in losses by identifying unauthorised activities, such as duplicate invoices or unusual payment patterns, before they escalate.

AI and ML also enhance the efficiency and accuracy of financial reporting. Producing timely, accurate reports is essential for stakeholder confidence and regulatory compliance. AI systems can automate the process of consolidating data, identifying discrepancies, and even generating narrative summaries for key financial metrics. This reduces the workload for finance teams while ensuring that reports are delivered faster and with fewer errors, allowing CFOs to focus on strategy rather than operational details.

Despite their advantages, adopting AI and ML is not without challenges. These technologies require significant investments in infrastructure, talent, and data governance. Ensuring data quality and managing ethical considerations, such as algorithmic bias, are critical to building trust in AI-driven systems. CFOs must also foster a culture of data literacy, equipping teams with the skills needed to interpret and act on AI-generated insights.

An inspiring example of AI's potential is seen in a global e-commerce company that used machine learning to optimise its supply chain. By analysing data from weather patterns, customer behaviour, and transportation logistics, the ML system identified bottlenecks and recommended dynamic adjustments to delivery routes. This led to a 15% reduction in shipping costs while improving delivery times, demonstrating the value of AI-driven decision-making.

In conclusion, AI and machine learning are reshaping the landscape of financial analytics, empowering CFOs to harness data more effectively than ever before. These technologies enable faster, more accurate decision-making, improve operational efficiency, and enhance risk management. While adoption requires careful planning and investment, the long-term benefits make AI and ML indispensable tools for organisations seeking to thrive in an increasingly data-driven world.

6.3 - Blockchain and Its Impact on Finance

Blockchain technology, often associated with cryptocurrencies, has emerged as a transformative force in finance, offering new ways to enhance transparency, efficiency, and security. For CFOs, understanding the potential of blockchain is crucial, as it holds the capacity to revolutionise traditional financial processes, disrupt established practices, and create new opportunities for value creation. While the adoption of blockchain is still evolving, its implications for finance are profound and far-reaching.

At its core, blockchain is a decentralised ledger that records transactions across a network of computers. Each transaction is grouped into a block, which is then cryptographically linked to the previous block, forming a chain. This structure ensures that the data is immutable and tamper-proof, providing a level of security and trust that surpasses traditional systems. Unlike centralised databases, where a single point of failure can compromise the entire system, blockchain's distributed nature makes it inherently resilient.

One of the most significant impacts of blockchain in finance is its ability to streamline and automate transactional processes. Traditional financial transactions often involve intermediaries, such as banks or clearinghouses, which add time, cost, and

Despite its benefits, the adoption of blockchain in finance is not without challenges. One of the primary obstacles is regulatory uncertainty, as governments and regulatory bodies grapple with the implications of decentralised systems. Additionally, the integration of blockchain into existing financial systems requires substantial investment in infrastructure and talent. Many organisations also face resistance to change, particularly when it comes to adopting a technology that fundamentally redefines established workflows.

However, the potential benefits of blockchain outweigh these challenges. Enhanced transparency, for instance, is invaluable in industries where compliance and accountability are critical. Consider an auditing scenario where blockchain provides an unalterable record of financial transactions. Auditors could access real-time data, reducing the time and cost of audits while improving accuracy. This capability has significant implications for sectors such as banking, healthcare, and real estate, where fraud and inefficiencies are persistent issues.

Blockchain's impact extends beyond operational improvements to new business models. Tokenisation, for example, allows assets such as real estate, art, or intellectual property to be represented digitally on a blockchain. This creates opportunities for fractional ownership and opens up investments to a broader audience. A CFO in the investment sector might explore tokenisation as a way to diversify offerings and attract new investors.

complexity. Blockchain eliminates the need for intermediaries by enabling peer-to-peer transactions example, in cross-border payments, blockchain can settlement times from several days to mere s significantly lowering transaction fees and improving ca for businesses.

Another area where blockchain is making strides is s chain financing. By providing a transparent and immu record of transactions, blockchain ensures that all particip in a supply chain, suppliers, manufacturers, and retailers, access to the same information. This transparency red disputes and accelerates processes such as invoice financin CFO overseeing a global supply chain might use blockchain verify the authenticity of invoices, ensuring that financing only extended to valid claims. This not only mitigates fraud b also builds trust among stakeholders.

Smart contracts, a feature of blockchain, are another game changer for finance. These are self-executing contracts with the terms of the agreement directly written into code. Smart contracts automatically enforce obligations, reducing the need for manual oversight and intermediaries. For instance, in insurance, a smart contract could automatically trigger a payout when predefined conditions, such as flight delays or weather events, are met. For CFOs, the ability to automate such processes translates into cost savings and operational efficiency.

A compelling example of blockchain in action is its use in trade finance. Traditionally, trade finance involves multiple parties, including exporters, importers, banks, and customs authorities, each maintaining their own records. This fragmented approach leads to inefficiencies, delays, and increased costs. By adopting a blockchain-based platform, a multinational corporation could streamline the process, ensuring that all parties have access to the same verified information. This reduces disputes, accelerates transaction times, and enhances trust across the supply chain.

In conclusion, blockchain technology has the potential to transform finance by enhancing transparency, automating processes, and enabling new business models. While adoption presents challenges, the opportunities it offers are too significant to ignore. For CFOs, embracing blockchain is not just about staying ahead of technological trends, it is about rethinking how value is created and delivered in a rapidly changing world. As technology continues to mature, its role in reshaping finance will only grow, making it a critical consideration for forward-thinking organisations.

6.4 - Cybersecurity Risks and Mitigation

As organisations increasingly rely on digital technologies to manage financial operations, cybersecurity risks have become one of the most pressing challenges for CFOs. Cyberattacks, data breaches, and system vulnerabilities not only threaten financial stability but also damage reputations and erode stakeholder trust. For CFOs, addressing these risks requires a proactive and strategic approach, combining robust defences with a culture of vigilance and preparedness.

The finance function is particularly vulnerable to cyber threats due to its reliance on sensitive data and high-value transactions. Attackers often target systems such as accounts payable, treasury management platforms, and ERP systems, seeking to exploit weaknesses for financial gain. For instance, phishing attacks, where fraudulent emails trick employees into divulging sensitive information or transferring funds, are a common threat faced by finance teams. Ransomware attacks, which lock users out of critical systems until a ransom is paid, have also surged in frequency, causing significant disruption and financial loss.

One of the most critical steps in mitigating cybersecurity risks is conducting a comprehensive risk assessment. CFOs must work closely with IT and security teams to identify vulnerabilities within their systems and processes. This involves evaluating the organisation's technology infrastructure, employee practices, and third-party vendor relationships. For example, a CFO might uncover that outdated software in the finance department lacks critical security updates, making it an easy target for attackers. Addressing these vulnerabilities through upgrades and patches is essential to reducing risk.

In addition to technology, employee training is a cornerstone of cybersecurity defence. Human error remains one of the leading causes of cyber incidents, with employees inadvertently falling victim to phishing schemes or using weak passwords. CFOs should ensure that all staff, particularly those in finance, receive regular training on recognising and responding to cyber threats. For example, simulated phishing exercises can help employees identify suspicious emails and improve their response to potential attacks.

Implementing multi-factor authentication (MFA) is another effective measure for protecting sensitive financial systems. MFA requires users to verify their identity through multiple factors, such as a password and a mobile device, significantly reducing the likelihood of unauthorised access. Similarly, encrypting financial data ensures that even if attackers gain access to systems, the data remains unreadable without the decryption key.

Collaboration with third parties is also crucial, as many organisations rely on external vendors for software, cloud services, and financial platforms. CFOs must ensure that vendors adhere to strict cybersecurity standards, conducting due diligence before entering into agreements and regularly reviewing compliance. For instance, a CFO might require a vendor to provide evidence of penetration testing or certification under recognised security frameworks such as ISO 27001.

Despite these measures, no system is entirely immune to cyberattacks. Therefore, having a response and recovery plan in place is essential. This plan should outline clear protocols for containing breaches, notifying stakeholders, and restoring operations. For example, a CFO might collaborate with the IT department to establish a rapid response team that includes legal, PR, and financial experts. This team would coordinate efforts to minimise damage and communicate transparently with affected parties.

A real-world example of effective cybersecurity measures can be seen in a global financial institution that experienced a phishing attack targeting its treasury team. By implementing a combination of MFA, employee training, and AI-powered monitoring tools, the organisation detected and thwarted the attack before any funds were transferred. Additionally, the CFO spearheaded a review of security practices, introducing stricter controls and regular audits to prevent future incidents.

In conclusion, cybersecurity risks pose a significant challenge to modern finance, but proactive mitigation strategies can minimise their impact. For CFOs, this involves not only investing in technology but also fostering a culture of vigilance and accountability. By addressing vulnerabilities, educating employees, and preparing for the unexpected, organisations can protect their financial systems and maintain stakeholder confidence in an increasingly digital world.

6.5 - Implementing Financial Automation

Financial automation has become an essential tool for CFOs aiming to enhance efficiency, reduce errors, and focus resources on strategic priorities. By automating repetitive and labour-intensive tasks, organisations can save time, lower costs, and improve overall accuracy. However, successful implementation of automation requires more than just adopting new technologies, it demands strategic planning, cross-departmental collaboration, and a commitment to fostering a culture of innovation.

At its core, financial automation involves using technology to streamline processes such as accounts payable, accounts receivable, payroll management, and financial reporting. These tasks, which were traditionally time-consuming and prone to human error, can now be executed with precision and speed through tools like robotic process automation (RPA) and intelligent automation systems. For instance, an organisation using RPA to manage accounts payable can automatically process invoices, match them with purchase orders, and approve payments without human intervention. This reduces processing time by up to 70%, eliminates manual errors, and allows finance teams to focus on more value-driven activities.

One of the most significant benefits of financial automation is its ability to improve data accuracy. Errors in financial reporting can lead to compliance issues, stakeholder mistrust, and even financial penalties. Automated systems minimise these risks by standardising processes, enforcing controls, and validating data in real-time. For example, a cloud-based financial platform can automatically flag discrepancies in expense reports or detect duplicate invoices, ensuring that only accurate information is recorded and processed.

Automation also enhances decision-making by providing real-time insights into key financial metrics. Traditional reporting methods often involve manual data consolidation, which can delay access to critical information. With automation, CFOs can generate up-to-date reports at the click of a button, allowing them to respond quickly to changes in market conditions or organisational needs. For instance, during a liquidity crunch, an automated cash flow forecasting tool can provide instant visibility into available funds, enabling the CFO to make informed decisions about resource allocation.

Despite its advantages, implementing financial automation comes with challenges. One of the most common barriers is resistance to change, particularly among employees who may fear job displacement or struggle to adapt to new systems. CFOs must address these concerns by emphasising that automation is not about replacing people but empowering them to focus on higher-value tasks. Providing comprehensive training and clear communication about the benefits of automation can help build trust and acceptance among team members.

Another challenge is ensuring that the chosen automation tools align with the organisation's specific needs and existing infrastructure. Not all systems are compatible with legacy platforms, and integrating new technologies can be complex and costly. CFOs should work closely with IT teams to conduct thorough assessments of potential solutions, prioritising scalability, security, and ease of integration. For example, a multinational corporation transitioning to an automated financial system might opt for a cloud-based platform that seamlessly integrates with its global ERP system, ensuring consistency across regions.

Financial automation also requires robust data security measures. Automated systems handle sensitive financial information, making them a target for cyberattacks. CFOs must ensure that all platforms comply with industry standards and employ advanced security features such as encryption, multi-factor authentication, and real-time threat monitoring. Regular audits and updates are essential to maintaining the integrity of automated systems.

A compelling example of financial automation in action is seen in a mid-sized manufacturing company that struggled with delayed financial reporting and high overhead costs in its accounts payable department. By implementing RPA, the CFO reduced the time required to process invoices from weeks to days, cutting administrative costs by 30%. The automation also improved reporting accuracy, enabling the organisation to identify and address inefficiencies in its procurement process. These improvements freed up resources that were reinvested in strategic initiatives, such as expanding production capacity and entering new markets.

In conclusion, implementing financial automation is a transformative step for organisations looking to optimise their finance functions and drive long-term success. While adoption requires careful planning, investment, and change management, the benefits, ranging from increased efficiency and accuracy to enhanced decision-making, make it an essential component of modern financial strategy. For CFOs, embracing automation is not just about keeping pace with technological advancements; it is about positioning the organisation to thrive in an increasingly competitive and data-driven world.

6.6 - Understanding Cloud-Based Solutions

The rise of cloud-based solutions has revolutionised the way organisations manage their financial operations. By enabling real-time access to data, seamless collaboration, and scalable infrastructure, cloud technology has become a cornerstone of modern finance. For CFOs, understanding the benefits and challenges of cloud adoption is essential for leveraging its full potential and driving organisational agility.

At its most basic level, a cloud-based solution refers to software or services hosted on remote servers and accessed over the Internet. Unlike traditional on-premises systems, which require significant upfront investment in hardware and ongoing maintenance, cloud solutions offer a subscription-based model, reducing capital expenditure and operational complexity. This affordability and flexibility have made cloud technology an attractive option for organisations of all sizes.

One of the primary advantages of cloud-based solutions is their ability to centralise financial data across departments, geographies, and business units. For organisations with operations in multiple locations, consolidating data into a single platform eliminates silos and ensures that all stakeholders have access to accurate, real-time information. For example, a CFO at a multinational corporation might use a cloud-based ERP system to monitor cash flow, revenue performance, and expenses across various subsidiaries in different countries. This level of visibility enhances decision-making and ensures that resources are allocated effectively.

Cloud technology also facilitates collaboration among teams. In traditional setups, sharing financial data often involves manual processes, such as exporting and emailing spreadsheets, which can lead to version control issues and delays. Cloud platforms, on the other hand, provide a shared workspace where multiple users can access and update information simultaneously. This is particularly valuable during financial planning cycles or audit processes, where cross-functional collaboration is essential. For instance, during budgeting season, finance, marketing, and operations teams can work together on a single platform, ensuring alignment and efficiency.

Another key benefit of cloud-based solutions is their scalability. As organisations grow or encounter fluctuations in demand, cloud platforms can easily adapt to changing requirements. Unlike on-premises systems, which often require costly upgrades to accommodate growth, cloud solutions allow organisations to scale up or down by adjusting subscription levels. For example, a fast-growing e-commerce company might increase its cloud storage capacity during peak shopping seasons, ensuring uninterrupted access to financial systems and data.

Despite these benefits, adopting cloud-based solutions requires careful consideration of potential challenges. Data security is one of the most significant concerns, as financial information stored in the cloud could be vulnerable to breaches if not adequately protected. CFOs must ensure that cloud providers adhere to strict security protocols, such as data encryption, multi-factor authentication, and compliance with regulatory standards. Conducting regular security audits and implementing backup and recovery solutions are essential for mitigating risks.

Integration is another challenge, particularly for organisations transitioning from legacy systems. Ensuring that cloud-based platforms can seamlessly integrate with existing tools and workflows is critical to avoiding disruptions and maximising value. CFOs should prioritise solutions that offer robust APIs and customisation options, enabling smooth integration with systems such as payroll, CRM, and supply chain management software.

A real-world example of the power of cloud-based solutions can be seen in a mid-sized professional services firm that struggled with inefficiencies in financial reporting. By migrating to a cloud-based financial management platform, the firm centralised its data, reduced reporting errors, and cut month-end closing times by 40%. The platform's scalability also allowed the organisation to expand its client base without needing significant infrastructure upgrades.

In conclusion, cloud-based solutions are transforming the finance function, offering unmatched flexibility, scalability, and collaboration capabilities. While adoption requires addressing challenges such as security and integration, the long-term benefits make cloud technology an indispensable tool for modern CFOs. By embracing the cloud, organisations can enhance efficiency, improve decision-making, and position themselves for sustainable growth in an increasingly digital world.

6.7 - Big Data and Predictive Analytics

The advent of big data and predictive analytics has revolutionised the finance function, empowering CFOs to make smarter, faster, and more informed decisions. By harnessing vast amounts of data and applying advanced analytical techniques, organisations can uncover trends, anticipate risks, and seize opportunities that were previously beyond reach. For CFOs, understanding and leveraging these tools is no longer optional, it is essential for navigating the complexities of modern business environments.

Big data refers to the massive volumes of structured and unstructured data generated by various sources, including transactions, customer interactions, and operational processes. While this data holds immense potential, its sheer volume and complexity often make it challenging to analyse using traditional methods. This is where predictive analytics comes into play. Predictive analytics involves using statistical algorithms and machine learning models to identify patterns and predict future outcomes, enabling CFOs to move from reactive to proactive decision-making.

One of the most powerful applications of predictive analytics in finance is revenue forecasting. Traditional forecasting methods often rely on historical data and static assumptions, which can fail to capture dynamic market conditions. Predictive analytics, on the other hand, incorporates a wide range of variables, such as economic indicators, customer behaviour, and industry trends, to generate more accurate and nuanced forecasts. For example, a CFO at a retail company might use predictive models to project sales during the holiday season, taking into account factors like weather patterns, consumer sentiment, and competitor promotions. This enables the organisation to optimise inventory, staffing, and marketing strategies, ultimately maximising profitability.

Another critical application is in risk management. Predictive analytics allows CFOs to identify and mitigate risks before they materialise. For instance, an insurance company might use predictive models to assess the likelihood of claims based on customer demographics, historical data, and external factors such as climate conditions. Similarly, a financial institution might employ predictive analytics to detect early warning signs of loan defaults, enabling it to take preemptive action and minimise losses.

Cost optimisation is another area where big data and predictive analytics create significant value. By analysing spending patterns across departments and geographies, CFOs can identify inefficiencies and implement targeted cost-saving measures. For example, a manufacturing firm might use predictive analytics to optimise energy consumption, reducing costs without compromising productivity. Similarly, a logistics company might analyse fuel usage and route efficiency to lower transportation expenses.

Despite their potential, implementing big data and predictive analytics comes with challenges. One of the primary hurdles is ensuring data quality. Predictive models are only as good as the data they rely on, making it essential to address issues such as incomplete, inconsistent, or outdated information. CFOs must invest in robust data governance frameworks, ensuring that data is accurate, consistent, and secure. Additionally, organisations often face a talent gap, as leveraging these tools requires expertise in data science, analytics, and machine learning. CFOs should consider upskilling their teams or partnering with external experts to bridge this gap.

Another challenge lies in integrating predictive analytics into existing workflows. Many organisations struggle to operationalise insights, with valuable predictions remaining underutilised due to siloed systems or resistance to change. CFOs must ensure that predictive analytics is embedded into decision-making processes across departments, fostering a culture of data-driven innovation. For example, a CFO could collaborate with marketing and sales teams to use predictive insights for customer segmentation and targeted campaigns, ensuring alignment with broader strategic goals.

A compelling example of big data and predictive analytics in action is seen in a global airline that used these tools to optimise pricing strategies. By analysing historical booking data, competitor pricing, and external factors such as fuel prices and weather conditions, the airline developed dynamic pricing models that maximised revenue per seat. This not only improved profitability but also enhanced customer satisfaction by offering competitive fares and personalised promotions.

In conclusion, big data and predictive analytics are transforming the finance function, providing CFOs with the tools to anticipate challenges, optimise performance, and drive innovation. While adoption requires addressing challenges such as data quality and integration, the long-term benefits are undeniable. For organisations willing to embrace these technologies, the possibilities for improving decision-making, enhancing efficiency, and gaining a competitive edge are virtually limitless.

6.8 - Driving Innovation in Finance Departments

The role of the CFO has evolved beyond managing budgets and overseeing financial reporting. Today, CFOs are expected to act as innovation leaders, fostering a culture of creativity and driving transformative change within their finance departments. By embracing new technologies, reimagining processes, and challenging traditional practices, CFOs can position their organisations for sustainable growth and resilience in an ever-changing business landscape.

Innovation in finance begins with a shift in mindset. Traditionally, finance departments have been viewed as cost centres focused on compliance, accuracy, and risk management. While these responsibilities remain critical, modern finance teams must also prioritise strategic value creation. This involves adopting a proactive approach to identifying opportunities for improvement, whether through process optimisation, technology adoption, or new ways of delivering insights to stakeholders.

One of the most impactful ways to drive innovation is by embracing emerging technologies. Tools such as artificial intelligence (AI), machine learning (ML), and robotic process automation (RPA) have already proven their ability to enhance efficiency and accuracy in finance. For example, an AI-powered expense management system can automatically categorise transactions, flag anomalies, and generate insights, significantly reducing the time spent on manual reviews. By integrating such technologies, CFOs can empower their teams to focus on strategic tasks rather than routine operations.

Another key area for innovation is data democratisation. Traditionally, access to financial data has been restricted to finance professionals, limiting its impact on decision-making across the organisation. By leveraging tools like self-service analytics platforms, CFOs can make financial insights accessible to non-financial stakeholders, enabling them to make data-driven decisions. For instance, a marketing manager could use a self-service dashboard to analyse campaign ROI in real time, aligning marketing efforts with the organisation's financial goals.

Driving innovation also involves rethinking how finance teams collaborate with other departments. Cross-functional collaboration is essential for aligning financial strategies with broader business objectives. CFOs can encourage this by creating integrated planning processes that bring together finance, operations, marketing, and IT teams. For example, during the budgeting process, finance teams can work closely with operations to identify cost-saving opportunities in production, ensuring that resources are allocated efficiently.

Fostering a culture of innovation requires investing in talent development. As finance roles evolve, traditional skill sets such as accounting and compliance must be complemented by expertise in data analytics, technology, and strategic thinking. CFOs should prioritise training programmes, mentorship opportunities, and recruitment strategies that attract and develop forward-thinking professionals. For example, partnering with universities to offer internships in fintech or data science can help build a pipeline of future-ready talent.

However, driving innovation is not without its challenges. Resistance to change, particularly among long-tenured employees, can slow progress. CFOs must address this by communicating the benefits of innovation clearly and consistently, highlighting how new tools and processes will improve efficiency and job satisfaction. Additionally, implementing innovative solutions often requires substantial investment, both in terms of financial resources and time. CFOs must build a strong business case for innovation, demonstrating the long-term ROI to secure buy-in from leadership and stakeholders.

A powerful example of innovation in finance can be seen in a global FMCG company that transformed its budgeting process using AI. By implementing an AI-driven forecasting tool, the finance team reduced the time required to create budgets by 50% while improving accuracy. This allowed the team to focus on scenario planning and strategic initiatives, enhancing the company's ability to respond to market changes.

In conclusion, driving innovation in finance departments is a critical responsibility for modern CFOs. By embracing new technologies, fostering collaboration, and investing in talent, CFOs can transform the finance function into a hub of creativity and strategic value. While challenges exist, the rewards, ranging from improved efficiency to enhanced decision-making, make innovation an essential priority for organisations seeking to thrive in a competitive and rapidly evolving world.

6.9 - CFO's Role in Organisational Digital Transformation

The Chief Financial Officer (CFO) has become a central figure in driving organisational digital transformation, a process that extends far beyond technology adoption to encompass cultural shifts, process optimisation, and strategic alignment. As organisations increasingly rely on digital tools to enhance operations and create value, the CFO's role evolves from that of a financial steward to a catalyst for change. For modern businesses, digital transformation is not merely a competitive advantage, it is a necessity for long-term survival and success.

At the heart of the CFO's role in digital transformation is the responsibility to align financial strategy with organisational goals. Digital transformation requires significant investment in technology, talent, and infrastructure. CFOs must ensure that these investments deliver measurable returns, balancing the need for innovation with the imperative to manage costs and risks. For example, a CFO in the healthcare sector overseeing the adoption of electronic medical records might evaluate the upfront costs against long-term benefits such as improved patient care, operational efficiency, and regulatory compliance.

One of the most critical contributions the CFO makes to digital transformation is resource allocation. By leveraging data and analytics, CFOs can prioritise investments in technologies that offer the highest return on investment (ROI) and align with strategic objectives. For instance, a retail CFO might allocate resources toward an omnichannel strategy, integrating e-commerce platforms with physical store operations to enhance customer experience and increase sales. This strategic allocation ensures that the organisation's digital initiatives are both effective and sustainable.

In addition to resource allocation, the CFO plays a pivotal role in risk management. Digital transformation introduces new risks, including cybersecurity threats, regulatory challenges, and implementation failures. CFOs must work closely with IT leaders to identify potential vulnerabilities and develop mitigation strategies. For example, when adopting cloud-based solutions, the CFO might ensure that the organisation complies with data protection regulations such as GDPR, safeguarding sensitive financial and customer information.

The CFO's influence also extends to change management, a critical component of successful digital transformation. Implementing new technologies often requires shifts in workflows, organisational structures, and employee roles. Resistance to change can derail even the most well-planned initiatives, making it essential for CFOs to foster a culture of innovation and adaptability. This involves communicating the benefits of digital transformation clearly and consistently, addressing employee concerns, and providing training to ensure a smooth transition.

Collaboration is another hallmark of the CFO's role in digital transformation. Digital initiatives often span multiple departments, requiring cross-functional coordination and alignment. CFOs must work closely with leaders in IT, operations, marketing, and HR to ensure that digital strategies are integrated into every aspect of the organisation. For instance, during the implementation of a customer relationship management (CRM) system, the CFO might collaborate with marketing to ensure that the platform supports customer segmentation and campaign tracking while also working with sales to streamline lead management.

A key aspect of the CFO's role is measuring and monitoring the success of digital initiatives. Unlike traditional projects, digital transformation often involves ongoing adaptation and optimisation. CFOs must establish metrics and KPIs to evaluate the impact of digital investments, such as cost savings, revenue growth, or customer satisfaction improvements. For example, a

CFO at a logistics company adopting AI-driven route optimisation tools might track reductions in fuel costs and delivery times as indicators of success.

One of the challenges CFOs face in leading digital transformation is addressing the cultural shift required for its success. Many employees are accustomed to traditional processes and may view new technologies as disruptive or intimidating. CFOs must take a leadership role in fostering a culture that embraces change, encouraging employees to view digital tools as enablers of efficiency and innovation. This can be achieved through training programmes, workshops, and open forums where employees can voice concerns and provide feedback.

A compelling example of the CFO's role in digital transformation is seen in a global manufacturing company that sought to digitise its supply chain. Under the CFO's leadership, the organisation adopted blockchain technology to enhance transparency and traceability across its supplier network. The CFO worked closely with IT and operations teams to implement the system, ensuring that it integrated seamlessly with existing workflows. The initiative resulted in a 20% reduction in supply chain costs and improved compliance with sustainability standards, highlighting the transformative potential of digital tools.

In conclusion, the CFO's role in organisational digital transformation is multifaceted, encompassing financial stewardship, strategic alignment, risk management, and change leadership. By driving innovation and fostering collaboration, CFOs can ensure that digital initiatives deliver measurable value and position the organisation for long-term success. In an increasingly digital world, the ability to lead transformation effectively is a defining trait of modern financial leadership.

6.10 - Case Study: Leading a Digital Finance Revolution

Digital transformation within the finance function is not merely about adopting new technologies, it requires a fundamental reimagining of how finance operates, delivers value, and supports organisational goals. This case study details how Susan, the CFO of a global retail company, successfully led a comprehensive digital finance transformation, illustrating the critical roles of leadership, strategy, and innovation in achieving impactful change.

The Context: A Need for Transformation

When Susan stepped into her role as CFO, she faced a department plagued by inefficiencies and limited by outdated processes. The finance function heavily relied on manual workflows, leading to delays in reporting and an inability to access real-time insights. Financial data was siloed across multiple legacy systems, creating inconsistencies and obstructing decision-making.

Susan recognised that these challenges were more than operational bottlenecks, they hindered the finance team's ability to support the company's strategic objectives. To address this, she envisioned a bold initiative to digitise the finance function, positioning it as a strategic enabler of growth and innovation.

Phase 1: Assessing the Current Landscape

The transformation began with a comprehensive audit of the finance function. Susan and her team identified several critical issues:

- Excessive time spent on repetitive transaction processing tasks.
- Fragmented data across departments, leading to inconsistencies and inefficiencies.
- Limited integration between financial and operational systems.
- Inadequate tools for real-time reporting and predictive analysis.

This assessment formed the foundation for a strategic roadmap prioritising high-impact initiatives, setting clear objectives for operational efficiency, data centralisation, and enhanced decision-making capabilities.

Phase 2: Implementing Digital Solutions

Susan's strategy revolved around three core pillars: data centralisation, automation, and advanced analytics. Each initiative was carefully designed to address specific pain points while aligning with the company's broader goals.

1. **Cloud-Based ERP Implementation:**
   - Susan led the deployment of a cloud-based enterprise resource planning (ERP) system, consolidating financial data into a single, accessible platform.
   - The ERP system facilitated real-time visibility into key metrics such as cash flow, revenue trends, and expense patterns. This improved decision-making speed and accuracy across departments.
   - Additionally, the centralised system fostered cross-functional collaboration, allowing finance, operations, and sales teams to work seamlessly with a unified source of truth.

2. **Robotic Process Automation (RPA):**
   - Susan introduced RPA to automate routine tasks, including accounts payable, payroll processing, and reconciliations.
   - By eliminating manual errors and reducing processing times, the finance team achieved a 60% improvement in efficiency. Suppliers benefited from faster payments, strengthening relationships across the supply chain.

3. **Advanced Analytics and Machine Learning:**
   - Susan invested in predictive analytics tools powered by machine learning, enabling the finance team to forecast trends and anticipate risks with greater precision.
   - For instance, predictive models helped optimise inventory management during peak seasons, ensuring better alignment with sales forecasts and improving profitability.

Phase 3: Driving Organisational Change

Recognising that technology alone could not drive transformation, Susan prioritised change management and employee engagement to ensure sustainable success:

- **Training and Upskilling:** A series of training programmes equipped employees with the skills needed to navigate new tools and processes. Emphasis was placed on fostering data literacy and analytical capabilities within the team.

- **Promoting Innovation**: Susan cultivated a culture of innovation, encouraging team members to identify inefficiencies and propose solutions. This empowered employees and instilled a sense of ownership in the transformation journey.

- **Stakeholder Engagement:** Regular updates were provided to senior leadership and other departments, ensuring alignment and transparency throughout the transformation process.

The Outcome: Tangible Results

The digital finance revolution led by Susan delivered remarkable outcomes:

1. **Operational Efficiency:** A 40% reduction in operational costs within the finance department was achieved through automation and process optimisation.
2. **Enhanced Decision-Making:** Real-time insights enabled faster, more informed decisions, supporting the company's strategic growth initiatives.
3. **Data Consistency:** Centralised data systems eliminated redundancies, improving reporting accuracy and reliability.
4. **Strategic Alignment:** The finance function transitioned from a transactional support role to a strategic partner, driving innovation and contributing to organisational goals.

Lessons Learned

Susan's success highlights key lessons for CFOs embarking on digital transformations:

1. **Comprehensive Assessment:** A detailed audit of existing systems and processes is essential for identifying pain points and setting priorities.
2. **Technology Integration:** The right mix of tools, from ERP systems to RPA and advanced analytics, can revolutionise efficiency and decision-making.
3. **Change Management:** Engaging employees and fostering a culture of innovation is critical for sustainable adoption.

4. **Measurable Impact:** Setting clear objectives and tracking outcomes ensures that digital initiatives deliver tangible value.

Conclusion

Susan's leadership exemplifies the transformative potential of digital finance. By combining strategic vision with innovative solutions and a strong focus on cultural change, she positioned the finance function as a catalyst for growth and success. This case study serves as an inspiring roadmap for CFOs aiming to lead similar revolutions in their organisations.

Chapter 7

Risk Management and Compliance

> *"The strength of an organisation lies not in avoiding risks but in its ability to face them with foresight, preparation, and resilience."*
> **Robert N. Jacobs**

Effective risk management and compliance are critical pillars of financial leadership, ensuring organisations navigate uncertainty while adhering to regulatory standards. For CFOs, the ability to identify, assess, and mitigate risks is essential for safeguarding assets, maintaining stakeholder trust, and achieving long-term stability. This chapter delves into the intricacies of managing financial risks and compliance, highlighting the strategies, tools, and leadership skills required to excel in these areas.

7.1 - Identifying Financial Risks

The process of identifying financial risks is a cornerstone of effective risk management. For CFOs, this task involves understanding the internal and external factors that could jeopardise the organisation's financial health. Financial risks take many forms, from market volatility and liquidity constraints to credit exposure and operational inefficiencies. A proactive approach to identifying these risks is essential to mitigate potential threats before they escalate.

Market risks are among the most significant financial threats that organisations face. These include fluctuations in interest rates, exchange rates, and commodity prices, all of which can have a direct impact on profitability. For example, a CFO at a manufacturing firm reliant on imported raw materials may face rising costs due to unfavourable currency movements. To mitigate this risk, the CFO might adopt hedging strategies, such as forward contracts or options, to stabilise costs and protect margins.

Liquidity risk is another critical concern, particularly for organisations operating in cash-intensive industries. Liquidity risk arises when an organisation is unable to meet its short-term financial obligations, such as payroll, supplier payments, or loan repayments. Identifying liquidity risks requires a comprehensive understanding of cash flow patterns, working capital requirements, and debt structures. CFOs can address these risks by maintaining adequate cash reserves, securing lines of credit, and implementing robust cash flow forecasting tools.

Credit risk is equally important, particularly for organisations that extend payment terms to customers or invest in financial instruments. The risk of default by customers or counterparties can lead to significant losses and disrupt cash flow. CFOs must assess the creditworthiness of clients and counterparties using tools such as credit ratings, financial analysis, and historical payment behaviour. Establishing clear credit policies and monitoring receivables closely are essential for minimising exposure to bad debts.

Operational risks are often overlooked but can have severe financial implications. These risks arise from internal processes, systems, or human errors that disrupt operations and incur costs. For example, a data breach due to weak cybersecurity measures could result in financial losses, regulatory penalties, and reputational damage. CFOs must work closely with IT and operations teams to identify vulnerabilities and implement preventive measures.

A proactive approach to identifying financial risks also involves scenario analysis and stress testing. These tools allow CFOs to model the impact of various risk scenarios, such as economic downturns, regulatory changes, or supply chain disruptions. For instance, a CFO in the retail sector might conduct a stress test to assess the organisation's resilience during a significant drop in consumer spending. The insights gained from these exercises enable organisations to prepare contingency plans and allocate resources effectively.

External risks, such as geopolitical instability or natural disasters, also require attention. While these risks are beyond the organisation's control, understanding their potential impact is crucial for building resilience. For example, a CFO in the energy sector might evaluate the financial implications of regulatory shifts aimed at reducing carbon emissions. By identifying these risks early, the organisation can adjust its strategy to align with changing external conditions.

An example of proactive risk identification can be seen in a global logistics company that faced significant volatility in fuel prices. The CFO implemented a risk management strategy that included fuel hedging, diversifying the company's fleet to include electric vehicles, and investing in predictive analytics to forecast price trends. This comprehensive approach allowed the organisation to maintain stable operating costs and protect its margins despite market fluctuations.

In conclusion, identifying financial risks is a foundational skill for CFOs, enabling them to anticipate threats and implement effective mitigation strategies. By adopting a proactive, data-driven approach and collaborating with cross-functional teams, CFOs can build resilience and safeguard the organisation's financial health in an increasingly complex and unpredictable world.

7.2 - Enterprise Risk Management (ERM) Frameworks

Enterprise Risk Management (ERM) frameworks provide a structured approach for organisations to identify, assess, and manage risks across all areas of their operations. For CFOs, ERM is not just about compliance or avoiding losses; it is a strategic tool for enhancing decision-making, improving resource allocation, and creating value. Implementing a robust ERM framework ensures that risks are managed holistically rather than in silos, enabling organisations to align their risk appetite with their strategic objectives.

At the core of an ERM framework is the principle of risk integration. Unlike traditional risk management, which often focuses on specific areas such as finance or operations, ERM considers the interdependencies between different types of risks. For example, a company expanding into a new market faces financial risks (such as currency fluctuations), operational risks (such as supply chain disruptions), and compliance risks (such as regulatory requirements). An ERM framework allows CFOs to assess how these risks interact and prioritise mitigation efforts accordingly.

One of the most widely used ERM models is the COSO ERM Framework, developed by the Committee of Sponsoring Organizations of the Treadway Commission. This framework emphasises the importance of integrating risk management into the organisation's culture and decision-making processes. It consists of components such as governance, strategy, performance, and review, providing a comprehensive guide for implementing risk management practices. For instance, the framework encourages CFOs to work closely with the board of directors to define the organisation's risk appetite and ensure that it aligns with strategic goals.

Another critical component of ERM is risk assessment and quantification. CFOs must evaluate the likelihood and impact of each risk using both qualitative and quantitative methods. Tools such as heat maps and risk matrices are commonly used to prioritise risks based on their severity. For example, a CFO in the hospitality industry might assess the financial impact of a potential cyberattack versus the impact of fluctuating occupancy rates. This analysis enables the organisation to allocate resources to the most critical risks and develop targeted mitigation plans.

Implementing an ERM framework also involves embedding risk management into daily operations. This requires collaboration across departments to ensure that risk considerations are factored into decision-making processes at all levels. For instance, during product development, the CFO might collaborate with marketing and R&D teams to assess risks related to consumer demand, regulatory compliance, and production costs. By integrating risk management into these processes, organisations can make more informed decisions and avoid costly missteps.

Effective ERM frameworks also emphasise continuous monitoring and adaptation. Risks are not static; they evolve over time due to changes in internal and external conditions. CFOs must establish mechanisms for monitoring key risk indicators and revising strategies as needed. For example, during the COVID-19 pandemic, many organisations had to adapt their risk management plans to address unprecedented challenges, such as remote work, supply chain disruptions, and shifting consumer behaviours. An ERM framework provides the flexibility and structure needed to respond to such changes effectively.

A practical example of ERM in action is seen in a global pharmaceutical company that faced significant risks related to regulatory compliance and supply chain disruptions. The CFO led the implementation of an ERM framework that integrated risk assessments into strategic planning. By collaborating with legal, operations, and compliance teams, the organisation identified critical vulnerabilities and developed mitigation strategies, such as diversifying suppliers and investing in compliance training. This approach not only reduced risks but also enhanced the organisation's ability to capitalise on growth opportunities in emerging markets.

In conclusion, Enterprise Risk Management frameworks are essential for modern organisations, providing a holistic approach to managing risks and aligning them with strategic goals. For CFOs, implementing ERM is a proactive step toward building resilience, improving decision-making, and driving long-term value creation. By fostering a culture of risk awareness and collaboration, CFOs can ensure that their organisations are prepared to navigate uncertainty and thrive in a complex business environment.

7.3 - Regulatory Compliance Overview

Regulatory compliance is an essential component of risk management and organisational integrity. For CFOs, ensuring compliance with local and international laws is not merely about avoiding fines or penalties; it is about safeguarding the organisation's reputation, fostering stakeholder trust, and maintaining a competitive advantage. As regulatory landscapes become increasingly complex, the ability to navigate compliance challenges effectively is a critical skill for financial leaders.

Compliance requirements vary widely across industries and geographies, encompassing areas such as financial reporting standards, tax laws, data protection regulations, and environmental mandates. For instance, organisations operating in the European Union must comply with the General Data Protection Regulation (GDPR), which governs the collection, storage, and processing of personal data. Failure to adhere to these regulations can result in substantial fines and reputational damage. Similarly, publicly traded companies must ensure compliance with financial reporting standards such as IFRS (International Financial Reporting Standards) or GAAP (Generally Accepted Accounting Principles), depending on their jurisdiction.

The CFO's role in regulatory compliance is multifaceted. At a fundamental level, CFOs are responsible for ensuring that the organisation's financial practices align with applicable laws and standards. This involves overseeing accurate and transparent financial reporting, ensuring that tax obligations are met, and maintaining detailed records to support audits. For example, a CFO in the retail sector might work with tax advisors to ensure compliance with VAT regulations across multiple jurisdictions, minimising the risk of penalties or disputes.

Beyond financial reporting, CFOs play a pivotal role in managing compliance risks related to anti-money laundering (AML) and anti-corruption laws. These areas have gained heightened attention from regulators in recent years, particularly for organisations operating in high-risk regions or industries. CFOs must implement robust controls to detect and prevent illicit activities, such as suspicious transactions or bribery. For instance, a multinational corporation expanding into emerging markets might establish strict due diligence procedures for vetting suppliers and business partners, ensuring compliance with anti-corruption frameworks such as the UK Bribery Act.

Another critical aspect of regulatory compliance is adapting to new and evolving regulations. Regulatory environments are constantly changing, driven by economic shifts, technological advancements, and societal expectations. CFOs must stay informed about these changes and assess their potential impact on the organisation. For example, the growing emphasis on Environmental, Social, and Governance (ESG) reporting has introduced new compliance requirements for organisations in many industries. CFOs must ensure that the organisation collects and reports accurate ESG data, aligning with emerging standards and stakeholder expectations.

To manage compliance effectively, CFOs must adopt a proactive approach to risk assessment and control implementation. This includes conducting regular compliance audits, establishing internal policies and procedures, and fostering a culture of accountability. For example, a CFO in the financial services sector might implement a compliance management system that automates the monitoring of regulatory requirements and alerts teams to potential breaches. These systems not only reduce the risk of non-compliance but also enhance efficiency and transparency.

Collaboration is another key element of compliance management. CFOs must work closely with legal, HR, and IT teams to ensure that compliance efforts are integrated across the organisation. For instance, during the implementation of a new data protection policy, the CFO might collaborate with the IT department to strengthen cybersecurity measures and with HR to provide employee training on data privacy practices. This cross-functional approach ensures that compliance is embedded into every aspect of the organisation's operations.

A practical example of effective compliance management can be seen in a global pharmaceutical company that faced increased scrutiny from regulators due to heightened safety concerns. The CFO led a comprehensive review of compliance processes, implementing stricter controls for clinical trials, enhancing reporting practices, and establishing a dedicated compliance team. These measures not only reduced regulatory risks but also improved stakeholder confidence, positioning the organisation as a leader in ethical and transparent practices.

In conclusion, regulatory compliance is a dynamic and multifaceted challenge that requires strategic oversight, cross-functional collaboration, and a commitment to continuous improvement. For CFOs, ensuring compliance goes beyond meeting legal obligations; it is about protecting the organisation's reputation, fostering trust, and enabling long-term success. By adopting a proactive and integrated approach, CFOs can navigate the complexities of regulatory environments and create a foundation for sustainable growth.

7.4 - Building a Risk-Aware Culture

Creating a risk-aware culture is one of the most effective ways to enhance an organisation's resilience and ensure that risk management becomes an integral part of daily operations. For CFOs, building such a culture requires not only implementing systems and processes but also influencing behaviours, mindsets, and attitudes at every level of the organisation. A risk-aware culture fosters proactive identification, assessment, and mitigation of risks, empowering employees to contribute to the organisation's stability and success.

At its core, a risk-aware culture is about embedding risk management principles into decision-making processes. This begins with leadership commitment. CFOs, along with other senior executives, must set the tone at the top by demonstrating their commitment to risk management and encouraging open dialogue about potential threats and challenges. For example, a CFO might regularly discuss risk factors during board meetings, ensuring that risk considerations are prioritised alongside strategic goals.

Employee engagement is another critical component of a risk-aware culture. To foster this, CFOs must ensure that employees at all levels understand the importance of risk management and their role in identifying and addressing risks. This involves providing comprehensive training programmes that equip employees with the knowledge and skills needed to recognise red flags, follow established protocols, and report concerns. For instance, a retail CFO might implement fraud prevention training for store managers, helping them identify and address suspicious activities such as theft or unauthorised discounts.

Transparency and communication are essential for building trust and promoting risk awareness. Employees must feel empowered to raise concerns without fear of retaliation or blame. CFOs can facilitate this by establishing whistleblower programmes and anonymous reporting channels, ensuring that potential risks are identified and addressed promptly. For example, an anonymous hotline might enable employees to report unethical practices, such as conflicts of interest or misuse of company funds, without fear of reprisal.

To reinforce a risk-aware culture, CFOs must also integrate risk management into performance metrics and reward systems. This might involve recognising teams or individuals who demonstrate exceptional risk awareness or contribute to the mitigation of critical risks. For instance, a CFO in the manufacturing industry might reward a supply chain manager who successfully identifies alternative suppliers during a disruption, ensuring continuity and minimising financial losses.

Technology plays a vital role in supporting a risk-aware culture. Advanced tools such as risk dashboards and data analytics platforms provide employees with real-time insights into potential risks, enabling proactive decision-making. For example, a CFO at an energy company might implement a risk dashboard that monitors fluctuations in oil prices, geopolitical developments, and regulatory changes, providing employees with the information needed to address risks effectively.

A compelling example of building a risk-aware culture can be seen in a financial services firm that faced reputational damage due to a high-profile compliance breach. The CFO spearheaded a cultural transformation initiative, introducing regular risk workshops, establishing clear accountability frameworks, and leveraging technology to enhance transparency. These efforts not only reduced compliance violations but also improved employee engagement, fostering a shared commitment to organisational integrity.

In conclusion, building a risk-aware culture is a strategic priority for CFOs seeking to enhance resilience and align risk management with organisational goals. By fostering transparency, engaging employees, and integrating risk considerations into daily operations, CFOs can create an environment where risks are identified and addressed proactively. In an era of increasing complexity and uncertainty, a risk-aware culture is not just a best practice; it is a competitive advantage.

7.5 - Managing Credit Risk

Credit risk is one of the most significant financial risks organisations face, particularly for those that extend credit to customers or invest in financial instruments. Managing credit risk effectively is essential to safeguarding the organisation's financial health, ensuring liquidity, and maintaining profitability. For CFOs, this involves a combination of strategic oversight, robust policies, and advanced analytical tools to minimise exposure while enabling growth.

At its core, credit risk refers to the potential for a borrower, customer, or counterparty to default on their obligations, leading to financial losses for the organisation. This risk is particularly pronounced in industries such as retail, manufacturing, and financial services, where large portions of revenue may depend on receivables or loans. For instance, a retail CFO extending credit to wholesale customers must evaluate their payment histories and financial stability to mitigate the risk of non-payment.

One of the foundational strategies for managing credit risk is establishing clear credit policies. These policies should define the criteria for extending credit, including customer creditworthiness, payment terms, and credit limits. CFOs must ensure these policies are applied consistently across the organisation, with regular reviews to adapt to changing market conditions. For example, during an economic downturn, a CFO might tighten credit terms or reduce exposure to high-risk customers to protect the organisation's cash flow.

Customer credit assessments are a critical component of credit risk management. These assessments evaluate a customer's ability to meet their financial obligations based on factors such as financial statements, credit ratings, and payment history. CFOs can leverage third-party credit agencies to access comprehensive reports or use internal analytics to assess risk levels. For instance, a CFO in the automotive industry might use predictive analytics to identify customers with a high likelihood of default, enabling the organisation to take proactive measures such as requiring upfront payments or adjusting payment terms.

Monitoring receivables is equally important in managing credit risk. CFOs must ensure that overdue payments are flagged promptly and that collections processes are efficient and effective. Automated systems can track receivables in real-time, providing alerts for overdue accounts and generating reports to guide decision-making. For example, a manufacturing CFO might use an accounts receivable dashboard to identify customers who consistently delay payments, enabling the organisation to address issues early and prevent further exposure.

Another strategy is diversifying the customer base to reduce dependency on a few high-risk clients. Over-reliance on a small number of customers can amplify credit risk, particularly if those customers experience financial difficulties. CFOs should work with sales and marketing teams to expand the customer base, focusing on attracting low-risk, high-value clients. For instance, a CFO in the technology sector might target stable, long-term contracts with government agencies or large enterprises to offset the risks associated with smaller, high-growth startups.

Hedging strategies can also play a role in managing credit risk. For example, trade credit insurance allows organisations to protect against losses from non-payment, providing financial security while enabling them to maintain competitive credit terms. CFOs must assess the cost-benefit of such insurance, ensuring that it aligns with the organisation's risk tolerance and financial goals.

Effective credit risk management also involves ongoing communication and collaboration with other departments. Sales teams, for instance, often have valuable insights into customer behaviours and market conditions that can inform credit decisions. Similarly, close coordination with legal teams ensures that contracts and payment terms are enforceable, reducing the risk of disputes. For example, a CFO in the construction industry might collaborate with project managers to ensure milestone-based payments are clearly defined and legally binding.

Despite proactive measures, defaults are sometimes unavoidable. In such cases, CFOs must implement effective recovery strategies, including negotiation, restructuring payment terms, or pursuing legal action. For example, during a temporary cash flow issue, a CFO might work with a customer to extend payment terms or establish a repayment plan, maintaining the relationship while ensuring the recovery of funds.

A practical example of successful credit risk management can be seen in a global FMCG company that faced rising bad debts due to economic instability. The CFO introduced a tiered credit policy based on customer risk profiles, combining stricter terms for high-risk clients with incentives for early payments from low-risk customers. By implementing advanced analytics tools to monitor receivables and collaborating closely with sales teams, the organisation reduced overdue accounts by 30% within a year, significantly improving cash flow and financial stability.

In conclusion, managing credit risk is a vital responsibility for CFOs, requiring a balance between caution and growth. By implementing robust credit policies, leveraging analytics, and fostering collaboration across departments, CFOs can minimise exposure while enabling the organisation to pursue opportunities confidently. In a world of increasing financial uncertainty, effective credit risk management is not just a defensive measure; it is a strategic advantage.

7.6 - Mitigating Operational Risks

Operational risks arise from internal processes, systems, or human factors, and they can significantly disrupt an organisation's operations and financial stability. For CFOs, mitigating these risks is a critical aspect of financial leadership, requiring a proactive and strategic approach. Effective operational risk management not only protects the organisation from financial losses but also enhances efficiency, resilience, and stakeholder confidence.

Operational risks encompass a wide range of issues, including process inefficiencies, system failures, human errors, and external disruptions. For example, a manufacturing company might face operational risks from equipment breakdowns, supply chain interruptions, or safety incidents. Similarly, a financial institution might encounter risks from cybersecurity breaches, regulatory non-compliance, or errors in transaction processing. Identifying and addressing these risks is essential for maintaining continuity and avoiding costly disruptions.

The first step in mitigating operational risks is conducting a comprehensive risk assessment to identify vulnerabilities across the organisation. CFOs must work with functional leaders to map out critical processes and evaluate potential failure points. For instance, in a retail organisation, the CFO might analyse risks associated with inventory management, identifying areas where stockouts or overstocking could impact revenue and profitability. This assessment provides a foundation for prioritising mitigation efforts and allocating resources effectively.

Technology plays a central role in addressing operational risks, particularly those related to process inefficiencies and system failures. Advanced tools such as enterprise resource planning (ERP) systems, automation, and predictive analytics can enhance operational reliability by streamlining workflows, reducing errors, and providing real-time insights. For example, an ERP system might automatically flag discrepancies in purchase orders and invoices, enabling the finance team to address issues before they escalate. Similarly, predictive maintenance tools can monitor equipment performance and predict failures, minimising downtime and repair costs.

CFOs must also focus on strengthening internal controls to mitigate operational risks. This includes implementing policies, procedures, and safeguards to prevent errors and fraud. For example, segregation of duties ensures that no single individual has control over multiple aspects of a financial transaction, reducing the risk of mismanagement. Regular audits and compliance checks further enhance accountability and identify areas for improvement.

Employee training is another critical element of operational risk management. Human error is a leading cause of operational failures, and equipping employees with the knowledge and skills to follow best practices can significantly reduce risks. For instance, a CFO in the logistics industry might provide training on safety protocols, ensuring that employees adhere to standards and minimise the risk of accidents. Similarly, cybersecurity training can help employees recognise and avoid phishing attacks, protecting the organisation from data breaches.

Resilience planning is essential for addressing external disruptions, such as natural disasters, geopolitical events, or pandemics. CFOs must ensure that the organisation has contingency plans in place to maintain operations during crises. This might involve diversifying suppliers, establishing backup systems, or implementing remote work capabilities. For example, during the COVID-19 pandemic, organisations with robust resilience plans were able to transition to remote operations seamlessly, minimising disruptions and maintaining productivity.

A notable example of effective operational risk mitigation can be seen in a global e-commerce company that faced risks from rapid growth and increasing order volumes. The CFO implemented automation tools to streamline order processing and invested in AI-driven inventory management systems to optimise stock levels. These initiatives reduced processing errors by 50% and improved order fulfilment rates, enabling the organisation to scale efficiently while maintaining operational integrity.

In conclusion, mitigating operational risks is a multifaceted challenge that requires a combination of technology, processes, and people. For CFOs, the key is to adopt a proactive approach, identifying vulnerabilities, implementing controls, and fostering a culture of accountability and continuous improvement. By addressing operational risks effectively, organisations can enhance resilience, protect their assets, and maintain stakeholder trust in an increasingly complex and dynamic environment.

7.7 - Financial Fraud Detection and Prevention

The risk of financial fraud is a persistent challenge for organisations, posing threats to their financial stability, reputation, and stakeholder trust. For CFOs, detecting and preventing fraud is not simply about safeguarding monetary assets; it is about creating a robust framework that fosters transparency, accountability, and trust. Financial fraud encompasses a range of activities, from internal embezzlement and expense falsification to external scams like phishing and invoice fraud. Tackling these risks requires a blend of advanced technology, proactive policies, and a commitment to ethical practices.

Financial fraud often arises from gaps in processes or a lack of oversight. For instance, employees with unchecked access to funds or financial systems may exploit vulnerabilities for personal gain. Similarly, external actors may target organisations through sophisticated schemes, such as impersonating suppliers or exploiting weaknesses in digital payment platforms. A proactive approach begins with recognising these vulnerabilities. CFOs must first conduct comprehensive fraud risk assessments, mapping out processes that involve cash flow, financial transactions, or vendor payments. For example, identifying that purchase orders and invoice approvals are managed by the same individual could signal a need for stronger segregation of duties.

The implementation of robust internal controls is essential for fraud prevention. These controls create an environment where fraud becomes both difficult to execute and easy to detect. Segregation of duties is a particularly effective strategy, ensuring that no single individual has complete control over financial transactions. For instance, an accounts payable process where one employee prepares invoices, another approves payments, and a third reconciles accounts reduces the likelihood of collusion or errors. Automated approval workflows further enhance this process by enforcing consistency and minimising human interference.

Advanced data analytics tools and artificial intelligence (AI) have revolutionised the detection of fraudulent activities. AI systems can analyse vast datasets to identify anomalies that human reviewers might miss. For example, a CFO may implement a fraud detection platform that flags duplicate payments or unusual patterns in expense claims. These tools can process data in real-time, allowing organisations to act swiftly when irregularities are detected. In one instance, a multinational logistics company used predictive analytics to uncover a pattern of small, repeated payments to a dormant supplier account, halting the fraudulent activity before it escalated.

Employee training is equally vital in combating financial fraud. Many cases of fraud stem from employees failing to recognise threats, such as phishing emails or dubious supplier requests. CFOs should invest in regular training programmes that educate employees about common fraud schemes and the importance of adhering to established processes. For example, a manufacturing firm might implement an annual fraud awareness week, complete with workshops, role-playing scenarios, and updates on emerging risks. By empowering employees with knowledge, organisations can strengthen their first line of defence against fraud.

A culture of transparency and accountability is essential for sustaining long-term fraud prevention efforts. CFOs must lead by example, demonstrating a commitment to ethical behaviour and encouraging open communication. Whistleblower programmes and anonymous reporting channels allow employees to voice concerns without fear of retaliation. For instance, an organisation with a confidential hotline for reporting suspicious activities may uncover fraudulent schemes that would otherwise remain hidden. Recognising and acting on such reports promptly reinforces the importance of integrity across the organisation.

In cases where fraud does occur, a well-defined response plan is crucial. CFOs must act decisively, coordinating investigations, assessing the financial and reputational impact, and implementing measures to prevent recurrence. Working closely with forensic accountants, legal teams, and external auditors can help organisations recover losses and restore confidence. Transparency with stakeholders, including clear communication about the steps being taken, further bolsters trust and credibility.

A real-world example of effective fraud prevention is seen in a retail chain that faced increasing losses from fake refunds processed by employees. The CFO introduced automated point-of-sale systems with built-in fraud detection capabilities alongside randomised audits of cash handling procedures. Within six months, fraudulent transactions decreased by 80%, saving the organisation significant revenue while reinforcing the importance of vigilance.

In conclusion, financial fraud detection and prevention is a dynamic challenge that requires a multifaceted approach. By implementing robust internal controls, leveraging technology, and fostering a culture of awareness and accountability, CFOs can protect their organisations from financial and reputational harm. In an era of increasingly sophisticated fraud schemes, proactive measures are not just a safeguard; they are a strategic imperative for ensuring long-term resilience and trust.

7.8 - Role of Internal Controls

Internal controls are the cornerstone of financial stability, ensuring that processes are executed efficiently, assets are safeguarded, and risks are minimised. For CFOs, the implementation and oversight of internal controls go beyond compliance; they are integral to maintaining organisational integrity, enhancing operational efficiency, and enabling informed decision-making. A strong internal control framework empowers organisations to identify potential vulnerabilities and address them proactively.

At their most fundamental level, internal controls are mechanisms that enforce checks and balances across an organisation's financial and operational activities. These mechanisms include policies, procedures, and technologies designed to reduce the likelihood of errors, fraud, and inefficiencies. For instance, a manufacturing company may implement mandatory reconciliation of inventory levels against sales data, ensuring discrepancies are flagged and investigated promptly. Such controls ensure that the organisation's resources are accurately accounted for, fostering accountability and reliability.

One of the most effective internal controls is the segregation of duties, which prevents any single individual from having complete control over a financial process. This practice minimises the risk of fraud and errors by requiring multiple employees to approve, execute, and review transactions. For example, in the procurement process, one employee might issue purchase orders, another approve them, and a third manage payments. This division of responsibilities not only enhances transparency but also ensures that irregularities are more likely to be detected.

Automation plays a pivotal role in strengthening internal controls, particularly in large organisations with complex financial operations. Automated systems can enforce compliance with policies, flag anomalies in real-time, and provide audit trails for every transaction. For instance, a cloud-based enterprise resource planning (ERP) system can generate alerts for transactions that exceed predefined limits, ensuring that unauthorised expenses are escalated for review. Automation also reduces reliance on manual processes, which are more prone to human error and manipulation.

Regular audits and reviews are another critical component of internal controls. These exercises provide an independent assessment of the organisation's adherence to policies and highlight areas for improvement. CFOs should prioritise both internal and external audits, ensuring a comprehensive evaluation of financial processes. For example, an internal audit might uncover gaps in expense tracking, prompting the implementation of tighter controls and automated expense reporting systems. External audits conducted by independent professionals further enhance credibility and provide assurance to stakeholders.

A strong internal control framework is not static; it must evolve in response to emerging risks and changing business conditions. CFOs must monitor the effectiveness of controls continuously, using key performance indicators (KPIs) such as the timeliness of reconciliations, the frequency of exceptions, or the results of audits. By analysing these metrics, organisations can identify weaknesses and adapt their control environment accordingly. For instance, a CFO noticing a rise in exceptions flagged by an automated accounts payable system may investigate root causes and implement corrective measures, such as additional training or process adjustments.

The success of internal controls also depends on fostering a culture of accountability and compliance. CFOs must emphasise the importance of adhering to established processes and encourage employees to report potential violations. For example, an organisation with a clear whistleblower policy and confidential reporting mechanisms is more likely to detect and address issues early, minimising financial and reputational risks.

A compelling example of internal controls in action is seen in a global logistics company that faced repeated losses due to unauthorised fuel purchases by drivers. The CFO implemented a fuel card system with real-time monitoring, restricting usage to approved locations and predefined limits. This measure reduced unauthorised purchases by 90% within six months, demonstrating the tangible benefits of robust internal controls.

In conclusion, the role of internal controls extends far beyond preventing fraud or meeting compliance requirements. They are critical enablers of operational efficiency, risk management, and stakeholder confidence. For CFOs, maintaining and continuously improving these controls is essential for ensuring financial stability and long-term organisational success.

7.9 - Navigating Legal and Tax Risks

Navigating legal and tax risks is a critical responsibility for CFOs, requiring a deep understanding of regulatory frameworks, proactive planning, and close collaboration with legal and tax professionals. These risks can arise from changes in legislation, non-compliance with regulations, or misinterpretation of complex tax codes. Mismanaging such risks can lead to significant financial penalties, reputational damage, and even legal disputes. For CFOs, addressing these risks effectively involves combining technical expertise with strategic foresight.

One of the most prominent legal risks for organisations is non-compliance with contractual obligations. Contracts govern relationships with suppliers, customers, and other stakeholders, and breaches can result in costly disputes. CFOs must ensure that contractual terms are clear, enforceable, and aligned with the organisation's objectives. For instance, in the construction industry, a CFO might work with legal counsel to structure contracts with subcontractors that include penalty clauses for missed deadlines, reducing the organisation's exposure to project delays.

Tax risks, on the other hand, often stem from the complexity and variability of tax codes across jurisdictions. For organisations operating in multiple countries, navigating differences in tax regulations, such as corporate income tax rates, transfer pricing rules, or VAT requirements, can be particularly challenging. CFOs must ensure that the organisation's tax strategy complies with local laws while optimising its overall tax position. For example, a CFO managing a multinational corporation might work with tax advisors to structure intercompany transactions in a way that complies with transfer pricing regulations while minimising tax liabilities.

Proactively managing tax risks also involves staying informed about changes in tax legislation and anticipating their potential impact. Governments worldwide are increasingly focusing on corporate taxation, introducing measures to combat tax avoidance and ensure transparency. For example, the OECD's Base Erosion and Profit Shifting (BEPS) initiative has prompted many countries to implement stricter rules on cross-border transactions. A CFO must monitor these developments closely, adapting the organisation's tax policies to remain compliant while maintaining competitiveness.

Data accuracy is another critical factor in managing legal and tax risks. Errors or inconsistencies in financial reporting can attract regulatory scrutiny, leading to audits, penalties, or legal action. CFOs must ensure that the organisation's accounting and reporting processes are robust, with adequate checks and balances to detect and rectify errors. For instance, implementing automated systems for tax calculations and reporting can reduce the risk of human error and ensure compliance with filing deadlines.

Collaboration is essential for navigating legal and tax risks effectively. CFOs must work closely with internal teams, including legal, tax, and compliance departments, as well as external advisors such as auditors and legal counsel. This collaborative approach ensures that all aspects of risk management are addressed comprehensively. For example, during a corporate restructuring, the CFO might coordinate with legal and tax experts to assess the implications of transferring assets, reorganising entities, or merging subsidiaries.

Another important consideration is dispute resolution. Despite best efforts, organisations may encounter legal or tax disputes, such as challenges to tax filings or breaches of contracts. CFOs must be prepared to manage these situations, working with legal teams to develop strategies for resolution. For instance, in the event of a tax audit, the CFO might provide detailed documentation to substantiate the organisation's position, engaging with tax authorities to negotiate settlements if necessary.

A practical example of navigating legal and tax risks can be seen in a global technology company facing scrutiny over its transfer pricing practices. The CFO led a comprehensive review of the company's pricing policies, aligning them with OECD guidelines and local regulations. By engaging external experts and enhancing internal documentation processes, the company successfully resolved disputes with tax authorities, avoiding substantial penalties and reputational damage.

Managing legal and tax risks also requires fostering a culture of compliance within the organisation. CFOs must emphasise the importance of ethical practices, ensuring that employees understand and adhere to relevant regulations. Regular training programmes and clear policies can help embed compliance into the organisation's operations. For instance, a CFO in the retail sector might implement mandatory training for finance and sales teams on VAT regulations, reducing the risk of non-compliance.

In conclusion, navigating legal and tax risks is a multifaceted challenge that demands vigilance, collaboration, and strategic planning. For CFOs, the ability to address these risks effectively is essential for protecting the organisation's financial health and reputation. By combining technical expertise with proactive risk management, CFOs can navigate complex regulatory landscapes and create a foundation for sustainable growth.

7.10 - Case Study: Overcoming a Risk Management Challenge

Risk management is often tested in times of crisis, and the ability to navigate these challenges effectively is a hallmark of strong financial leadership. This case study examines how the CFO of a global manufacturing company successfully led the organisation through a significant risk management challenge, showcasing the importance of preparation, adaptability, and collaboration.

The Context: A Crisis in the Supply Chain

The organisation, a global manufacturing company with operations across multiple regions, faced an unprecedented crisis when its largest supplier unexpectedly declared bankruptcy. This event disrupted the company's supply chain, jeopardising its ability to meet production schedules and fulfil customer orders.

The financial and operational impact was immediate:

- Rising Costs: Sourcing alternative suppliers required premium pricing, while penalties for delayed deliveries added further financial strain.
- Reputation at Risk: Customers began to question the company's reliability, potentially damaging long-term relationships.
- Operational Vulnerabilities: Critical production lines faced shutdowns due to raw material shortages.

The CFO recognised the severity of the situation and took swift, decisive action to stabilise operations and protect the organisation's financial health.

Phase 1: Immediate Response and Stabilisation

The CFO's first priority was to stabilise the organisation and address the immediate financial and operational challenges. Key actions included:

1. **Comprehensive Risk Assessment:**
    - The CFO worked closely with procurement, operations, and sales teams to evaluate the full scope of the disruption.

- Critical vulnerabilities were identified, such as production lines at risk of halting and contracts with strict delivery deadlines.
- A rapid analysis of financial exposure helped quantify the immediate cost implications.

2. **Cost Control Measures:**
   - Non-essential capital expenditures were deferred to conserve cash.
   - Payment terms with other suppliers were renegotiated to ease financial pressure.
   - The CFO leveraged relationships with banking partners to secure a revolving credit facility, ensuring the organisation maintained liquidity to cover increased costs.

3. **Supplier Diversification:**
   - The CFO and procurement team conducted expedited due diligence to onboard alternative suppliers that met quality and pricing standards.
   - To avoid over-reliance on a single supplier in the future, the organisation implemented a diversification strategy, sourcing critical components from multiple suppliers across different regions.

Phase 2: Rebuilding and Mitigating Future Risks

Once the immediate crisis was under control, the CFO turned their attention to longer-term recovery and resilience-building initiatives.

1. **Strengthening the Supply Chain:**

- A supplier diversification strategy was formally integrated into procurement policies, ensuring the organisation was no longer overly dependent on single vendors.
- Advanced supply chain analytics were introduced to monitor supplier health, providing early warnings of potential financial or operational risks.
- Contingency agreements were established with backup suppliers to ensure production continuity in case of future disruptions.

2. **Technology Adoption:**
   - Predictive analytics tools were implemented to enhance scenario planning capabilities and identify risks proactively.
   - The CFO invested in a supply chain risk management platform that provided real-time visibility into supplier performance, inventory levels, and potential bottlenecks.

3. **Scenario Planning and Contingency Framework:**
   - The risk management framework was overhauled to include detailed contingency plans for high-risk areas.
   - Cross-functional crisis response protocols were established, ensuring all departments were prepared to act swiftly and cohesively in the event of future disruptions.

Phase 3: Communication and Stakeholder Engagement

Effective communication played a pivotal role in navigating the crisis and maintaining stakeholder trust.

1. **Customer Communication:**
   - Customers were promptly informed of potential delays and offered alternative solutions, such as expedited shipping or partial deliveries.
   - Proactive updates reassured clients of the company's commitment to resolving the issue and maintaining service quality.

2. **Internal Communication:**
   - Transparent updates were shared with employees, fostering a sense of shared purpose and resilience.
   - Cross-functional meetings ensured alignment between teams, streamlining efforts to address the crisis.

3. **Supplier Relationships:**
   - The CFO worked closely with alternative suppliers to build strong partnerships and negotiate favourable terms, ensuring long-term stability and mutual trust.

The Outcome: A Remarkable Recovery

Through swift and strategic action, the CFO guided the organisation to recovery and strengthened its long-term resilience:

1. Production Restoration: Within six months, the organisation returned to full production capacity.
2. Cost Reductions: Improved procurement practices achieved a 20% reduction in supply chain costs.

3. Customer Confidence: Transparent communication and on-time recovery efforts preserved key customer relationships, with many clients expressing increased trust in the company's ability to navigate challenges.

4. Risk Management Leadership: The company emerged as a leader in risk management within its industry, setting new benchmarks for supply chain resilience.

Lessons Learned

This case study offers valuable lessons for CFOs and financial leaders:

1. Proactive Risk Management: Diversifying suppliers and enhancing scenario planning can mitigate the impact of unexpected disruptions.

2. Swift Action: Timely decisions, such as securing financing and onboarding alternative suppliers, are critical in a crisis.

3. Collaboration: Cross-functional teamwork ensures comprehensive solutions and strengthens organisational resilience.

4. Stakeholder Trust: Transparent communication with customers, employees, and partners is essential to maintaining confidence during turbulent times.

Conclusion

The CFO's leadership during this crisis exemplifies the importance of adaptability, foresight, and collaboration in effective risk management. By turning a challenging situation into an opportunity for growth and innovation, the organisation not only recovered but also emerged stronger and better prepared for future uncertainties. This case serves as an inspiring example of how financial leaders can navigate crises and deliver long-term value through strategic risk management.

Chapter 8

Building and Leading High-Performance Teams

> *"Leadership is not about commanding greatness but creating an environment where greatness thrives naturally."*
> **Robert N. Jacobs**

Building and leading a high-performance finance team is a fundamental responsibility for CFOs. Beyond financial expertise, successful CFOs must demonstrate leadership, vision, and an ability to inspire their teams. This chapter explores how CFOs can build cohesive, motivated, and effective teams by addressing key aspects of leadership, talent management, collaboration, and recognition.

8.1 - Importance of Leadership in Finance

Leadership in finance goes beyond managing numbers; it involves inspiring individuals, fostering collaboration, and ensuring alignment with organisational goals. A CFO's ability to lead effectively determines the finance team's performance and its impact on broader business objectives. Leadership in finance is about creating clarity, accountability, and a shared sense of purpose.

Successful leadership begins with a clear vision. A CFO must articulate the finance team's role within the organisation and how it aligns with strategic objectives. For instance, in a rapidly growing technology company, the CFO might define the team's vision as transitioning from a transactional function to a strategic partner, focusing on areas such as financial forecasting and market analysis. By clearly outlining this purpose, the CFO ensures that every team member understands their contribution to the organisation's success.

Accountability and trust are essential components of leadership. CFOs must create an environment where team members feel empowered to take ownership of their responsibilities while maintaining high ethical standards. This involves implementing transparent processes, encouraging collaboration, and recognising contributions. For example, acknowledging an analyst for identifying cost-saving opportunities reinforces accountability and highlights the importance of proactive problem-solving.

Emotional intelligence (EI) is equally critical for effective leadership. CFOs must support their teams through challenges, demonstrating empathy and active listening. For example, during a stressful budgeting cycle, a CFO who takes the time to understand their team's concerns and provides encouragement fosters resilience and morale. By balancing technical expertise with emotional intelligence, CFOs can lead with both authority and compassion. Leadership also involves fostering adaptability and innovation. In a rapidly changing business landscape, CFOs must encourage their teams to embrace new technologies, processes, and strategies. For instance, introducing automation for routine tasks allows the team to focus on strategic initiatives, promoting a culture of continuous improvement.

Communication is a hallmark of great leadership. CFOs must effectively convey complex financial information to diverse audiences, from board members to team members. Tailoring communication to the audience ensures clarity and engagement. For instance, presenting financial results to the board might focus on high-level insights, while discussions with the finance team delve into detailed analysis.

A practical example of leadership in action can be seen in a global retail company where the CFO transformed the finance function during a period of rapid expansion. By articulating a clear vision, fostering collaboration, and embracing innovation, the CFO empowered the team to meet the challenges of scaling operations while maintaining accuracy and efficiency.

In conclusion, leadership in finance is about more than managing numbers; it is about inspiring and enabling teams to achieve their best. By combining strategic vision, emotional intelligence, and effective communication, CFOs can create high-performing teams that drive organisational success.

8.2 - Hiring and Retaining Top Talent

Attracting and retaining top talent is a cornerstone of building a high-performance finance team. In an increasingly competitive job market, CFOs must develop strategies that go beyond offering competitive salaries to create an environment where skilled professionals want to join and remain. This involves aligning recruitment with organisational goals, crafting a compelling employer value proposition, and fostering a supportive work culture.

The process begins with a clear understanding of the organisation's needs. CFOs must identify the skills and capabilities required to achieve the finance team's objectives. For instance, a company undergoing digital transformation may prioritise hiring professionals with expertise in financial technology and data analytics. By aligning hiring strategies with these priorities, CFOs ensure that the team's skills remain relevant and forward-focused.

Recruitment processes must reflect the organisation's commitment to excellence. Structured interviews, case studies, and skills assessments can identify candidates who excel both technically and culturally. For example, a CFO hiring for a financial planning and analysis role might assess a candidate's ability to model complex scenarios while evaluating their communication and teamwork skills.

Once top talent is hired, retention becomes the focus. Creating opportunities for growth and development is a key retention strategy. CFOs can invest in training programmes, certifications, and mentorship initiatives to enhance employee skills. For instance, sponsoring a team member's enrolment in a data analytics certification programme recognises their contributions and prepares them for future challenges.

Recognition and rewards also play a crucial role. Monetary incentives, such as performance-based bonuses, should be complemented by non-monetary rewards, such as professional development opportunities or public acknowledgement. For example, recognising a team for successfully completing an audit ahead of schedule during a company-wide meeting highlights their achievements and reinforces the value of teamwork.

Flexibility is another important factor in retaining talent. Offering remote work options, flexible schedules, and work-life balance initiatives can enhance job satisfaction. For instance, allowing a finance manager to work from home part-time demonstrates the organisation's commitment to employee well-being.

A practical example of effective hiring and retention can be seen in a global pharmaceutical company that reduced turnover by implementing career development plans and emphasising work-life balance. These initiatives positioned the company as an employer of choice, attracting and retaining top talent.

In conclusion, hiring and retaining top talent requires a strategic approach that prioritises growth, recognition, and flexibility. By creating an environment where employees feel valued and supported, CFOs can build a finance team that drives organisational success.

8.3 - Developing Future Finance Leaders

The development of future finance leaders ensures the sustainability and long-term success of the finance function. Leadership succession is not just about filling roles; it is about nurturing talent, fostering innovation, and preparing individuals to navigate the complexities of modern finance. CFOs play a pivotal role in identifying high-potential employees, providing development opportunities, and creating a culture of continuous learning.

Leadership development begins with identifying potential candidates. High-potential employees often exhibit a combination of technical expertise, strategic thinking, and emotional intelligence. For instance, an analyst who consistently delivers insightful recommendations and collaborates effectively may be a strong candidate for leadership development.

Mentorship is a cornerstone of leadership development. Pairing emerging leaders with experienced mentors facilitates the transfer of knowledge and skills. For example, a CFO mentoring a junior manager might guide them on managing stakeholder relationships or navigating organisational politics.

Formal training programmes enhance both technical and soft skills. CFOs can provide workshops on areas such as risk management, financial modelling, and leadership communication. Encouraging certifications, such as Chartered Financial Analyst (CFA), adds credibility to the team's expertise.

Exposure to cross-functional experiences broadens perspectives and enhances problem-solving abilities. For instance, involving a finance professional in a cross-departmental initiative, such as launching a new product, helps them understand how finance integrates with other functions.

A practical example of leadership development can be seen in a logistics company where the CFO introduced mentorship programmes and rotational assignments, resulting in a 40% increase in internal promotions.

In conclusion, developing future finance leaders is a critical responsibility for CFOs. By investing in mentorship, training, and cross-functional experiences, CFOs can build a pipeline of capable leaders who drive success and innovation.

8.4 - Managing Diverse Teams

Managing diverse teams is a crucial aspect of leadership in the modern workplace. For CFOs, diversity within the finance function is not just a matter of representation but a source of competitive advantage. Teams that include individuals with varied backgrounds, experiences, and perspectives are more innovative, creative, and effective at problem-solving. However, to fully harness the benefits of diversity, CFOs must intentionally foster an environment where everyone feels valued, respected, and empowered to contribute.

Diversity in finance teams can take many forms, including differences in cultural backgrounds, educational experiences, professional expertise, and even generational perspectives. For example, a team might include seasoned accountants with decades of experience, data analysts skilled in artificial intelligence, and team members from international markets with a deep understanding of local regulations. This mix of skills and perspectives can lead to richer discussions, more balanced decision-making, and improved organisational outcomes.

The foundation of managing diverse teams is creating a culture of inclusion. While diversity refers to the presence of differences, inclusion ensures that these differences are valued and leveraged effectively. CFOs must actively promote a culture where team members feel comfortable sharing their ideas, asking questions, and challenging assumptions. For example, a CFO might establish regular team meetings where all members are encouraged to contribute, ensuring that quieter voices are heard and respected.

Communication is a critical component of managing diversity. Team members from different cultural or professional backgrounds may have varying communication styles, which can sometimes lead to misunderstandings. CFOs must adapt their communication methods to ensure clarity and alignment. For instance, using clear and concise language, avoiding jargon, and employing visual aids can help bridge gaps in understanding. Additionally, fostering open channels of communication where team members can express concerns or provide feedback is essential for building trust.

Empathy and cultural awareness are equally important. CFOs must understand and appreciate the unique perspectives and experiences that each team member brings to the table. This requires not only sensitivity to cultural norms but also a willingness to learn and adapt. For instance, in an international finance team, recognising different approaches to time management or decision-making can help avoid conflicts and build stronger working relationships.

Equitable performance evaluations are another critical aspect of managing diverse teams. Bias, whether conscious or unconscious, can undermine efforts to create an inclusive environment. CFOs should implement clear, objective criteria for assessing performance, focusing on measurable outcomes rather than subjective impressions. For example, instead of evaluating an employee based on their "fit" within the team, assessments should centre on their contributions to achieving financial targets or improving processes.

Technology can also play a significant role in managing diverse teams, particularly in remote or hybrid work environments. Collaborative tools such as project management software, cloud platforms, and video conferencing enable team members to work together seamlessly across geographies. For instance, a CFO overseeing a global finance team might use shared dashboards to track budgets and forecasts in real-time, ensuring transparency and alignment.

Fostering collaboration among diverse team members is essential for maximising their potential. CFOs can encourage cross-functional projects that bring together individuals with complementary skills and perspectives. For example, involving a financial analyst, a compliance officer, and a tax expert in a strategic planning initiative ensures that all relevant angles are considered, leading to more robust outcomes.

A compelling example of managing diverse teams successfully can be seen in a multinational company where the CFO implemented a rotating meeting schedule to accommodate team members in different time zones. This simple yet effective strategy demonstrated respect for the team's diversity and improved participation and collaboration across the board.

In conclusion, managing diverse teams requires intentional effort, empathy, and strategic leadership. By fostering inclusion, adapting communication, and leveraging technology, CFOs can create an environment where diversity thrives. A diverse finance team is not only better equipped to tackle challenges but also drives innovation and supports organisational success.

8.5 - Building a Culture of Collaboration

Collaboration is the backbone of any successful team, and in a finance function where precision and coordination are paramount, a culture of collaboration is essential. CFOs play a pivotal role in fostering an environment where team members work together effectively, share knowledge, and align their efforts toward common goals. Collaboration enhances problem-solving, boosts efficiency, and ensures that the finance team operates as a cohesive unit.

The foundation of collaboration lies in open communication. CFOs must ensure that team members feel comfortable sharing ideas, asking questions, and providing feedback. This begins with setting the tone at the top. For instance, during budgeting sessions, a CFO might encourage input from all team members, from junior analysts to senior managers, emphasising that diverse perspectives strengthen decision-making. Such inclusivity not only improves outcomes but also builds trust within the team.

Trust is a cornerstone of collaboration. Without it, team members may hesitate to rely on one another or share information freely. CFOs can build trust by fostering transparency, ensuring that processes are fair, and recognising contributions. For example, if a team successfully implements a new financial reporting process, publicly acknowledging their collective effort reinforces the value of collaboration.

Cross-functional collaboration is another critical element of a collaborative culture. CFOs should encourage their teams to work closely with other departments, such as marketing, operations, or IT. For example, during a product launch, the finance team might collaborate with marketing to forecast sales, optimise pricing strategies, and track ROI. These cross-departmental efforts not only enhance outcomes but also help finance professionals understand how their work impacts the broader organisation.

Technology can be a powerful enabler of collaboration. Tools such as cloud-based platforms, real-time dashboards, and project management software allow teams to work together seamlessly, even in remote or hybrid settings. For example, a CFO might implement a collaborative budgeting tool that enables team members to update forecasts in real-time, ensuring that everyone has access to the latest information and can contribute to collective decision-making.

Recognising and rewarding collaboration is vital for sustaining a collaborative culture. CFOs should highlight and celebrate team achievements, ensuring that collective success is valued as much as individual performance. For instance, organising a team lunch or sharing a message of appreciation after completing a major project reinforces the importance of working together.

Conflict resolution is also a key component of fostering collaboration. Disagreements are inevitable in any team, but they can be opportunities for growth if handled constructively. CFOs must model effective conflict resolution, encouraging open dialogue and finding solutions that satisfy all parties. For example, if two team members have differing approaches to a financial analysis project, the CFO might facilitate a discussion to align their perspectives and ensure that the final output meets the team's goals.

A practical example of fostering collaboration can be seen in a logistics company where the CFO introduced a shared knowledge repository for best practices and tools. This resource allowed team members to learn from each other's experiences and enhanced efficiency across the department.

In conclusion, building a culture of collaboration is essential for creating a high-performing finance team. By fostering trust, leveraging technology, and recognising teamwork, CFOs can create an environment where collaboration flourishes. Collaboration is not just a skill; it is a mindset that empowers teams to achieve more together than they could individually.

8.6 - Communication Skills for CFOs

For a CFO, communication skills are as vital as technical expertise. Finance is a complex domain filled with numbers, metrics, and strategies that require clear explanation and contextualisation. A CFO's ability to effectively communicate with diverse audiences, including their finance team, the executive board, investors, and other departments, can shape how decisions are made and how the finance function is perceived across the organisation. Communication is more than just transmitting information; it involves inspiring confidence, fostering collaboration, and ensuring alignment with strategic goals.

One of the CFO's most important communication responsibilities is translating complex financial data into actionable insights. Financial jargon, detailed reports, and intricate analyses can overwhelm non-financial stakeholders, such as marketing or operations teams. A skilled CFO simplifies this complexity, presenting information in a clear, concise, and relevant way. For example, when explaining quarterly financial results to the board, the CFO might focus on key figures such as profit margins, cash flow, and future projections while using visuals like charts or dashboards to make the data more digestible.

Adapting communication to suit different audiences is another essential skill. A CFO's tone, depth, and focus must shift depending on whether they are addressing their finance team, external investors, or the CEO. For instance, while a CEO may require a high-level overview of financial performance and strategic recommendations, finance team members may need detailed guidance on executing budget plans or managing variances. Tailoring communication ensures that messages are impactful and understood by all recipients.

Listening skills are equally critical in effective communication. CFOs must actively listen to their teams and stakeholders, seeking to understand their concerns, perspectives, and priorities. For example, during a discussion about a cost-cutting initiative, listening to feedback from department heads might reveal potential risks or opportunities that had not been considered. This two-way exchange not only improves decision-making but also builds trust and collaboration.

Clarity and brevity are paramount in written communication. Whether drafting reports, emails, or memos, CFOs must ensure their writing is precise, professional, and free of ambiguity. A well-written report outlining a new financial strategy can inspire confidence and prompt action, while a poorly worded one might lead to confusion or hesitation. For example, in a budget proposal, the CFO should clearly outline objectives, expected outcomes, and justifications, ensuring that all stakeholders are aligned.

Another key aspect of communication is persuasion. CFOs often need to advocate for specific strategies or initiatives, such as securing investment for a new technology platform or gaining approval for a restructuring plan. Persuasion involves presenting a compelling argument supported by data, logic, and anticipated benefits. For example, when recommending a shift to cloud-based financial systems, the CFO might emphasise the long-term cost savings, increased scalability, and enhanced data security these systems offer.

Storytelling is an increasingly valuable tool for CFOs. Numbers alone rarely inspire action, but embedding them in a narrative makes them more relatable and memorable. For instance, rather than merely stating that operational costs have been reduced by 15%, a CFO might explain how a new procurement strategy saved resources while maintaining supplier relationships. This storytelling approach not only highlights the team's success but also connects the achievement to the organisation's broader goals.

Effective communication also requires non-verbal cues. Body language, tone of voice, and eye contact can reinforce or undermine a message. For example, during a high-stakes presentation to investors, maintaining steady eye contact, using open gestures, and speaking with confidence signals competence and assurance. Conversely, appearing distracted or uncertain might cast doubt on the CFO's credibility.

Technology can enhance communication, particularly in global or hybrid work environments. Tools like video conferencing, collaborative platforms, and real-time dashboards enable CFOs to engage with stakeholders more effectively. For instance, using interactive dashboards to present financial data during a virtual meeting ensures that participants remain engaged and informed.

An excellent example of exceptional communication is seen in a retail CFO who successfully navigated a merger. By holding regular town hall meetings, sharing progress updates through newsletters, and directly addressing employee concerns, the

CFO maintained transparency and trust throughout the process. This communication strategy ensured alignment and morale, ultimately contributing to the merger's success.

In conclusion, communication skills for CFOs are critical for bridging the gap between financial expertise and organisational strategy. By mastering clear, adaptive, and persuasive communication, CFOs can inspire confidence, foster collaboration, and drive alignment. In a role where precision and influence are paramount, effective communication is the foundation of strong financial leadership.

8.7 - Conflict Resolution in Finance Teams

Conflict is an inevitable part of any workplace, especially in finance teams, where high-pressure environments, tight deadlines, and differing priorities often create tension. However, when addressed constructively, conflict can lead to innovation, improved relationships, and stronger team dynamics. For CFOs, the ability to identify, manage, and resolve conflicts effectively is a crucial leadership skill that ensures the finance team operates cohesively.

The first step in resolving conflict is identifying its root cause. Conflicts can stem from various sources, such as miscommunication, competing goals, or personality differences. CFOs must approach these situations with curiosity and a commitment to understanding all perspectives. For example, a disagreement over resource allocation might arise from differing views on departmental priorities. By facilitating an open dialogue, the CFO can uncover the underlying concerns and work toward a resolution.

Empathy and active listening are essential for managing conflict. CFOs must create a safe space where team members feel heard and respected. This involves listening without interruption, acknowledging emotions, and asking clarifying questions. For instance, if two employees disagree about a financial forecast's assumptions, the CFO might encourage each to present their rationale, fostering mutual understanding and collaboration.

Transparency and constructive feedback are critical during conflict resolution. CFOs should focus on facts rather than assigning blame, guiding the conversation toward solutions. For example, instead of criticising an employee for a missed deadline, the CFO might explore whether unclear expectations or resource constraints contributed to the issue and propose improvements for future projects.

Collaboration is key to resolving conflicts sustainably. CFOs should involve all parties in developing solutions, ensuring their voices are heard and respected. This collaborative approach not only resolves the immediate issue but also strengthens trust and accountability. For example, during a dispute over workload distribution, a CFO might facilitate a team discussion to reassign tasks equitably, ensuring buy-in from all members.

In some cases, conflicts may require mediation or external support. CFOs can act as impartial mediators or enlist HR professionals to guide the discussion. For instance, if a conflict involves accusations of bias or misconduct, involving HR ensures that the resolution process is fair and compliant with organisational policies.

Finally, CFOs must address systemic issues that contribute to recurring conflicts. For example, if disagreements frequently arise during budgeting cycles, it may signal a need for clearer processes or better communication. Proactively resolving these underlying challenges reduces the likelihood of future disputes.

A compelling example of effective conflict resolution is seen in a global finance team where tensions arose between the forecasting and reporting functions. The CFO introduced regular cross-functional workshops to improve communication, resulting in enhanced collaboration and fewer disputes.

In conclusion, conflict resolution in finance teams is a vital skill for CFOs, requiring empathy, transparency, and a focus on collaboration. By addressing issues constructively, CFOs can transform conflict into an opportunity for growth, ensuring that the team operates harmoniously and achieves its goals.

8.8 - Leading Through Change

Change is an inevitable part of business, and for CFOs, leading through change is one of the most challenging yet essential responsibilities. Whether driven by market conditions, technological advancements, or internal restructuring, change can evoke uncertainty and resistance within teams. A skilled

CFO not only navigates these challenges but also inspires confidence fosters adaptability and ensures a smooth transition toward the desired outcomes.

The cornerstone of leading through change is clarity of vision. Employees are more likely to embrace change when they understand its purpose and potential benefits. CFOs must articulate why the change is necessary, what it aims to achieve, and how it aligns with the organisation's strategic goals. For instance, during the implementation of a new financial reporting system, the CFO might explain how the system will streamline processes, improve accuracy, and provide actionable insights. Providing a clear roadmap with defined milestones and timelines helps employees see the bigger picture and understand their roles within the transition.

Communication is paramount in times of change. Uncertainty often leads to fear, which can hinder progress. CFOs must address concerns openly, share regular updates, and provide forums for discussion. Tailoring communication to different audiences ensures that messages resonate effectively. For example, while the finance team might require detailed technical guidance on a new system, the executive team may only need an overview of its strategic impact. Using multiple communication channels, such as town halls, emails, and one-on-one meetings, ensures that everyone stays informed and engaged.

Empathy is another critical quality for leading through change. CFOs must acknowledge the challenges and emotions their teams face during transitions. Change often disrupts established routines, creating anxiety and discomfort. For example, employees transitioning to a new budgeting tool may feel overwhelmed by the learning curve. A CFO who listens to these concerns provides reassurance, and offers additional training demonstrates care and commitment to their team's success. Empathy fosters trust and helps build resilience during periods of uncertainty.

Empowering employees is key to building ownership and commitment to the change process. CFOs can involve team members in decision-making, giving them a sense of control and responsibility. For example, when restructuring the finance department, the CFO might invite team members to contribute ideas for improving workflows. This collaborative approach not only generates valuable insights but also increases buy-in by showing that employees' voices are heard and valued.

Training and support are essential for equipping teams to adapt to change. CFOs must ensure that employees have the resources and knowledge needed to navigate new systems, processes, or roles. This might include workshops, online tutorials, or mentorship opportunities. For instance, during the rollout of automation tools, the CFO could organise hands-on training sessions and provide access to a dedicated helpdesk for troubleshooting. Ongoing support ensures that employees feel confident and capable, reducing resistance and enhancing productivity.

Flexibility and adaptability are also crucial. Even the best-laid plans may need adjustments in response to unforeseen challenges. CFOs must remain open to feedback and willing to revise strategies as necessary. For example, if a new workflow proves inefficient, the CFO might work with the team to identify bottlenecks and implement improvements. This iterative approach demonstrates agility and reinforces trust in leadership.

Celebrating progress is another important aspect of leading through change. Recognising milestones and achievements, whether large or small, boosts morale and maintains momentum. For example, after completing the first phase of a restructuring initiative, the CFO might host a team lunch or send a congratulatory email highlighting the team's efforts. These gestures show appreciation and reinforce a sense of accomplishment.

A real-world example of effective change leadership can be seen in a manufacturing company where the CFO led a digital transformation initiative. The shift to cloud-based financial systems initially faced resistance from employees accustomed to traditional methods. By clearly communicating the benefits, involving the team in testing and implementation, and providing comprehensive training, the CFO overcame these challenges. The transformation not only improved efficiency but also enhanced the team's confidence in their ability to adapt to new technologies.

In conclusion, leading through change requires vision, empathy, and adaptability. CFOs must guide their teams with clarity and compassion, ensuring they feel supported and empowered throughout the transition. By fostering trust, providing resources, and celebrating progress, CFOs can transform resistance into resilience, enabling their teams to navigate change successfully and thrive in an ever-evolving business landscape.

8.9 - Recognizing and Rewarding Success

Recognition and rewards are powerful tools for driving engagement and fostering a high-performance culture. For CFOs, acknowledging the achievements of their finance teams is more than a courtesy; it's a strategic necessity. Celebrating success reinforces positive behaviours, motivates employees, and builds a sense of pride and belonging within the team. In a demanding field like finance, where precision and deadlines are paramount, recognising accomplishments helps sustain morale and commitment.

Recognition begins with identifying what constitutes success. While meeting deadlines and achieving targets are common metrics, CFOs should also celebrate behaviours that align with organisational values, such as innovation, collaboration, and resilience. For example, recognising a team for successfully navigating a challenging audit not only highlights their technical expertise but also reinforces the importance of perseverance and teamwork.

Timely and specific recognition is essential for maximum impact. Generic praise like "Good job!" is less effective than tailored feedback that highlights the specific contributions of an individual or team. For instance, a CFO might say, "Your analysis of cash flow trends enabled us to secure favourable loan terms, which directly supported our expansion plans." Such recognition not only validates the employee's efforts but also shows how their work contributes to the organisation's success.

Public recognition amplifies the value of acknowledgement. Sharing achievements during team meetings, in newsletters, or on internal platforms ensures that successes are visible across the organisation. For example, a CFO might spotlight a finance manager who led a successful cost-reduction initiative, showcasing their work as an example of excellence. Public recognition not only motivates the individual but also inspires others to strive for similar achievements.

Monetary rewards like bonuses, raises, or performance incentives are effective ways to reward success. However, they should be complemented by non-monetary recognition, which can be equally impactful. Offering opportunities for professional growth, such as training programmes or conference attendance, demonstrates an investment in employees' futures. For instance, sponsoring a high-performing analyst to attend an industry workshop acknowledges their contributions while enhancing their skills.

Tailoring rewards to individual preferences ensures that recognition feels meaningful. Some employees may value public acknowledgement, while others might prefer private praise or increased responsibilities. For example, promoting a finance professional to lead a high-profile project not only rewards their hard work but also fosters their career development.

Building a culture of peer-to-peer recognition further reinforces success. CFOs can create platforms where team members can acknowledge each other's contributions, fostering camaraderie and mutual respect. For instance, a CFO might implement a recognition programme where employees nominate colleagues for quarterly awards, strengthening team bonds and morale.

Celebrating team successes is as important as recognising individual achievements. Organising events like team lunches, outings, or virtual celebrations provide an opportunity to reflect on shared accomplishments and strengthen relationships. For example, after completing a major system upgrade, the CFO could host a team celebration to acknowledge everyone's efforts and highlight the collective impact of their work.

A practical example of effective recognition can be seen in a pharmaceutical company where the CFO introduced a quarterly recognition programme. High-performing employees were acknowledged during company-wide meetings, featured in newsletters, and received personalised thank-you notes from the CFO. This programme boosted morale and reduced turnover by creating a culture where contributions were consistently valued.

In conclusion, recognising and rewarding success is a critical leadership responsibility for CFOs. By celebrating achievements, tailoring rewards, and fostering a culture of appreciation, CFOs can motivate their teams, enhance engagement, and drive performance. Recognition is more than a gesture; it's a cornerstone of a thriving and high-performing finance function.

8.10 - Case Study: Transforming a Finance Team

Transforming a finance team into a high-performing, strategic unit is a defining achievement for any CFO. This case study examines how Sarah, the CFO of a mid-sized technology company, revitalised her finance department, turning it from a reactive and fragmented group into a proactive, collaborative, and impactful function.

The Context: A Struggling Finance Function

When Sarah joined the company, she was confronted with a series of challenges:

- **Outdated Processes:** Manual workflows caused inefficiencies and frequent errors, leading to delays and frustration.
- **Fragmented Communication:** Team members operated in silos, resulting in a lack of cohesion and poor collaboration.

- **Low Morale:** Employees felt disengaged and disconnected from the organisation's strategic goals, which stifled motivation and innovation.

These issues hindered the finance team's ability to deliver value, limiting its effectiveness in supporting the company's growth and resilience. Recognising the need for transformative change, Sarah set out to overhaul the finance function, addressing operational inefficiencies, cultural barriers, and strategic misalignment.

Phase 1: Conducting a Thorough Assessment

The transformation began with a comprehensive evaluation of the finance function. Sarah employed a two-pronged approach:

1. **Individual Conversations:** Sarah held one-on-one meetings with team members to understand their perspectives, frustrations, and aspirations.
2. **Team Workshops:** Collaborative sessions were conducted to identify bottlenecks, clarify pain points, and gather input on potential solutions.

This assessment revealed three critical areas requiring immediate attention:

1. Inefficient workflows due to reliance on manual processes and outdated tools.
2. A lack of professional development opportunities, which left employees feeling undervalued.
3. Weak alignment between the finance team's activities and the company's overarching strategy.

Armed with these insights, Sarah crafted a transformation plan focused on three pillars: technology modernisation, cultural improvement, and strategic alignment.

Phase 2: Implementing Modern Technology

The first step in Sarah's transformation plan was addressing inefficiencies through technology. She secured funding to implement an enterprise resource planning (ERP) system that would automate repetitive tasks and enhance data accuracy.

Key steps included:

1. **Team Involvement:** Sarah engaged team members in the system selection and testing process, ensuring that the final solution met their needs and addressed pain points.
2. **Comprehensive Training:** Employees received hands-on training sessions, equipping them with the skills needed to confidently use the new tools.
3. **Streamlined Processes:** The ERP system automated critical workflows, such as accounts payable, financial reporting, and budgeting.

The impact was significant:

- Routine task times were reduced by 30% within six months, freeing up employees to focus on higher-value activities.
- Reporting accuracy improved dramatically, enabling more reliable decision-making across the organisation.

Phase 3: Building a Collaborative Team Culture

Recognising that technology alone could not drive transformation, Sarah focused on fostering a cohesive and motivated team culture.

1. **Improved Communication:**
   - Regular team meetings were introduced to encourage open dialogue and collaboration.
   - Cross-functional updates ensured that the finance team remained connected to broader organisational developments.

2. **Professional Development:**
   - Sarah launched a mentorship programme, pairing junior staff with experienced mentors to accelerate skill development.
   - Employees were provided access to professional training and certifications, enabling them to enhance their technical and strategic expertise.

3. **Recognition and Morale Boosting:**
   - A recognition programme celebrated individual and team achievements, fostering a culture of appreciation.
   - For example, a team that successfully streamlined the month-end close process was publicly acknowledged during an all-hands meeting, boosting morale and engagement.

These initiatives created a more cohesive, motivated, and capable team, transforming the department's dynamic.

Phase 4: Aligning Finance with Strategic Goals

Sarah recognised that the finance team's impact could only be maximised if their efforts aligned with the organisation's strategic objectives. She implemented several measures to bridge the gap:

1. **Involvement in Cross-Functional Projects:**
   - Finance team members were embedded in key initiatives, such as product launches and market expansions, to show how their work contributed to the company's success.
   - This exposure helped employees build relationships with other departments and gain a deeper understanding of the business.

2. **Strategic KPIs:**
   - New performance metrics were introduced, focusing on outcomes that aligned with organisational goals, such as profitability, efficiency, and growth.

- Regular progress reviews ensured accountability and clarity around how the finance team's efforts supported the company's vision.

By aligning finance with strategy, Sarah elevated the team's role from a support function to a strategic partner.

The Outcome: A High-Performing Finance Team

The transformation delivered remarkable results:

- Operational Efficiency: Reporting accuracy improved by 50%, and budgeting cycles were reduced by 25%.

- Employee Satisfaction: Employee engagement scores increased significantly, reflecting higher morale and motivation.

- Strategic Agility: The finance team's enhanced capabilities enabled the company to navigate a challenging economic period with confidence, identifying cost-saving measures that preserved profitability.

- Organisational Impact: The finance team became a key contributor to organisational success, strengthening cross-functional collaboration and delivering actionable insights.

Lessons Learned

This case study highlights key lessons for CFOs seeking to transform their finance teams:

1. Holistic Approach: Addressing technology, culture, and strategic alignment is essential for lasting impact.

2. Team Involvement: Engaging employees in decision-making fosters buy-in and accelerates the adoption of new tools and processes.

3. Continuous Development: Investing in professional growth boosts morale and enhances team capabilities.

4. Strategic Integration: Aligning finance with organisational goals positions the team as a critical driver of success.

Conclusion

Sarah's leadership exemplifies the power of strategic transformation in finance. By modernising technology, fostering a collaborative culture, and aligning the team's efforts with broader objectives, she turned a struggling finance function into a high-performing, strategic powerhouse. This case serves as a blueprint for CFOs aiming to create lasting value and elevate the role of finance within their organisations.

Chapter 9

Global CFO Challenges

> *"The global CFO must think like a strategist, act like a diplomat, and plan like an economist."*
> **Robert N. Jacobs**

As businesses expand their reach across borders, CFOs face increasingly complex challenges that require both strategic foresight and operational dexterity. Operating on a global stage demands an understanding of diverse markets, regulatory environments, and cultural dynamics. This chapter explores the critical responsibilities of CFOs managing multinational organisations and the skills required to navigate these challenges successfully.

9.1 - Managing Multinational Operations

The role of a CFO in managing multinational operations is multifaceted, encompassing financial oversight, compliance, and strategic alignment across multiple geographies. Operating in diverse markets means dealing with varying tax laws, regulatory frameworks, and business practices. The complexity increases when organisations operate in regions with differing economic conditions, currencies, and political landscapes. For CFOs, balancing these elements while maintaining financial health and operational efficiency is a constant challenge.

At the heart of managing multinational operations is financial consolidation. CFOs must ensure that financial data from subsidiaries in different countries is accurate, timely, and aligned with global reporting standards. This requires robust systems and processes to consolidate data effectively. For instance, implementing a centralised enterprise resource planning (ERP) system allows the finance team to collect, standardise, and analyse data from all regions. Such systems enable the CFO to provide a comprehensive view of the organisation's financial position, facilitating informed decision-making.

Compliance is another critical area for CFOs managing multinational operations. Each jurisdiction has its own set of regulations, from accounting standards to tax requirements. Failing to comply with these regulations can result in financial penalties and reputational damage. For example, a CFO operating in the United States and Europe must navigate both Generally Accepted Accounting Principles (GAAP) and International Financial Reporting Standards (IFRS). Ensuring compliance across multiple jurisdictions often involves working closely with local finance teams and external advisors.

Communication and alignment are essential for managing teams spread across different locations. Cultural differences, time zones, and language barriers can create challenges in coordination and collaboration. CFOs must foster open communication channels and establish clear expectations for regional teams. For instance, regular global finance meetings, both virtual and in-person, can help ensure alignment and provide opportunities for knowledge sharing. By promoting a unified vision and encouraging collaboration, CFOs can create a cohesive finance function despite geographical distances.

Another challenge is managing currency exchange risks. Operating in multiple currencies exposes organisations to fluctuations in exchange rates, which can impact profitability. CFOs must develop strategies to mitigate these risks, such as using forward contracts or natural hedging techniques. For example, a CFO in a manufacturing company might align revenue and expenses in the same currency to reduce exposure. Effective currency risk management ensures that the organisation remains financially stable despite volatile market conditions.

Talent management is also crucial for multinational operations. CFOs must build and maintain high-performing finance teams in different regions while ensuring consistency in skills and values. Recruiting local talent provides valuable insights into regional markets while implementing global training programmes ensures that all team members adhere to the same standards and practices. For instance, a CFO might develop a leadership programme to identify and nurture potential finance leaders across the organisation, fostering a pipeline of talent that understands both local and global dynamics.

A practical example of managing multinational operations can be seen in a global retail company where the CFO implemented a centralised reporting system while empowering regional teams with decision-making autonomy. This balance allowed the organisation to maintain compliance and efficiency while adapting to local market conditions, ultimately driving growth and profitability.

In conclusion, managing multinational operations requires a combination of technical expertise, strategic vision, and strong leadership. CFOs must navigate the complexities of global markets while fostering collaboration and ensuring financial integrity. By leveraging technology, aligning teams, and mitigating risks, CFOs can create a finance function that supports the organisation's international ambitions.

9.2 - Understanding Global Financial Markets

For CFOs operating in a multinational environment, understanding global financial markets is not just an advantage, it is a necessity. The interconnected nature of today's economy means that events in one region can ripple across the globe, impacting currency values, commodity prices, interest rates, and investor sentiment. A deep understanding of these markets allows CFOs to make informed decisions that safeguard the organisation's financial health and capitalise on emerging opportunities.

At its core, understanding global financial markets involves staying attuned to macroeconomic trends. CFOs must monitor factors such as inflation rates, economic growth, central bank policies, and geopolitical developments. For instance, a rise in interest rates by the US Federal Reserve could increase borrowing costs for companies with dollar-denominated debt, while a slowdown in China's economy might reduce demand for raw materials. By analysing these trends, CFOs can anticipate risks and adjust strategies accordingly.

One of the most critical aspects of global financial markets is foreign exchange (FX) management. Currency fluctuations can significantly affect the profitability of multinational companies, especially those with revenues or expenses in multiple currencies. CFOs must implement strategies to mitigate FX risk, such as forward contracts, currency swaps, or natural hedging. For example, a CFO at an export-driven company might use hedging instruments to lock in favourable exchange rates, protecting the organisation from adverse currency movements.

Global financial markets also play a key role in capital allocation and fundraising. CFOs must evaluate opportunities to raise capital through equity or debt in different regions, considering factors such as market liquidity, regulatory requirements, and investor appetite. For instance, listing on a stock exchange in a high-growth market might attract investors who understand the company's regional potential. Similarly, issuing bonds in markets with low interest rates can reduce borrowing costs.

Another important consideration is the impact of global markets on investment portfolios. Multinational companies often hold diversified investments, from equities and bonds to commodities and derivatives. CFOs must ensure that these portfolios are optimised for risk and return, taking into account global market conditions. For example, during periods of market volatility, reallocating investments to safer assets like government bonds can preserve capital while maintaining liquidity.

Regulatory environments in global financial markets are another area of focus for CFOs. Different regions have varying requirements for financial reporting, capital markets, and taxation. Staying compliant while navigating these complexities requires collaboration with local advisors and a thorough understanding of market-specific regulations. For instance, a CFO raising capital in Europe might need to adhere to strict ESG (Environmental, Social, Governance) disclosure requirements, reflecting the region's emphasis on sustainability.

The increasing influence of technology and digitalisation in global financial markets presents both opportunities and challenges. Advanced tools such as predictive analytics, blockchain, and algorithmic trading enable CFOs to make data-driven decisions and improve efficiency. For example, using real-time market data platforms allows CFOs to monitor currency movements and interest rate changes, enabling faster responses to market developments.

A practical example of navigating global financial markets is seen in a multinational technology company where the CFO successfully raised $1 billion through a combination of euro-denominated bonds and a secondary stock offering in Asia. By leveraging favourable interest rates in Europe and strong investor interest in Asian markets, the CFO optimised the organisation's capital structure while minimising costs.

In conclusion, understanding global financial markets is essential for CFOs to manage risks, allocate resources effectively, and drive growth. By staying informed about macroeconomic trends, implementing robust FX management strategies, and leveraging technology, CFOs can navigate the complexities of global markets with confidence. In a world where financial landscapes are constantly shifting, this expertise is a cornerstone of effective global leadership.

9.3 - Addressing Cultural Differences in Finance

Cultural differences can have a profound impact on how finance teams operate within multinational organisations. From decision-making processes to communication styles and attitudes toward risk, cultural nuances shape behaviours and expectations. For CFOs, recognising and addressing these differences is essential to building cohesive, high-performing teams and ensuring that the finance function operates smoothly across borders.

One of the most noticeable cultural differences in finance is approaches to decision-making. In some cultures, decisions are made collaboratively, with input from multiple stakeholders, while in others, decision-making is hierarchical, with authority concentrated at the top. For example, in Japan, consensus-building (nemawashi) is often a critical part of the decision-making process, requiring time and extensive discussions. In contrast, Western cultures like the United States may prioritise speed and individual accountability. A CFO managing teams across these regions must adapt their leadership style to accommodate these differences, balancing efficiency with cultural sensitivity.

Communication styles also vary widely across cultures. Some cultures, such as those in Scandinavia, value direct and straightforward communication, while others, such as those in Southeast Asia, emphasise indirect communication to maintain harmony and avoid confrontation. For instance, a finance team in India might use nuanced language when discussing sensitive topics, requiring the CFO to read between the lines. Understanding these differences enables CFOs to foster effective communication and avoid misunderstandings.

Risk tolerance is another area where cultural differences manifest. Certain cultures are more risk-averse, prioritising stability and caution, while others embrace calculated risks to pursue growth and innovation. For example, German finance professionals may favour conservative financial strategies, focusing on long-term sustainability, while their American counterparts might be more open to aggressive investments. A CFO leading a multinational finance team must find a balance that aligns with the organisation's overall risk appetite while respecting regional preferences.

Workplace expectations and attitudes toward hierarchy can also influence team dynamics. In cultures with high power distance, such as many Asian and Middle Eastern countries, employees may defer to authority and avoid questioning their leaders. In contrast, teams in countries with low power distance, such as the Netherlands, may expect a more egalitarian approach, with open discussions and shared decision-making. CFOs must adapt their leadership style to suit these cultural norms while fostering a sense of inclusivity and collaboration.

Training and education can play a significant role in addressing cultural differences. CFOs can implement cross-cultural training programmes to help team members understand and appreciate diverse perspectives. For instance, organising workshops on cultural intelligence (CQ) can enhance awareness and build skills for navigating cultural complexities. This not only improves collaboration within the finance team but also strengthens relationships with external stakeholders, such as global clients and partners.

A practical example of addressing cultural differences can be seen in a multinational consumer goods company where the CFO introduced cultural sensitivity training for finance teams across Europe, Asia, and the Americas. By enhancing understanding and fostering open dialogue, the initiative reduced conflicts and improved the efficiency of cross-border projects.

In conclusion, addressing cultural differences in finance requires awareness, adaptability, and proactive leadership. By recognising and respecting these differences, CFOs can build cohesive teams that leverage cultural diversity as a strength. In a globalised world, understanding cultural nuances is not just a soft skill; it is a strategic advantage that drives collaboration and success.

9.4 - Taxation Challenges Across Borders

For CFOs of multinational organisations, managing cross-border taxation is one of the most complex and critical responsibilities. Tax regulations vary widely across jurisdictions, with differing rates, rules, and compliance requirements. Navigating these complexities while minimising tax liabilities, ensuring compliance, and avoiding reputational risks requires strategic planning, local expertise, and a robust understanding of global tax trends.

At the heart of cross-border taxation is the issue of transfer pricing. This refers to the pricing of goods, services, and intellectual property exchanged between related entities in different countries. Tax authorities closely scrutinise transfer pricing arrangements to ensure that they reflect market conditions and do not artificially shift profits to low-tax jurisdictions. For CFOs, ensuring that transfer pricing policies align with regulatory expectations is essential to avoid audits, fines, or disputes. For example, a CFO of a global software company might need to justify the royalties charged by a subsidiary for using patented technology, ensuring the rates are consistent with those charged to third parties.

Double taxation is another major challenge for multinational companies. When income is taxed in multiple jurisdictions, it can erode profitability and create cash flow issues. CFOs must navigate bilateral tax treaties and foreign tax credit mechanisms to mitigate this risk. For instance, a CFO operating in both the United States and Germany might leverage a tax treaty between the two countries to avoid paying taxes on the same income in both jurisdictions. This requires careful planning and close collaboration with local tax advisors.

The rise of digital taxation has added a new layer of complexity. As governments seek to tax revenues generated by digital services, multinational companies face evolving rules that often conflict between jurisdictions. For example, countries in the European Union have implemented digital services taxes targeting revenues from online advertising and marketplaces, even if the companies are headquartered elsewhere. CFOs must stay updated on these developments and assess their impact on revenue streams and compliance obligations.

Tax compliance across borders involves adhering to a myriad of reporting and documentation requirements. Each country has its own deadlines, formats, and regulations, which can be overwhelming for finance teams. Technology can help streamline compliance with tools that automate data collection, calculation, and reporting. For instance, a CFO might implement tax compliance software that consolidates data from subsidiaries and generates reports tailored to each jurisdiction's requirements.

Tax audits and disputes are an inherent risk of cross-border operations. CFOs must be prepared to respond to inquiries from tax authorities, providing documentation that demonstrates compliance and substantiates the organisation's tax positions. This requires meticulous record-keeping and a proactive approach to risk management. For example, maintaining detailed transfer pricing documentation and engaging in advance pricing agreements (APAs) with tax authorities can minimise disputes and provide certainty.

In addition to compliance, CFOs must consider tax optimisation strategies that align with business objectives. This might involve structuring operations to take advantage of favourable tax regimes, such as using regional hubs in low-tax jurisdictions for supply chain management. However, CFOs must balance optimisation with ethical considerations and the organisation's reputation. Aggressive tax planning strategies that prioritise short-term savings over long-term sustainability can attract public criticism and regulatory scrutiny. For instance, CFOs should ensure that strategies align with OECD guidelines under the Base Erosion and Profit Shifting (BEPS) framework, which aims to prevent tax avoidance.

A practical example of managing cross-border taxation can be seen in a multinational pharmaceutical company where the CFO centralised tax functions to improve efficiency and compliance. By leveraging shared services and implementing transfer pricing policies consistent with OECD guidelines, the organisation reduced tax risks while streamlining reporting processes.

In conclusion, taxation challenges across borders require CFOs to navigate a complex web of regulations, treaties, and compliance requirements. By adopting proactive strategies, leveraging technology, and collaborating with local experts, CFOs can manage tax liabilities effectively while supporting the organisation's global ambitions. In a world of increasing scrutiny and regulatory changes, mastering cross-border taxation is a critical skill for global CFOs.

9.5 - Global Supply Chain Management

Global supply chains are the backbone of multinational businesses, enabling the production and delivery of goods across continents. For CFOs, managing supply chains is not just an operational concern; it is a financial imperative. Supply chain disruptions can have a cascading impact on costs, revenues, and profitability, requiring CFOs to adopt a proactive and strategic approach to minimise risks and ensure efficiency.

One of the most significant challenges in global supply chain management is cost control. Supply chains involve multiple layers of expenses, from raw material procurement and transportation to warehousing and distribution. These costs can fluctuate due to factors such as fuel price volatility, tariffs, and currency exchange rates. CFOs must work closely with supply chain managers to optimise costs without compromising quality or service. For example, a CFO might negotiate long-term contracts with key suppliers to lock in stable pricing or explore nearshoring options to reduce transportation expenses.

Disruptions are an ever-present risk in global supply chains. Events such as natural disasters, geopolitical conflicts, or pandemics can disrupt production and delay deliveries, impacting revenues and customer satisfaction. CFOs must build resilience into supply chains by diversifying suppliers, maintaining safety stock, and developing contingency plans. For instance, during the COVID-19 pandemic, many CFOs re-evaluated their reliance on single-source suppliers and sought alternative vendors to mitigate risks.

Technology and data analytics play a pivotal role in supply chain management. Real-time visibility into supply chain operations allows CFOs to identify bottlenecks, optimise inventory levels, and respond to disruptions more effectively. For example, implementing a supply chain management platform that tracks shipments, monitors inventory, and forecasts demand can reduce waste and improve efficiency. CFOs can also use predictive analytics to anticipate risks and plan accordingly, such as adjusting procurement schedules based on seasonal demand patterns.

Sustainability is an increasingly important consideration in global supply chain management. Consumers and investors are demanding greater transparency and accountability regarding environmental and social impacts. CFOs must work with supply chain teams to ensure compliance with sustainability standards, such as reducing carbon emissions, minimising waste, and sourcing materials ethically. For example, a CFO might collaborate with suppliers to transition to renewable energy sources or adopt circular economy practices, such as recycling and reusing materials.

Managing supplier relationships is another critical aspect of supply chain management. Strong partnerships with suppliers can improve reliability, reduce costs, and foster innovation. CFOs must ensure that contracts are structured to incentivise performance while protecting the organisation from risks. For instance, including clauses that require suppliers to meet delivery deadlines or adhere to quality standards ensures accountability.

A practical example of effective supply chain management is seen in a global electronics manufacturer where the CFO implemented a dual-sourcing strategy for critical components. By sourcing from multiple suppliers in different regions, the company reduced its reliance on single vendors and mitigated risks associated with geopolitical tensions.

In conclusion, global supply chain management is a complex but essential responsibility for CFOs. By focusing on cost control, resilience, technology, and sustainability, CFOs can ensure that supply chains support the organisation's financial and strategic objectives. In a world of increasing uncertainties, effective supply chain management is a competitive advantage that drives long-term success.

9.6 - Exchange Rate Volatility

Exchange rate volatility is a constant concern for CFOs operating in a global environment. Fluctuating currency values can significantly impact revenues, costs, and profitability, especially for organisations conducting transactions in multiple currencies. Managing these risks requires a proactive approach, leveraging financial tools, and aligning strategies with the organisation's operational goals.

At the core of managing exchange rate volatility is understanding its impact on the organisation's financial performance. Currency fluctuations can affect several aspects of the business, including revenue streams, procurement costs, and balance sheet items. For instance, an exporter earning revenue in a foreign currency may see reduced profitability if the local currency strengthens against the foreign currency. Conversely, a weaker local currency could increase the cost of imported raw materials, squeezing margins.

To mitigate these risks, CFOs must employ hedging strategies. Hedging involves using financial instruments to lock in exchange rates, providing predictability and stability. Common hedging tools include forward contracts, options, and swaps. For example, a CFO of a multinational manufacturing company might use forward contracts to secure a fixed exchange rate for purchasing raw materials six months in advance. This approach ensures that fluctuations in currency values do not impact procurement costs.

Natural hedging is another effective strategy. This involves aligning revenues and expenses in the same currency to offset exchange rate impacts. For instance, a CFO operating in both the US and European markets might source materials locally in Europe to match revenue earned in euros. By balancing currency exposure, the organisation reduces its vulnerability to volatility.

Technology plays a critical role in managing exchange rate risks. Modern treasury management systems can provide real-time insights into currency exposures, enabling CFOs to act swiftly. For example, a dashboard showing exchange rate movements alongside cash flow forecasts allows CFOs to make informed decisions about hedging or adjusting financial strategies. Predictive analytics tools can also help CFOs anticipate currency trends and prepare for potential fluctuations.

In addition to hedging, CFOs must consider pricing strategies to address exchange rate volatility. Dynamic pricing, which adjusts product or service prices based on currency fluctuations, can help maintain profitability. For example, a global e-commerce company might update its prices in real-time to reflect changes in exchange rates, ensuring competitive pricing without eroding margins.

Collaboration with stakeholders is essential for effective exchange rate management. CFOs must work closely with procurement, sales, and treasury teams to align financial strategies with operational needs. For instance, during a period of currency volatility, the CFO might coordinate with the sales team to renegotiate payment terms with international clients, reducing exposure to fluctuating rates.

Geopolitical and economic monitoring is another critical aspect of managing exchange rate volatility. Political events, such as elections or trade disputes, can trigger currency fluctuations, as can economic factors like interest rate changes or inflation. CFOs must stay informed about these developments and assess their potential impact on currency markets. For example, anticipating an interest rate hike by a major central bank might prompt a CFO to hedge currency exposures in advance.

A compelling example of effective exchange rate management can be seen in a global automotive company where the CFO implemented a comprehensive hedging strategy to protect the organisation from currency risks associated with Brexit. By securing forward contracts and diversifying supplier locations, the company maintained stable costs and profitability despite significant fluctuations in the pound sterling.

In conclusion, managing exchange rate volatility is a critical responsibility for CFOs operating in global markets. By employing hedging strategies, leveraging technology, and aligning financial practices with operational goals, CFOs can mitigate currency risks and maintain financial stability. In a world of unpredictable markets, mastering exchange rate management is essential for sustaining global competitiveness.

9.7 - Political and Economic Risks

Political and economic risks are inherent challenges for CFOs managing multinational operations. From regulatory changes and trade restrictions to economic downturns and geopolitical tensions, these risks can disrupt supply chains, increase costs, and impact revenues. Navigating such uncertainties requires strategic foresight, scenario planning, and proactive risk management.

One of the most significant political risks is regulatory change. Governments frequently update laws and regulations that affect taxation, trade, and investment. For example, a sudden increase in import tariffs can raise costs for companies reliant on international supply chains. CFOs must monitor regulatory developments in the regions where their organisations operate and work with local advisors to ensure compliance. For instance, when the European Union introduced new data protection laws (GDPR), CFOs in global organisations had to assess the financial implications and allocate resources for compliance.

Geopolitical tensions are another source of risk. Trade wars, sanctions, and political instability can disrupt operations and impact market access. For example, a CFO managing operations in both the US and China might face challenges from escalating trade disputes, including increased tariffs or restrictions on technology exports. In such cases, CFOs must explore strategies to diversify markets, source alternative suppliers, or restructure supply chains to minimise exposure.

Economic risks, such as recessions and inflation, also pose significant challenges. Economic downturns can reduce consumer spending and demand, while inflation erodes purchasing power and increases costs. CFOs must develop contingency plans to address these scenarios. For instance, during an economic slowdown, a CFO might focus on cost control measures, such as renegotiating supplier contracts or delaying non-essential capital expenditures.

Scenario planning is a critical tool for managing political and economic risks. By modelling potential scenarios and their financial impacts, CFOs can prepare for a range of outcomes and develop response strategies. For example, a CFO might create scenarios based on varying levels of tariff increases, analysing how each scenario would affect profitability and cash flow. This preparation allows the organisation to act swiftly and minimise disruption.

Collaboration with risk management teams is essential for addressing these challenges. CFOs must work closely with internal and external experts to assess risks and implement mitigation strategies. For example, engaging with geopolitical analysts or industry associations can provide valuable insights into emerging threats and opportunities.

Insurance and financial instruments can also help mitigate political and economic risks. Trade credit insurance protects against payment defaults from international customers, while political risk insurance covers losses from events like expropriation or civil unrest. CFOs can also use financial derivatives to hedge against economic risks, such as interest rate fluctuations or commodity price volatility.

A practical example of navigating political and economic risks is seen in a global energy company where the CFO established a risk committee to monitor geopolitical developments and economic trends. By diversifying operations across regions and securing insurance coverage, the company reduced its exposure to external shocks and maintained stability.

In conclusion, political and economic risks are an unavoidable aspect of global business. CFOs must adopt a proactive approach to identify, assess, and mitigate these risks, ensuring the organisation's resilience in an unpredictable environment. Through strategic planning, collaboration, and financial safeguards, CFOs can navigate uncertainties and protect their organisations from potential disruptions.

9.8 - Sustainability and ESG (Environmental, Social, Governance)

The growing importance of sustainability and ESG (Environmental, Social, Governance) factors has transformed the role of CFOs in multinational organisations. Once considered peripheral concerns, ESG metrics are now central to strategic decision-making, investor relations, and long-term organisational resilience. CFOs must integrate sustainability into financial strategies, ensuring the organisation not only complies with regulatory requirements but also meets the expectations of stakeholders such as investors, employees, and customers.

Environmental considerations are a critical component of ESG. CFOs must evaluate how the organisation's operations impact the environment and identify opportunities to reduce its carbon footprint. This could involve investments in renewable energy, sustainable sourcing, or waste reduction programmes. For instance, a manufacturing company might install solar panels at its facilities to lower energy costs while demonstrating a commitment to sustainability. CFOs play a key role in analysing the financial implications of such initiatives and ensuring they align with the organisation's long-term goals.

Social factors focus on how the organisation interacts with its employees, communities, and supply chain. CFOs must ensure that financial decisions promote inclusivity, fairness, and ethical practices. For example, ensuring that suppliers adhere to fair labour practices or investing in community development programmes can strengthen the organisation's reputation and relationships. CFOs might also collaborate with HR and other departments to support diversity and inclusion initiatives, such as training programmes or equitable hiring practices.

Governance is the third pillar of ESG, addressing transparency, accountability, and ethical decision-making. CFOs are responsible for ensuring that financial reporting is accurate, compliant, and reflective of the organisation's ESG commitments. This may include incorporating ESG metrics into financial statements, such as carbon emissions reductions or progress toward diversity targets. Transparent reporting demonstrates accountability and builds trust with stakeholders.

One of the most pressing challenges in ESG is navigating regulatory requirements. Governments and regulatory bodies worldwide are increasingly mandating ESG disclosures, requiring organisations to provide detailed information on their environmental and social impacts. For instance, the European Union's Corporate Sustainability Reporting Directive (CSRD) requires organisations to disclose ESG metrics alongside financial data. CFOs must ensure that the organisation's systems and processes are equipped to meet these requirements. This could involve implementing ESG reporting software or working with external consultants to validate data accuracy.

CFOs must also consider the growing influence of ESG-focused investors. Institutional investors, such as pension funds and mutual funds, are prioritising organisations with strong ESG performance, viewing them as more resilient and better positioned for long-term growth. For example, a CFO preparing for an investor roadshow might highlight the organisation's progress on reducing emissions or improving employee satisfaction alongside traditional financial metrics such as revenue growth or profitability.

Cost-benefit analysis is an essential tool for integrating ESG initiatives. While sustainable practices often require upfront investment, they can yield significant long-term benefits, including cost savings, risk reduction, and enhanced brand loyalty. For instance, transitioning to energy-efficient machinery might involve higher initial costs but result in lower utility bills and reduced regulatory risks over time. CFOs must evaluate these trade-offs carefully, ensuring that ESG initiatives deliver both financial and non-financial value.

Technology and data analytics can enhance ESG reporting and performance. For example, using digital platforms to track energy usage, waste generation, or supplier compliance provides real-time insights that inform decision-making. CFOs can also leverage predictive analytics to model the financial impact of ESG initiatives, such as forecasting the savings from adopting renewable energy sources.

A real-world example of ESG leadership is seen in a global consumer goods company where the CFO spearheaded a sustainability initiative to eliminate single-use plastics from its supply chain. By investing in biodegradable packaging and collaborating with eco-friendly suppliers, the company not only reduced its environmental impact but also enhanced its brand reputation, attracting environmentally conscious consumers and investors.

In conclusion, sustainability and ESG are no longer optional for multinational organisations; they are essential for long-term success. CFOs must lead the integration of ESG factors into financial strategies, balancing regulatory compliance, stakeholder expectations, and financial performance. By embracing sustainability, CFOs can position their organisations as leaders in a rapidly changing world, creating value for both shareholders and society.

9.9 - Corporate Social Responsibility (CSR) Reporting

Corporate Social Responsibility (CSR) has evolved from a public relations exercise into a strategic priority for organisations operating in the global marketplace. CSR reporting, which communicates an organisation's social and environmental impact, is now a key responsibility for CFOs. Transparent and accurate reporting not only builds trust with stakeholders but also demonstrates accountability and aligns with the growing demand for ethical business practices.

CSR reporting involves disclosing information on a wide range of activities, from community engagement and charitable donations to environmental conservation and workplace diversity. For CFOs, the challenge lies in ensuring that these reports are not only comprehensive but also credible. Stakeholders, including investors, customers, and regulators, increasingly scrutinise CSR reports, expecting detailed insights into the organisation's contributions to society.

The foundation of effective CSR reporting is data collection and verification. CFOs must establish robust systems to track metrics such as greenhouse gas emissions, energy consumption, employee volunteer hours, or philanthropic contributions. For example, a CFO at a retail company might implement software that monitors supply chain sustainability, providing data on supplier compliance with environmental and labour standards. Ensuring the accuracy and reliability of this data is essential to maintaining credibility.

Standardised frameworks play a crucial role in CSR reporting. International guidelines such as the Global Reporting Initiative (GRI) or the United Nations Sustainable Development Goals (SDGs) provide benchmarks for measuring and disclosing CSR performance. CFOs must align their organisation's reporting practices with these frameworks to meet stakeholder expectations and ensure comparability with peers. For instance, using the GRI standards might involve reporting on metrics such as water usage, gender pay equity, or anti-corruption policies.

Integration with financial reporting is another important aspect of CSR reporting. CFOs should consider presenting CSR metrics alongside traditional financial data, highlighting the connection between sustainability and profitability. For example, reporting on cost savings achieved through energy-efficient operations demonstrates the financial benefits of CSR initiatives. This integrated approach provides stakeholders with a holistic view of the organisation's performance.

Transparency is key to building trust through CSR reporting. CFOs must disclose both successes and areas for improvement, avoiding the temptation to present an overly polished picture. For example, acknowledging challenges in reducing carbon emissions while outlining specific plans for improvement enhances credibility and shows a commitment to continuous progress.

Stakeholder engagement is a critical element of CSR reporting. CFOs should seek input from employees, customers, communities, and investors to ensure that the organisation's CSR efforts align with their priorities. For instance, conducting surveys or focus groups can provide insights into stakeholder expectations, guiding the development of meaningful initiatives and reports.

A practical example of impactful CSR reporting is seen in a global technology company where the CFO introduced an annual sustainability report detailing the organisation's progress on renewable energy adoption, workforce diversity, and community development programmes. By aligning the report with GRI standards and engaging stakeholders through public forums, the company enhanced its reputation and strengthened relationships with investors and customers.

In conclusion, CSR reporting is a vital tool for demonstrating an organisation's commitment to ethical and sustainable practices. CFOs play a central role in ensuring that these reports are accurate, transparent, and aligned with global standards. By integrating CSR reporting into the organisation's broader strategy, CFOs can build trust, enhance stakeholder relationships, and position the organisation as a leader in corporate responsibility.

9.10 - Case Study: Leading in a Globalised Economy

In today's interconnected world, CFOs of multinational organisations must balance complex financial, cultural, and regulatory challenges to drive growth and resilience. This case study explores how Mark, the CFO of a multinational logistics company, successfully navigated these challenges to build a robust and competitive finance function, ensuring sustained success in a globalised economy.

The Context: Challenges of Rapid Global Expansion

Mark joined the organisation during a period of rapid expansion into emerging markets. While these markets offered significant growth opportunities, they introduced unique challenges:

- **Currency Volatility:** Fluctuating exchange rates threatened to erode profit margins.
- **Regulatory Uncertainty:** Diverse and evolving compliance requirements across jurisdictions increased operational complexity.
- **Supply Chain Disruptions:** Entering new markets exposed the organisation to risks such as inconsistent infrastructure and political instability.
- **Cultural Barriers:** Differences in business practices, languages, and workplace norms created challenges in fostering collaboration across regions.

Recognising that these challenges could jeopardise the organisation's growth trajectory, Mark developed a comprehensive strategy to address them while capitalising on global opportunities.

Phase 1: Managing Currency Volatility

Operating in multiple currencies exposed the organisation to significant financial risks. To address this, Mark implemented a robust foreign exchange (FX) risk management strategy, which included:

1. **Hedging Instruments:**

- Mark utilised forward contracts to lock in favourable exchange rates, minimising the impact of fluctuations on revenue and costs.
- Currency swaps were used to manage cross-border transactions effectively, aligning cash flows with operational needs.

2. **Natural Hedging:**
   - By aligning revenues and expenses in the same currency within key markets, Mark reduced the organisation's vulnerability to exchange rate movements.
   - For example, sourcing materials locally in emerging markets balanced the company's currency exposure, ensuring financial stability.

3. **Monitoring and Analytics:**
   - Advanced treasury management systems provided real-time insights into currency exposure, enabling proactive decision-making.
   - Predictive analytics tools helped anticipate market trends, allowing the organisation to adjust its strategies ahead of potential currency shifts.

These measures ensured the organisation could maintain profitability despite unpredictable economic conditions.

Phase 2: Fostering Cultural Integration

Mark recognised that a diverse workforce spanning multiple regions could be a competitive advantage if managed effectively. To foster collaboration and cultural alignment, he introduced the following initiatives:

1. **Cross-Cultural Training:**
   - Training programmes were developed to enhance employees' cultural intelligence (CQ), equipping them with the skills to navigate differences in communication styles, decision-making processes, and workplace norms.
   - Workshops and team-building activities encouraged knowledge-sharing and collaboration across regions.

2. **Inclusive Leadership:**
   - Mark encouraged regional leaders to adopt inclusive practices, ensuring that employees from all backgrounds felt valued and heard.
   - Regular global finance meetings provided a platform for sharing insights, aligning strategies, and addressing challenges collectively.

3. **Employee Engagement:**
   - A global mentorship programme connected employees from different regions, fostering professional development and strengthening the company's cultural fabric.
   - Recognising and celebrating cultural events across regions helped build a sense of unity within the organisation.

By fostering an inclusive environment, Mark ensured that the organisation's diverse workforce was aligned with its strategic objectives.

Phase 3: Streamlining Global Financial Operations

To enhance operational efficiency, Mark leveraged technology to integrate and standardise financial processes across regions:

1. **Centralised ERP System:**
   - A cloud-based enterprise resource planning (ERP) system was implemented to consolidate financial data from all regions.
   - The system provided real-time insights into performance metrics, enabling data-driven decision-making at both local and global levels.

2. **Standardised Reporting:**
   - Reporting templates and processes were standardised to ensure consistency and accuracy across regions.
   - Automation reduced manual errors and expedited the reporting cycle, improving the speed and reliability of financial insights.

3. **Optimised Workflows:**
   - Finance teams in different regions were empowered with tools to manage local operations effectively while adhering to global standards.

- A shared services model was introduced for transactional tasks, such as accounts payable and receivable, reducing costs and improving efficiency.

These initiatives streamlined financial operations, allowing the organisation to scale efficiently as it expanded into new markets.

Phase 4: Embedding Sustainability into Strategy

As part of the organisation's commitment to environmental, social, and governance (ESG) principles, Mark spearheaded a sustainability initiative that aligned with global trends and customer expectations:

1. **Green Logistics:**
   - Investments were made in fuel-efficient vehicles and alternative energy sources to reduce the organisation's carbon footprint.
   - Delivery routes were optimised using data analytics, minimising fuel consumption and improving operational efficiency.

2. **Sustainability Metrics:**
   - Key performance indicators (KPIs) were introduced to track progress in reducing emissions, waste, and energy consumption.
   - Sustainability metrics were integrated into financial reporting, demonstrating the organisation's commitment to transparency and accountability.

3. **Stakeholder Engagement:**

- Mark collaborated with customers and investors to highlight the organisation's ESG efforts, enhancing its reputation and market position.
- Partnerships with environmentally conscious suppliers further reinforced the organisation's commitment to sustainability.

These initiatives not only reduce environmental impact but also attract environmentally conscious customers and investors, strengthening the organisation's competitive edge.

The Outcome: Transformational Success

Mark's strategic leadership delivered exceptional results:

- **Financial Stability:** Currency risk mitigation ensured stable profitability, even in volatile markets.
- **Operational Efficiency:** Global financial processes were streamlined, leading to a 20% improvement in efficiency.
- **Cultural Alignment:** Cross-cultural initiatives enhanced collaboration and employee engagement, creating a unified global workforce.
- **Sustainability Leadership:** The organisation reduced its carbon footprint and achieved industry recognition for its ESG efforts.
- **Market Growth:** The company achieved double-digit revenue growth in emerging markets, reinforcing its position as a global leader in logistics.

Lessons Learned

This case study highlights key lessons for CFOs managing multinational organisations:

1. **Proactive Risk Management:** Implementing robust FX and operational risk strategies is essential for navigating global uncertainties.

2. **Cultural Sensitivity:** Recognising and addressing cultural differences fosters collaboration and strengthens organisational cohesion.

3. **Technology Integration:** Leveraging advanced systems enhances efficiency, accuracy, and decision-making in global operations.

4. **Sustainability Alignment:** Embedding ESG principles into strategy creates long-term value for stakeholders and the organisation.

Conclusion

Leading in a globalised economy requires a blend of financial acumen, cultural intelligence, and strategic vision. Mark's ability to address complex challenges while driving innovation and alignment exemplifies the critical role of CFOs in multinational organisations. This case serves as a blueprint for navigating the complexities of global operations while creating lasting value in an interconnected world.

Chapter 10

Becoming a Visionary CFO

> *"Long-term value is built by those who invest in purpose as much as profit."*
> **Robert N. Jacobs**

The role of the CFO has evolved far beyond financial oversight, encompassing strategic leadership, innovation, and the ability to drive transformative change. To thrive in this dynamic environment, CFOs must cultivate a visionary mindset that enables them to anticipate challenges, seize opportunities, and inspire their teams. This chapter explores the attributes, practices, and philosophies that define a visionary CFO, offering insights for those who aspire to lead with purpose and impact.

10.1 - The CFO as a Change Agent

The modern CFO is no longer confined to managing budgets and analysing financial statements. Instead, they are expected to act as a change agent, driving innovation and transformation across the organisation. In a rapidly evolving business landscape, where technological advancements and market disruptions are the norm, the ability to lead change is a defining characteristic of a successful CFO.

At the heart of this role is the CFO's capacity to identify areas ripe for improvement and implement solutions that deliver lasting impact. This might involve introducing new technologies, optimising processes, or redefining business models. For example, a CFO in a retail company might spearhead the adoption of data analytics to enhance inventory management, reducing waste and improving profitability. By challenging the status quo and embracing innovation, the CFO positions the organisation for sustained growth.

Driving change also requires effective communication and collaboration. CFOs must engage stakeholders at all levels, from board members to frontline employees, to ensure alignment and buy-in. This involves articulating a clear vision, outlining the benefits of proposed changes, and addressing concerns transparently. For instance, during a digital transformation initiative, the CFO might hold workshops to explain how new systems will streamline workflows and enhance decision-making.

Resilience and adaptability are critical qualities for CFOs as change agents. Transformational efforts often encounter resistance, setbacks, and unforeseen challenges. A visionary CFO remains steadfast in their commitment to the organisation's goals, adjusting strategies as needed while maintaining focus on the bigger picture. For example, if initial attempts to implement automation tools face technical difficulties, the CFO might explore alternative solutions or allocate additional resources to address the issues.

The leading change also involves empowering others. CFOs must cultivate a culture of innovation within their teams, encouraging employees to experiment, take risks, and contribute ideas. This might include creating innovation hubs, offering training programmes, or recognising individuals who propose successful initiatives. For instance, a finance analyst who develops a new forecasting model that improves accuracy could be celebrated publicly, reinforcing the value of creative thinking.

A practical example of a CFO as a change agent can be seen in a global logistics company where the CFO led a sustainability initiative that redefined operations. By transitioning to electric vehicles and optimising delivery routes, the CFO not only reduced environmental impact but also achieved significant cost savings. This transformative approach enhanced the organisation's reputation and positioned it as an industry leader.

In conclusion, the CFO as a change agent is an indispensable force in modern organisations. By driving innovation, fostering collaboration, and demonstrating resilience, CFOs can lead their teams and businesses through transformation, creating value that extends far beyond financial performance.

10.2 - Developing a Personal Leadership Style

A visionary CFO's effectiveness is deeply rooted in their personal leadership style, which reflects their values, strengths, and approach to guiding others. Leadership is not a one-size-fits-all concept; it requires authenticity, adaptability, and continuous refinement. Developing a personal leadership style enables CFOs to inspire trust, build strong relationships, and navigate the complexities of their role with confidence and clarity.

The foundation of a strong leadership style is self-awareness. CFOs must take the time to understand their own strengths, weaknesses, and core values. This involves reflecting on past experiences, seeking feedback from colleagues, and identifying patterns in how they approach challenges and opportunities. For instance, a CFO who excels at analytical thinking but struggles with delegation might work on trusting their team to handle certain responsibilities, freeing themselves to focus on strategic initiatives.

Authenticity is equally important. A CFO's leadership style should be a genuine reflection of who they are rather than an attempt to mimic someone else's approach. Employees and stakeholders are more likely to trust and respect leaders who are consistent and transparent. For example, a CFO who values collaboration might actively involve their team in decision-making processes, demonstrating their commitment to shared success.

Adaptability is a hallmark of effective leadership. Different situations, teams, and challenges require varying approaches. A CFO leading a team through a crisis might adopt a more directive style, providing clear instructions and quick decisions to maintain stability. Conversely, during periods of growth and innovation, a more empowering style that encourages creativity and autonomy may be appropriate. The ability to pivot between leadership styles as circumstances evolve is a key skill for visionary CFOs.

Empathy and emotional intelligence (EI) are critical components of a personal leadership style. CFOs must understand and address the emotions, motivations, and concerns of their teams. This requires active listening, open communication, and a genuine commitment to supporting others. For instance, during a stressful budgeting cycle, a CFO who recognises the pressure their team is under might offer additional resources or extend deadlines to ensure well-being and productivity.

Visionary CFOs also focus on building relationships. A personal leadership style that prioritises connection fosters trust and collaboration. This includes not only relationships within the finance team but also with other departments, external partners, and stakeholders. For example, a CFO who regularly engages with marketing, operations, and IT teams ensures alignment and breaks down silos, creating a more cohesive organisation.

Continuous learning and growth are essential for refining a personal leadership style. CFOs must seek out opportunities to develop new skills, gain fresh perspectives, and adapt to changing circumstances. This might involve attending leadership workshops, reading books on management practices, or participating in executive coaching programmes. For instance, a CFO aiming to improve their public speaking skills might enrol in a communication course, enhancing their ability to present confidently to the board or investors.

A practical example of personal leadership development can be seen in the CFO of a global technology company that transitioned from a command-and-control approach to a more collaborative style. By seeking feedback from their team, investing in leadership training, and implementing regular check-ins to understand employee needs, the CFO significantly improved team morale and performance.

In conclusion, developing a personal leadership style is a journey of self-discovery, authenticity, and growth. By embracing self-awareness, adaptability, empathy, and continuous learning, CFOs can cultivate a leadership style that inspires trust, drives results, and supports the organisation's long-term success. Visionary CFOs lead not just with their expertise but with their humanity, creating a legacy of positive impact.

10.3 - Long-Term Value Creation

For a visionary CFO, the goal is not just short-term profitability but long-term value creation that benefits all stakeholders, shareholders, employees, customers, and communities. This requires a forward-thinking approach that balances financial performance with strategic investments in innovation, sustainability, and organisational resilience. Long-term value creation is about building a business that thrives not only today but also into the future.

One of the key principles of long-term value creation is strategic foresight. CFOs must anticipate market trends, technological advancements, and societal shifts, aligning the organisation's financial strategy with these changes. For instance, a CFO in the automotive industry might invest in electric vehicle technology and infrastructure, recognising the growing demand for sustainable transportation. By making decisions with the future in mind, the CFO ensures that the organisation remains competitive and relevant.

Sustainability and ESG initiatives are integral to long-term value creation. CFOs must prioritise environmental and social responsibility, recognising that these factors directly impact reputation, customer loyalty, and investor confidence. For example, reducing carbon emissions, improving diversity and inclusion, and adopting ethical supply chain practices are not just good for the planet; they also enhance the organisation's brand and attract socially conscious consumers and investors.

Innovation and adaptability are critical for sustaining long-term value. CFOs must support investments in research and development, digital transformation, and talent development, even when these initiatives require upfront costs. For instance, implementing artificial intelligence in financial forecasting might involve initial expenses, but the long-term benefits of improved accuracy and efficiency outweigh the investment. Visionary CFOs understand that innovation is not a cost; it is an asset that drives future growth.

Long-term value creation also involves engaging stakeholders. CFOs must balance the needs and expectations of shareholders, employees, customers, and communities, ensuring that the organisation creates value for all. Transparent communication, active listening, and inclusive decision-making build trust and foster stronger relationships. For instance, involving employees in discussions about sustainability goals or engaging customers to understand their evolving preferences demonstrates the organisation's commitment to shared success.

Risk management is another pillar of long-term value creation. CFOs must identify and mitigate risks that could undermine the organisation's future performance. This includes financial risks, such as currency volatility and interest rate fluctuations, as well as non-financial risks, such as cybersecurity threats and supply chain disruptions. For example, a CFO might implement a comprehensive risk management framework that includes scenario planning and stress testing, ensuring the organisation's resilience.

A practical example of long-term value creation can be seen in a multinational consumer goods company where the CFO led a five-year strategic initiative to transition to sustainable packaging. By investing in research and collaborating with suppliers, the organisation reduced costs, enhanced brand loyalty, and positioned itself as a leader in sustainability.

In conclusion, long-term value creation is about more than financial metrics; it is about building a resilient, innovative, and purpose-driven organisation. By prioritising strategic foresight, sustainability, and stakeholder engagement, visionary CFOs ensure that their decisions create enduring value for all. This holistic approach is the hallmark of financial leadership that stands the test of time.

10.4 - Navigating Disruptive Trends

The rapid pace of technological advancements, evolving market dynamics, and global economic shifts have introduced a wave of disruptive trends that are reshaping the business landscape. For visionary CFOs, navigating these disruptions is a critical responsibility that requires adaptability, foresight, and strategic leadership. The ability to identify emerging trends, assess their impact, and position the organisation to thrive in a changing environment is what sets exceptional CFOs apart.

One of the most prominent disruptive trends is digital transformation. Technologies such as artificial intelligence (AI), blockchain, and cloud computing are revolutionising how organisations operate, analyse data, and engage with stakeholders. For CFOs, adopting these technologies can drive efficiency, enhance decision-making, and unlock new opportunities. For instance, implementing AI-driven predictive analytics in financial forecasting can improve accuracy and provide deeper insights into future trends. However, embracing digital transformation also requires significant investment, cultural change, and upskilling within the finance team.

E-commerce and digital platforms are another trend reshaping industries. As consumer preferences shift toward online shopping and digital experiences, organisations must adapt their strategies to remain competitive. CFOs play a key role in allocating resources to develop robust e-commerce capabilities, such as optimising logistics, enhancing cybersecurity, and integrating customer relationship management (CRM) systems. For example, a CFO in the retail sector might support the development of an omnichannel strategy that combines physical stores with online platforms, ensuring seamless customer experiences across all touchpoints.

Globalisation and localisation are intertwined trends that present both opportunities and challenges. While global markets offer access to new customers and resources, localised strategies are essential for addressing regional preferences and regulations. CFOs must strike a balance between standardisation and customisation, ensuring that the organisation can scale effectively while remaining relevant in local markets. For instance, a CFO expanding operations into Asia might allocate funds to tailor marketing campaigns and adapt product offerings to align with cultural preferences.

The rise of sustainability and ESG (Environmental, Social, Governance) considerations is another major trend disrupting traditional business models. Stakeholders now demand greater accountability and transparency regarding environmental and social impacts. CFOs must lead efforts to integrate sustainability into the organisation's financial strategies, such as investing in renewable energy, reducing waste, and promoting diversity and inclusion. For example, a CFO in the manufacturing industry might champion the adoption of circular economy practices, reducing reliance on raw materials while enhancing the organisation's reputation.

Workforce transformation is also reshaping the role of the CFO. The shift toward remote and hybrid work models, coupled with the need for digital skills, requires CFOs to rethink talent management strategies. This includes investing in training programmes, leveraging technology to enable collaboration, and fostering a culture that supports flexibility and innovation. For instance, a CFO might implement virtual collaboration tools and organise regular online workshops to ensure that the finance team remains engaged and productive, regardless of location.

Disruptive trends also bring heightened cybersecurity risks, particularly as organisations adopt digital solutions and expand their online presence. CFOs must allocate resources to safeguard sensitive data, prevent breaches, and comply with data protection regulations. For example, a CFO might work with IT leaders to implement robust cybersecurity measures, conduct regular audits, and invest in employee training to mitigate risks.

Scenario planning and risk management are essential for navigating disruptive trends. CFOs must anticipate potential disruptions and develop strategies to mitigate their impact. This involves analysing best-case and worst-case scenarios, assessing financial implications, and creating contingency plans. For example, during the COVID-19 pandemic, CFOs who proactively developed cash flow strategies and diversified supply chains were better equipped to weather the crisis.

A real-world example of navigating disruptive trends can be seen in a global technology company where the CFO led a comprehensive digital transformation initiative. By adopting cloud-based financial systems, implementing AI for analytics, and prioritising cybersecurity, the organisation improved efficiency, enhanced decision-making, and maintained a competitive edge in a rapidly changing market.

In conclusion, navigating disruptive trends requires visionary CFOs to be proactive, adaptable, and forward-thinking. By embracing technology, fostering innovation, and aligning strategies with emerging market dynamics, CFOs can position their organisations to thrive in an era of constant change. This ability to turn disruption into opportunity is a defining characteristic of financial leadership in the modern world.

10.5 - Balancing Stakeholder Expectations

One of the most challenging aspects of a CFO's role is balancing the expectations of diverse stakeholders, including shareholders, employees, customers, and communities. Each group has unique priorities, and meeting these demands requires careful planning, transparent communication, and strategic decision-making. A visionary CFO must navigate these competing interests while maintaining alignment with the organisation's long-term goals.

For shareholders, the primary expectation is financial performance. They seek strong returns on their investments, often measured through metrics such as revenue growth, profitability, and share price appreciation. CFOs must deliver consistent results while providing clear insights into the organisation's financial health. For instance, a CFO presenting quarterly earnings to investors might emphasise key achievements, such as cost-saving initiatives or successful market expansions, while outlining future growth strategies.

Employees, on the other hand, prioritise job security, fair compensation, and opportunities for growth. CFOs play a key role in shaping policies that address these needs, such as budgeting for training programmes, offering performance-based incentives, and ensuring competitive salaries. For example, during a restructuring initiative, a CFO might work closely with HR to provide transparent communication and support for affected employees, demonstrating a commitment to their well-being.

For customers, the expectation is value, whether through high-quality products, competitive pricing, or exceptional service. CFOs must ensure that financial strategies support these objectives without compromising profitability. This might involve allocating resources to enhance product innovation, improve supply chain efficiency, or expand customer support capabilities. For instance, a CFO in the tech industry might invest in research and development to deliver cutting-edge solutions that meet evolving customer needs.

Communities and societal stakeholders increasingly expect organisations to prioritise sustainability and corporate social responsibility (CSR). CFOs must balance these expectations with financial goals, integrating ESG considerations into the organisation's strategy. For example, a CFO might allocate funds to reduce carbon emissions, support local charities, or adopt ethical sourcing practices, reinforcing the organisation's commitment to social and environmental impact.

Balancing these expectations requires effective communication and stakeholder engagement. CFOs must ensure that all stakeholders understand the organisation's priorities and how decisions align with their interests. This involves crafting tailored messages for each audience, using clear language and relevant data. For instance, a CFO preparing a sustainability report might highlight progress on environmental goals for investors while emphasising community impact for local stakeholders.

Trade-offs are inevitable in balancing stakeholder expectations, and CFOs must make decisions that align with the organisation's values and long-term vision. For example, prioritising investments in renewable energy might reduce short-term profits but enhance the organisation's reputation and resilience in the face of climate risks. By demonstrating transparency and accountability, CFOs can build trust and foster collaboration among stakeholders.

A compelling example of balancing stakeholder expectations can be seen in a global retail company where the CFO successfully navigated conflicting demands during a market expansion. By engaging with shareholders to secure funding, collaborating with employees to ensure a smooth transition, and addressing community concerns through local hiring initiatives, the CFO achieved alignment and drove sustainable growth.

In conclusion, balancing stakeholder expectations is a complex but essential responsibility for visionary CFOs. By addressing the needs of shareholders, employees, customers, and communities with transparency and strategic foresight, CFOs can create value for all stakeholders while positioning their organisations for long-term success.

10.6 - Continuous Learning and Growth

In the ever-evolving landscape of global business and finance, a visionary CFO recognises that continuous learning and growth are not optional, they are imperative. The complexities of managing a modern organisation require CFOs to stay ahead of industry trends, technological advancements, and evolving regulatory frameworks. By committing to lifelong learning, CFOs enhance their ability to adapt, innovate, and lead with confidence.

Continuous learning begins with a mindset of curiosity and openness. CFOs who actively seek out new knowledge and perspectives are better equipped to identify opportunities, solve problems, and navigate challenges. This involves not only staying informed about the latest financial tools and strategies but also exploring areas beyond traditional finance, such as technology, marketing, and sustainability. For instance, a CFO might delve into the principles of blockchain technology to understand its potential impact on supply chain transparency and transaction security.

Formal education plays a crucial role in lifelong learning. CFOs can benefit from enrolling in executive education programmes, earning advanced certifications, or pursuing specialised courses. For example, a CFO aiming to strengthen their expertise in data analytics might enrol in a course focused on predictive modelling and machine learning. These structured learning opportunities provide both theoretical knowledge and practical skills that can be applied directly to the organisation's needs.

Equally important is informal learning, which involves staying updated on industry news, attending conferences, and engaging with peers. CFOs can gain valuable insights by participating in finance leadership forums, joining professional associations, or networking with other executives. For example, attending a global CFO summit might expose a finance leader to best practices in risk management or strategies for navigating economic uncertainty. These interactions foster knowledge exchange and build connections that can prove invaluable in the future.

Mentorship and coaching are powerful tools for personal and professional growth. CFOs can benefit from both receiving and providing mentorship. Engaging with a mentor offers guidance, feedback, and perspectives that help refine leadership skills and navigate complex decisions. Conversely, mentoring emerging finance leaders provide opportunities to reflect on their experiences, reinforce key principles, and give back to the profession. For instance, a CFO mentoring a high-potential finance manager might discuss strategies for managing cross-functional teams or handling boardroom dynamics.

Technology has significantly enhanced opportunities for continuous learning. Online platforms, webinars, and virtual communities enable CFOs to access knowledge anytime and anywhere. For example, participating in an online course on ESG reporting standards allows a CFO to stay informed about evolving regulations and stakeholder expectations. Additionally, leveraging tools like podcasts, e-books, and industry blogs ensures that learning becomes an integrated part of daily life.

Self-reflection and feedback are integral to continuous growth. CFOs must regularly evaluate their performance, identify areas for improvement, and set goals for development. This might involve seeking feedback from colleagues, engaging in self-assessment exercises, or using performance reviews as opportunities for growth. For instance, a CFO who recognises a gap in public speaking skills might take deliberate steps to improve their presentation techniques through practice and coaching.

Continuous learning also involves embracing emerging trends and preparing for future disruptions. CFOs must stay informed about developments such as artificial intelligence, automation, and global economic shifts. By anticipating these changes, CFOs can position their organisations to remain competitive and resilient. For example, a CFO who explores the potential of AI-powered financial planning tools can lead the implementation of such solutions, driving efficiency and innovation.

A practical example of continuous learning can be seen in a multinational retail CFO who dedicated time each quarter to attend industry-specific workshops and engage with thought leaders. By staying updated on trends in consumer behaviour and e-commerce, the CFO introduced initiatives that improved customer engagement and increased revenue by 15% within two years.

In conclusion, continuous learning and growth are essential for CFOs to remain effective, innovative, and forward-thinking leaders. By embracing a mindset of curiosity, leveraging educational opportunities, and staying attuned to emerging trends, CFOs can enhance their expertise and adapt to the complexities of their role. Lifelong learning is not just a professional obligation; it is the foundation of visionary leadership.

10.7 - Building a Legacy as a CFO

A visionary CFO's impact extends far beyond their tenure in the organisation. Building a legacy involves leaving behind a lasting imprint that reflects the CFO's leadership, values, and contributions to the organisation's success. A strong legacy is not only measured by financial metrics but also by the culture, processes, and innovations established under their guidance.

The first step in building a legacy is defining a clear vision. CFOs must articulate the long-term goals they aim to achieve and align their actions with these objectives. For instance, a CFO committed to sustainability might prioritise initiatives that reduce the organisation's environmental footprint, ensuring that these efforts continue to shape corporate strategy long after they leave. By setting a bold and inspiring vision, the CFO creates a roadmap for enduring impact.

Empowering the finance team is a cornerstone of a strong legacy. CFOs must focus on developing high-performing teams that can sustain success and adapt to future challenges. This involves identifying and nurturing talent, providing opportunities for growth, and fostering a culture of collaboration and innovation. For example, a CFO who invests in leadership development programmes ensures that the next generation of finance leaders is well-prepared to carry forward the organisation's mission.

Institutionalising best practices is another critical aspect of legacy-building. CFOs must implement systems, processes, and frameworks that drive efficiency, transparency, and accountability. For instance, introducing robust financial reporting tools and standardised procedures ensures consistency and accuracy across the organisation. These practices not only improve day-to-day operations but also create a foundation for long-term success.

Building a legacy also requires a focus on culture and values. CFOs who lead with integrity, empathy, and a commitment to diversity and inclusion inspire their teams and shape the organisation's identity. For example, a CFO who champions ethical decision-making and equitable workplace practices leaves behind a culture that prioritises doing what is right over what is expedient.

Innovation and adaptability are hallmarks of a lasting legacy. CFOs must embrace change and encourage their teams to think creatively and challenge conventional wisdom. This might involve exploring new technologies, adopting agile methodologies, or fostering a mindset of continuous improvement. For instance, a CFO who drives the adoption of AI-powered financial analytics not only enhances current capabilities but also positions the organisation for future advancements.

A legacy is also about the relationships and trust built over time. CFOs who engage effectively with stakeholders, whether board members, employees, investors, or customers, create networks of support that benefit the organisation in the long run. Transparent communication, collaborative problem-solving, and genuine care for stakeholder needs leave an indelible mark on the organisation's reputation and credibility.

A real-world example of legacy-building is seen in the CFO of a global healthcare company that established a fund to support employee innovation projects. By empowering employees to develop and implement ideas, the CFO not only enhanced operational efficiency but also instilled a culture of ownership and creativity that continues to define the organisation's success.

In conclusion, building a legacy as a CFO is about more than achieving short-term goals; it is about creating a foundation for enduring success. By focusing on vision, team development, best practices, and values, CFOs can leave a meaningful and lasting impact. A legacy is not just what a CFO achieves during their tenure but the positive change they inspire for years to come.

10.8 - Mentorship and Giving Back

For visionary CFOs, the journey to leadership is not just about personal success but also about mentorship and giving back to the profession. The ability to guide, inspire, and empower others not only strengthens the next generation of finance leaders but also enhances the CFO's own legacy. Mentorship is a powerful tool for fostering talent, driving organisational growth, and contributing to the broader business community.

The foundation of effective mentorship lies in authentic relationships. CFOs must take the time to understand their mentees' aspirations, strengths, and challenges, tailoring their guidance to meet individual needs. For example, mentoring a young finance analyst might involve providing technical advice on financial modelling, while mentoring an aspiring CFO might focus on leadership development and strategic thinking. By building genuine connections, mentors create an environment of trust and support.

Sharing experiences and lessons learned is a cornerstone of mentorship. CFOs can draw on their own career journeys to provide valuable insights, helping mentees navigate complex situations and avoid common pitfalls. For instance, a CFO who has successfully managed organisational change might share strategies for fostering alignment and addressing resistance, equipping their mentee with practical tools for similar challenges.

Mentorship is not just about providing answers; it is about empowering mentees to find their own solutions. Effective mentors ask thought-provoking questions, encourage critical thinking, and foster confidence. For example, instead of prescribing a course of action for a budgeting dilemma, a CFO might guide their mentee through the decision-making process, helping them evaluate options and anticipate outcomes. This approach develops problem-solving skills and promotes independence.

Providing opportunities for growth is another essential aspect of mentorship. CFOs can identify and create pathways for their mentees to expand their skills, gain experience, and build networks. This might involve assigning stretch assignments, such as leading a cross-functional project or presenting to the board. For instance, a CFO might encourage a high-potential finance manager to spearhead a new initiative, providing guidance and support along the way. These opportunities not only enhance the mentee's capabilities but also prepare them for future leadership roles.

Mentorship extends beyond the organisation to the broader finance community. CFOs can give back by participating in industry associations, speaking at conferences, or supporting educational initiatives. For example, serving as a guest lecturer at a university finance programme allows CFOs to share their expertise with aspiring professionals, inspiring the next generation of leaders. Additionally, contributing to initiatives that promote diversity and inclusion in finance ensures that the profession becomes more equitable and representative.

Reverse mentorship is an increasingly valuable practice for CFOs. Engaging with younger or less experienced professionals provides fresh perspectives and insights, particularly in areas such as technology, social media, or emerging cultural trends. For example, a CFO might partner with a tech-savvy junior employee to better understand the potential applications of blockchain or AI in finance. This exchange of knowledge benefits both the mentor and the mentee, fostering mutual learning and collaboration.

The impact of mentorship extends far beyond individual relationships. A culture of mentorship within the organisation creates ripple effects, enhancing team cohesion, employee engagement, and talent retention. CFOs who prioritise mentorship inspire others to do the same, creating a self-sustaining cycle of development and growth.

A real-world example of mentorship and giving back is seen in the CFO of a multinational FMCG company that established a mentorship programme for underrepresented groups in finance. By pairing senior leaders with junior professionals from diverse backgrounds, the programme not only advanced individual careers but also enriched the organisation with varied perspectives and ideas.

In conclusion, mentorship and giving back are integral to a visionary CFO's role. By guiding and empowering others, CFOs contribute to the success of their teams, organisations, and the broader profession. Mentorship is not just an act of generosity, it is an investment in the future, fostering a legacy of leadership, inclusivity, and continuous growth.

10.9 - Future of the CFO Role

The role of the CFO has undergone significant transformation over the past few decades, evolving from a primarily accounting-focused position to one of strategic leadership and innovation. As organisations face an increasingly dynamic and complex business landscape, the future of the CFO role will continue to expand, requiring adaptability, forward-thinking, and a commitment to lifelong learning.

One of the most defining aspects of the future CFO role is the increasing integration of technology and data analytics. CFOs will need to harness the power of artificial intelligence (AI), machine learning, and predictive analytics to drive decision-making and improve efficiency. For example, AI-powered financial planning tools can analyse vast amounts of data to identify trends, forecast outcomes, and recommend strategies, enabling CFOs to make more informed and agile decisions. As technology advances, CFOs must embrace their role as champions of digital transformation, ensuring that their organisations remain competitive in a tech-driven world.

The focus on sustainability and ESG (Environmental, Social, and Governance) will also shape the future of the CFO role. Stakeholders are demanding greater accountability and transparency regarding environmental and social impacts, and CFOs will play a central role in integrating ESG metrics into financial strategies. This might involve developing sustainability budgets, implementing circular economy practices, or aligning corporate goals with global frameworks such as the United Nations Sustainable Development Goals (SDGs). For example, a CFO in the manufacturing sector might lead efforts to reduce carbon emissions while ensuring that these initiatives enhance long-term profitability.

Globalisation and geopolitical risks will further expand the CFO's responsibilities. As organisations operate in an increasingly interconnected world, CFOs will need to navigate regulatory complexities, currency fluctuations, and supply chain disruptions. This requires a deep understanding of international markets, as well as the ability to anticipate and respond to global economic trends. For instance, a CFO managing operations in both emerging and developed markets might need to balance growth opportunities with risk mitigation strategies.

The future CFO will also take on an enhanced role as a strategic partner to the CEO and board of directors. Beyond financial expertise, CFOs will be expected to provide insights into market dynamics, competitive positioning, and organisational innovation. For example, during a major acquisition, the CFO might analyse synergies, assess cultural alignment, and evaluate integration plans, contributing to both the financial and strategic aspects of the deal.

Leadership and talent development will remain a cornerstone of the CFO role. As finance teams adapt to new technologies and ways of working, CFOs will need to cultivate a culture of innovation, collaboration, and continuous learning. This involves recruiting diverse talent, fostering inclusivity, and providing opportunities for professional growth. For instance, a CFO might implement a leadership pipeline programme to prepare the next generation of finance professionals for the challenges of a digital economy.

A real-world example of the evolving CFO role is seen in a global e-commerce company where the CFO took the lead on implementing blockchain technology for supply chain transparency. By leveraging this innovative solution, the CFO not only enhanced operational efficiency but also strengthened customer trust and loyalty.

In conclusion, the future of the CFO role is one of increasing complexity and opportunity. As technology, sustainability, and globalisation redefine business priorities, CFOs must embrace their roles as strategic leaders, innovators, and change agents. The ability to adapt, collaborate, and drive value across all aspects of the organisation will be the hallmark of a successful CFO in the years to come.

10.10 - Case Study: Inspiring Leadership in Finance

Leadership in finance is about more than mastering numbers; it's about creating vision, fostering collaboration, and delivering meaningful impact. This case study explores how Maria, the CFO of a global technology company, transformed the finance function through innovation, inclusion, and alignment with sustainability goals. Her leadership elevated the organisation's performance and reputation, setting a benchmark for visionary financial leadership.

The Context: Challenges in a Dynamic Landscape

When Maria joined the organisation, the finance function faced several pressing issues:

1. **Outdated Processes:** Manual workflows led to inefficiencies and limited the team's ability to focus on strategic initiatives.

2. **Fragmented Collaboration:** Cross-departmental collaboration was weak, creating silos and slowing decision-making.

3. **Stakeholder Pressure:** Investors and customers increasingly demanded greater transparency and alignment with environmental, social, and governance (ESG) principles.

Maria recognised these challenges as opportunities to transform the finance team into a strategic enabler of growth, innovation, and sustainability.

Phase 1: Embracing Technology and Innovation

Maria's first step was modernising the finance function through digital transformation. Her technology-focused initiatives included:

1. **Automation of Routine Tasks:**
   - Maria introduced robotic process automation (RPA) to handle repetitive tasks such as accounts payable and financial reporting.
   - This freed up the team to focus on value-added activities, such as strategic forecasting and performance analysis.

2. **AI-Driven Predictive Analytics:**
   - By implementing advanced analytics tools, the finance team gained the ability to forecast trends and identify risks with greater accuracy.
   - For example, AI-driven models enabled the team to anticipate market shifts, providing actionable insights for strategic planning.

3. **Cloud-Based ERP System:**
   - A cloud-based enterprise resource planning (ERP) system improved data accessibility and enabled real-time collaboration across global offices.
   - Standardised processes and enhanced reporting capabilities streamlined decision-making at all levels.

These technological advancements enhanced efficiency, improved accuracy, and positioned the organisation as a leader in financial innovation.

Phase 2: Fostering Inclusion and Collaboration

Maria understood that a high-performing finance team required not only technological capabilities but also a strong, inclusive culture. To foster collaboration and engagement, she implemented several initiatives:

1. **Mentorship Programme:**

   - Maria launched a mentorship initiative pairing junior employees with senior leaders to facilitate knowledge sharing and career development.
   - This programme not only empowered emerging talent but also strengthened relationships within the team.

2. **Cross-Functional Workshops:**

   - Regular workshops brought together finance, marketing, operations, and IT teams to address organisational challenges collectively.
   - During a product launch, for instance, the finance team collaborated with marketing to develop a pricing strategy that balanced profitability with market competitiveness.

3. **Recognition and Rewards:**

   - Maria introduced a recognition programme to celebrate individual and team achievements, boosting morale and reinforcing positive behaviours.

- After the successful implementation of the ERP system, the team was publicly acknowledged, fostering a sense of accomplishment and motivation.

These efforts created a cohesive and engaged finance team that actively contributed to the organisation's strategic goals.

Phase 3: Aligning Financial Strategy with Sustainability

Sustainability became a cornerstone of Maria's leadership as she aligned the organisation's financial strategy with its ESG commitments. Her initiatives included:

1. **Reducing the Carbon Footprint:**
   - Maria spearheaded a transition to renewable energy sources for the organisation's facilities, significantly lowering emissions.
   - Supply chain logistics were optimised to reduce waste and fuel consumption, enhancing both sustainability and cost efficiency.

2. **Integrating ESG Metrics:**
   - A sustainability dashboard was introduced to track progress on key ESG goals, including emissions reduction, workforce diversity, and community engagement.
   - These metrics were incorporated into financial reporting, providing stakeholders with a holistic view of the organisation's performance.

3. **Stakeholder Engagement:**
   - Maria collaborated with investors and customers to highlight the organisation's ESG initiatives,

reinforcing its commitment to transparency and ethical practices.
- These efforts attracted socially conscious investors and improved customer loyalty.

Maria's leadership in sustainability strengthened the organisation's reputation and positioned it as a responsible industry leader.

Phase 4: Leading Through Crisis

Maria's ability to navigate crises further showcased her inspiring leadership. During a global economic downturn, she took decisive actions to protect the organisation's financial health while maintaining its long-term vision:

1. **Cost Management:**
   - Maria renegotiated supplier contracts and deferred non-essential expenditures to preserve cash flow.
   - Essential investments, such as technology upgrades, were prioritised to ensure continued growth and innovation.

2. **Transparent Communication:**
   - Town hall meetings were held to address employee concerns and provide updates on the organisation's financial position.
   - This transparent approach fostered trust and unity among stakeholders, reinforcing confidence in the organisation's leadership.

Maria's crisis management not only stabilised the organisation but also enhanced its resilience to future challenges.

The Outcome: Transformational Success

Under Maria's leadership, the finance function achieved remarkable results:

1. **Operational Efficiency:** Automation and process improvements reduced operational costs by 20%.
2. **Employee Engagement:** Satisfaction scores increased significantly, reflecting higher morale and motivation.
3. **Sustainability Leadership:** The organisation earned industry recognition for its ESG performance, attracting investors and customers alike.
4. **Strategic Impact:** The finance team evolved into a strategic partner, contributing directly to the organisation's growth and innovation.

Lessons Learned

This case study highlights the qualities of inspiring leadership in finance:

1. **Visionary Thinking:** Transforming challenges into opportunities requires foresight and bold decision-making.
2. **Inclusive Culture:** Fostering collaboration and inclusion empowers teams and drives engagement.
3. **Sustainability Alignment:** Integrating ESG goals into financial strategy creates long-term value for all stakeholders.

4. **Adaptability:** Navigating crises with resilience and transparency strengthens organisational stability and trust.

Conclusion

Maria's leadership exemplifies the transformative potential of a visionary CFO. By combining innovation, inclusion, and sustainability, she redefined the role of finance within the organisation, delivering lasting value and impact. This case serves as a blueprint for CFOs seeking to inspire, lead, and leave a legacy of growth, trust, and excellence.

Final Word

Inspiring a New Era of CFO Leadership

"The future demands CFOs who are unafraid to reimagine the boundaries of their role, blending financial acumen with bold, strategic leadership."

Robert N. Jacobs

The journey of a Chief Financial Officer is one of evolution, resilience, and vision. Throughout the pages of this book, we have uncovered not only the technical expertise required of a CFO but also the leadership qualities and strategic mindset that distinguish an extraordinary financial leader from an ordinary one. The role of the CFO today transcends the traditional boundaries of financial oversight, encompassing strategic leadership, technological innovation, and the ability to navigate complex global challenges. This journey is not linear; it is a dynamic and multifaceted path that demands continuous learning, adaptability, and a commitment to creating long-term value.

The story of the modern CFO begins with reimagining the fundamentals of the role. Gone are the days when a CFO was confined to managing budgets and financial statements. Today, a CFO is expected to be a strategic partner to the CEO and board, aligning financial strategies with broader business objectives. This expanded role requires a keen ability to see beyond the numbers and anticipate opportunities and challenges that lie ahead. Visionary CFOs understand that their work is not confined to spreadsheets; it is embedded in the decisions that shape the organisation's future.

From this foundation, the importance of strategic financial planning emerges as a core responsibility. Effective planning is not a static exercise but a dynamic process that accounts for growth, market conditions, and unforeseen disruptions. A CFO must be both a planner and a navigator, ensuring that financial strategies remain flexible while aligned with the organisation's long-term goals. This duality of precision and adaptability becomes the cornerstone of financial leadership, enabling organisations to thrive in the face of uncertainty.

Budgeting and forecasting are natural extensions of this strategic mindset. Far from being mere exercises in cost control, these processes are opportunities for organisations to unlock potential and pursue bold ambitions. Accurate forecasting enables a CFO to anticipate risks, allocate resources effectively, and empower teams to achieve operational excellence. In this way, budgets are transformed from constraints into enablers of growth and innovation.

The focus on financial optimisation continues with the imperative of cost management. The ability to identify inefficiencies and implement strategies that optimise resources without stifling innovation is a hallmark of exceptional CFOs. The art of cost management lies in balancing short-term efficiency with long-term value creation. It is not merely about cutting expenses; it is about uncovering opportunities to maximise impact. Whether by adopting automation, streamlining supply chains, or renegotiating vendor contracts, the CFO must approach cost management as a strategic endeavour, always mindful of its implications for the organisation's broader goals.

In every decision, the CFO must navigate the tension between immediate needs and future ambitions. Strategic decision-making demands a holistic perspective, one that balances tactical execution with a long-term vision. A CFO must weigh the trade-offs inherent in every choice, ensuring that today's actions align with tomorrow's outcomes. This capacity for strategic foresight distinguishes the CFO as not just a steward of the present but a leader of the future.

Technology has emerged as a transformative force in the CFO's journey. The integration of artificial intelligence, machine learning, blockchain, and predictive analytics has revolutionised the finance function, enabling faster, more accurate decision-making. The ability to harness these tools is no longer optional; it is essential for driving efficiency, enhancing insight, and maintaining a competitive edge. Yet, the adoption of technology is not without challenges. It requires cultural shifts, substantial investments, and the ability to inspire teams to embrace change. A visionary CFO leads this transformation with clarity and conviction, positioning the organisation to thrive in a digital-first world.

But even as technology transforms the role, the essence of leadership remains deeply human. The CFO's ability to inspire, engage, and empower their team is critical to building a high-performance finance function. Leadership is not about command and control; it is about fostering collaboration, trust, and a shared sense of purpose. The most effective CFOs prioritise diversity, inclusion, and professional growth, creating teams that are not only capable but also motivated to drive innovation and success.

Globalisation adds another layer of complexity to the CFO's responsibilities. Operating in multinational environments requires an understanding of diverse markets, regulatory landscapes, and cultural dynamics. The ability to navigate cross-border taxation, manage currency volatility, and address geopolitical risks distinguishes the global CFO as a diplomat and strategist. Yet, amid these challenges, the global stage also offers opportunities to leverage cultural diversity, foster cross-border collaboration, and position the organisation as a leader in an interconnected world.

As the journey progresses, the focus shifts from managing complexities to embracing the qualities of visionary leadership. A visionary CFO is more than a financial expert; they are a change agent who drives innovation, champions sustainability, and leaves a legacy of positive impact. Long-term value creation becomes their guiding principle, influencing every decision they make. Whether by prioritising ESG initiatives, supporting innovation, or fostering stakeholder trust, the visionary CFO ensures that their work creates enduring value for all.

This journey culminates in the recognition that the role of the CFO is not static but dynamic. It is a journey of constant growth, learning, and reinvention. A visionary CFO embraces this evolution with curiosity, courage, and conviction, knowing that their impact extends far beyond the numbers. They are mentors, leaders, and stewards of transformation, shaping not only the future of their organisation but also the future of the profession.

As we conclude this exploration, the message is clear: the path to becoming a visionary CFO is one of purpose and progress. It is a journey that demands both technical mastery and human connection, strategic foresight, and operational excellence. For aspiring CFOs, this book serves as a guide and inspiration. For experienced CFOs, it is a call to reflect, adapt, and continue pushing the boundaries of what is possible. The future belongs to those who embrace the challenge, lead with integrity, and dare to envision a better tomorrow.

The journey does not end here; it begins anew with every challenge, every decision, and every opportunity. For the visionary CFO, the possibilities are limitless. May you rise to meet them.

Printed in Great Britain
by Amazon

e961e4d8-1f91-47b5-9d50-0323e5bd8cc7R01